NEITHER
VICTOR
NOR
VANQUISHED

NEITHER VICTOR NOR VANQUISHED

America in the War of 1812

WILLIAM WEBER

Potomac Books
Washington, D.C.

Copyright © 2013 by the Board of Regents of the University of Nebraska
Potomac Books is an imprint of the University of Nebraska Press

Library of Congress Cataloging-in-Publication Data
Weber, William, 1951–
    Neither victor nor vanquished : America in the War of 1812 / William Weber. —
First edition.
        pages cm
    Includes bibliographical references and index.
    ISBN 978-1-61234-607-6 (hardcover : alk. paper)
    ISBN 978-1-61234-608-3 (electronic)
    1. United States—History—War of 1812. I. Title.
    E354.W44 2013
    973.5'2—dc23
                            2013001472

Printed in the United States of America on acid-free paper that meets the American
National Standards Institute Z39-48 Standard.

Potomac Books
22841 Quicksilver Drive
Dulles, Virginia 20166

First Edition

10 9 8 7 6 5 4 3 2 1

CONTENTS

ILLUSTRATIONS

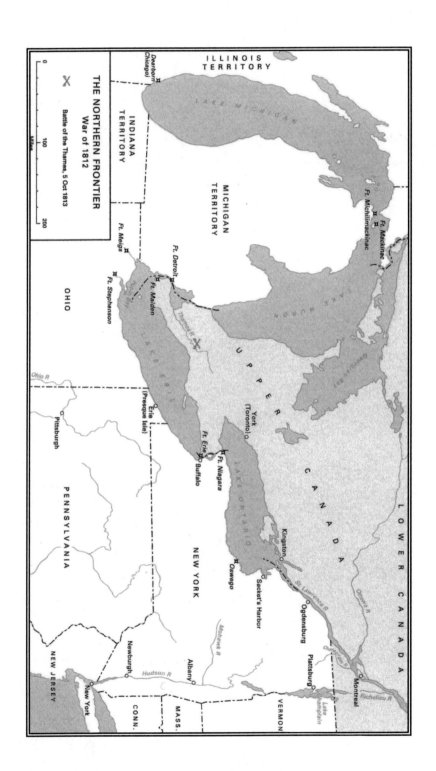

THE NORTHERN FRONTIER
War of 1812

✗ Battle of the Thames, 5 Oct 1813

Miles
0   100   200

ILLINOIS
TERRITORY

INDIANA
TERRITORY

MICHIGAN
TERRITORY

OHIO

PENNSYLVANIA

NEW YORK

UPPER CANADA

LOWER CANADA

NEW JERSEY

CONN.

MASS.

VERMONT

LAKE MICHIGAN

LAKE HURON

LAKE ERIE

LAKE ONTARIO

Georgian Bay

Dearborn
(Chicago)

Ft. Mackinac

Ft. Michilimackinac

Ft. Meigs

Ft. Detroit

Ft. Malden

Ft. Stephenson

Thames R.

York
(Toronto)

Erie
(Presqu'isle)

Pittsburgh

Ft. Erie

Ft. Niagara

Buffalo

Kingston

Oswego

Sacket's Harbor

Ogdensburg

Plattsburg

Montreal

St. Lawrence R.

Ottawa R.

Richelieu R.

Lake Champlain

Mohawk R.

Albany

Newburgh

Hudson R.

New York

Ohio R.

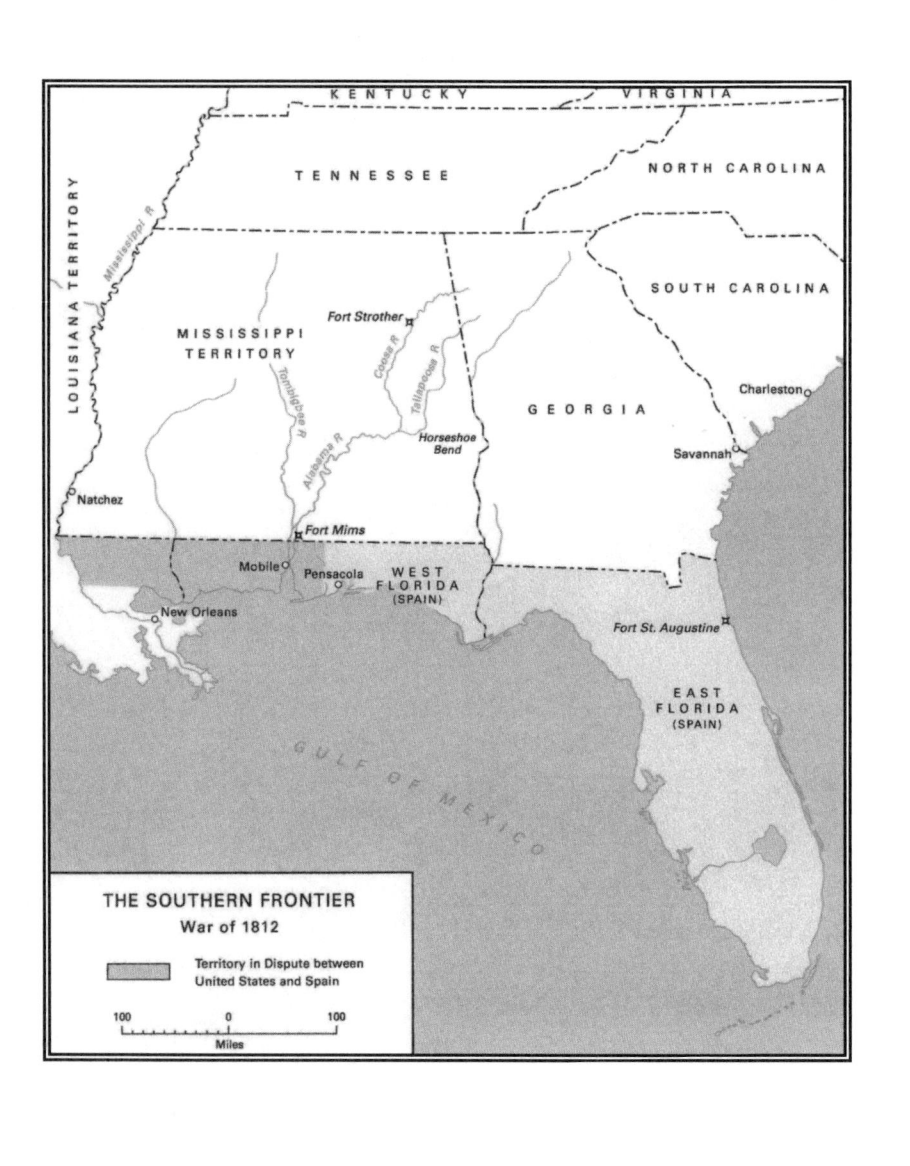

THE SOUTHERN FRONTIER
War of 1812

Territory in Dispute between
United States and Spain

100 0 100
Miles

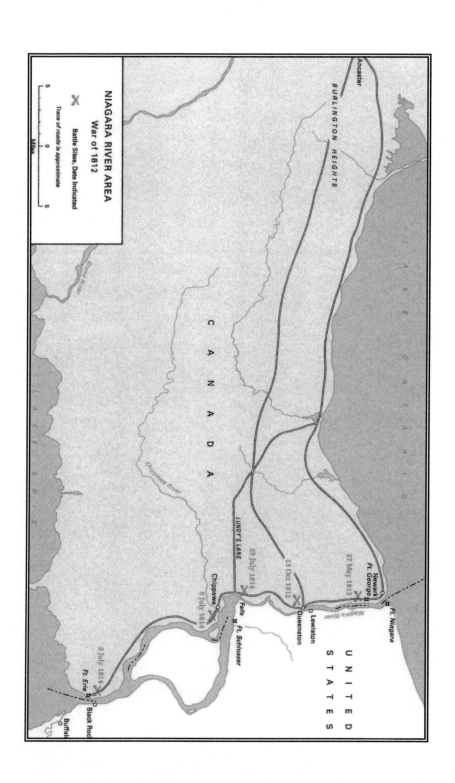

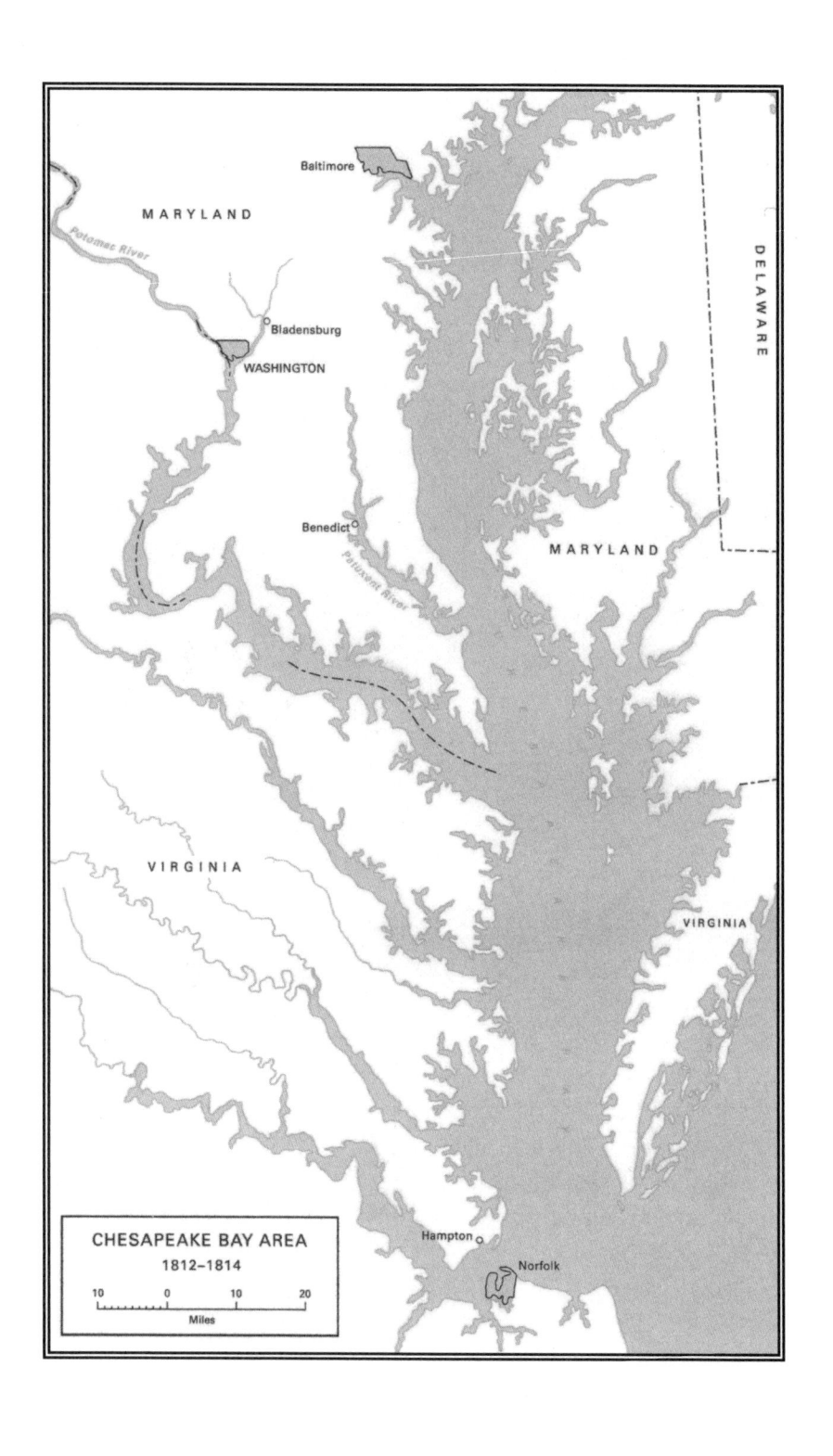

MARYLAND

Baltimore

Potomac River

Bladensburg
WASHINGTON

Benedict

Patuxent River

MARYLAND

DELAWARE

VIRGINIA

VIRGINIA

Hampton
Norfolk

CHESAPEAKE BAY AREA
1812–1814

10   0   10   20
Miles

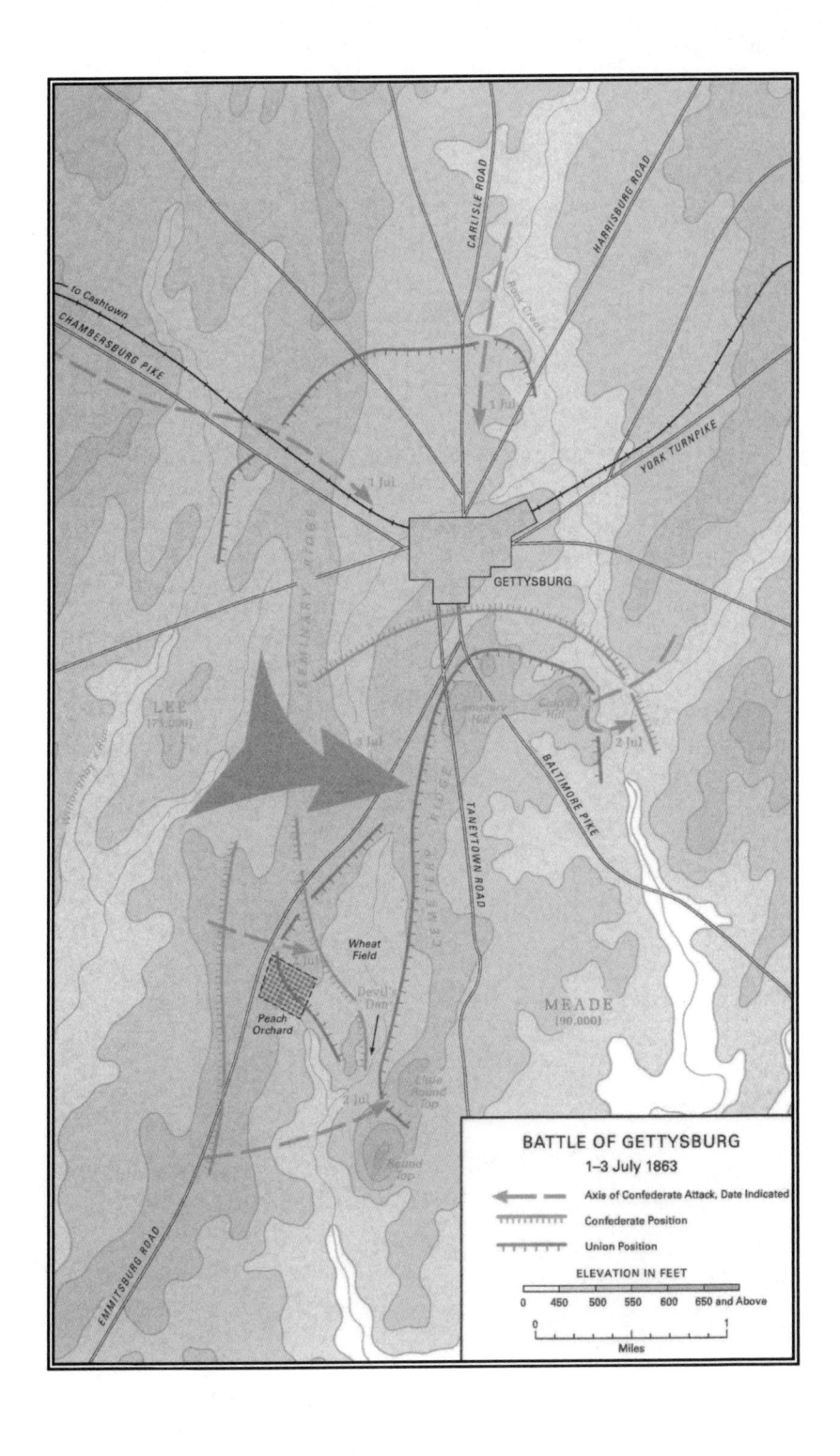

BATTLE OF GETTYSBURG

1–3 July 1863

Axis of Confederate Attack, Date Indicated

Confederate Position

Union Position

ELEVATION IN FEET

| 0 | 450 | 500 | 550 | 600 | 650 and Above |

0   1

Miles

ACKNOWLEDGMENTS

I owe many people a debt of gratitude for their assistance in writing this book. My parents, Jack and Fran, began my lifelong interest in history. Not a Christmas passed without another history book from the Landmark Books series that my siblings and I shared and fought over. Many years later, they also supported my undergraduate education at Canisus College, where I majored in history and benefited greatly from the honors program run by Dr. James Valone and Dr. Walter Sharrow. Both professors taught me about the craft of history and discipline of historiography.

My particular interest in the War of 1812 stems from having lived the majority of my life in Buffalo, New York, and Washington, D.C. Long aware that the British Army had captured both "villages" during the war sparked my interest in the conflict. Pierre Berton's *The Invasion of Canada, 1812–1813* was the first of many volumes that now occupy my shelves. I have enjoyed learning about the war through the writings of many other authors, such as Donald Hickey, J. Mackay Hitsman, Donald Graves, and J. C. A. Stagg—just to name a few.

Several people were instrumental in the production of this book. Dr. Roger George of National Defense University provided a useful critique on an earlier draft, making suggestions for which I am truly grateful. At Potomac Books, Dr. Elizabeth Demers, Amanda Irle, Laura Briggs, Vicki Chamlee, and Elizabeth Norris were instrumental in turning my manuscript into a book. Ms. Beth F. MacKenzie, U.S. Army Center for Military History, pointed me to American Military History, Volume 1, *The United States Army and the Forging of a Nation, 1775–1971* for the maps that appear in this book.

Most important, this book would not have been possible without the patience and love of my wife, Pam, to whom it is dedicated. With two careers and two sons, Sam and Daniel, consuming most of our waking moments, she provided the time and encouragement needed to research and write this volume. Any errors of fact, interpretation, and omission in the pages that follow are, of course, mine.

INTRODUCTION

The bicentennial commemoration of the War of 1812 has raised popular awareness of this often forgotten and unappreciated conflict. Americans are already familiar with some basic facts. Francis Scott Key penned the lyrics of the "Star-Spangled Banner" as he stood on the deck of a British warship observing the ferocious bombardment of Fort McHenry in 1814. The Battle of New Orleans, the Americans' most decided victory, took place shortly after the British and the Americans signed the Treaty of Ghent, an agreement to end the conflict, on Christmas Eve 1814. The War of 1812 is also the source of two of the most famous quotes in American naval history: "Don't give up the ship" (or words to that effect), which a dying Capt. James Lawrence uttered aboard the frigate USS *Chesapeake*; and "We have met the enemy and they are ours," which began Commodore Oliver Hazard Perry's report of his victory on Lake Erie. His flagship, the brig USS *Lawrence*, also flew a banner honoring its namesake's last words.

Government and private organizations have undertaken much of this public education effort. Fort McHenry, for example, distributes a brochure listing thirty historic locations in the District of Columbia, Maryland, and Virginia along a Star-Spangled Banner Driving Tour, as well as nineteen related organizational websites. At many of these and similar locations in other states, reenactments of battles draw participants and onlookers alike. Frigates such as the USS *Chesapeake* in Baltimore and USS *Constitution* in Boston also provide comparable educational experiences.

Despite these well-conceived and executed efforts, the War of 1812 will likely slip back into the recesses of national memory after the anniversary. For one, public attention will be diverted to a plethora of other historic anniversaries. The bicentennial of the War of 1812 coincides with the sesquicentennial of the

American Civil War. In the national imagination, Gettysburg receives more attention than Baltimore, Vicksburg more than New Orleans, and Robert E. Lee and Ulysses S. Grant far more than Andrew Jackson and Jacob Brown. The centennial anniversary of World War I, the Great War, begins in 2014. The sinking of RMS *Lusitania* on May 7, 1915, is a particularly somber mark, and the deaths of 128 (out of 139) American passengers tipped American sentiments toward Britain. In 2015, attention (particularly that of grognards, or war game aficionados) will shift from the Battle of New Orleans to the 200th commemoration of the Battle of Waterloo, where the Duke of Wellington's victory sent Napoleon Bonaparte into exile, and to the 50th anniversary of the introduction of major U.S. ground forces into Vietnam.

Attention to the War of 1812 struggles against the larger and continually growing literature devoted to other American conflicts. Despite a steady stream of books and articles that cover the war's major campaigns, battles, and personalities, far more has been written on World War II, the American Civil War, the Gulf War, and the American Revolutionary War as a visit to any online or brick-and-mortar bookstore will attest. *The Oxford Companion to American Military History* provides summary articles on all U.S. conflicts among its more than one thousand entries, but the volume has only one entry on a specific battle from the War of 1812, the Battle of New Orleans. Similarly, John Keegan's *Fields of Battle: The Wars for North America* focuses on James Wolfe's capture of Quebec, the Battle of Yorktown, the Peninsular Campaign of 1862, and the Battle of the Little Bighorn. The War of 1812 receives only a passing glance from this eminent historian. Finally, Kevin Phillips's *The Cousins' Wars: Religion, Politics, and the Triumph of Anglo-America* provides modest coverage of 1812 in its detailed and compelling analysis of the linkage between three major civil wars: the English Civil War, the American Revolutionary War, and the American Civil War.[1]

This relative neglect seems odd given Gordon S. Wood's succinct assessment of the war in his history of the early American republic, *Empire of Liberty: A History of the Early Republic, 1789–1815*: "The War of 1812 is the strangest war in American history . . . it was nonetheless one of the most important wars in American history."[2] Wood argues that the War of 1812 was more important to the development of the United States than its reputation for "strangeness" suggests. Far from being a footnote to the Napoleonic wars in Europe, the War of 1812 played a vital role in setting the stage for the Civil War by securing the Louisiana Purchase, crippling the Federalist Party, bringing to power Andrew

Jackson and his like-minded protégés, accelerating the spread of Jeffersonian democracy, and opening the fertile lands of the Southeast to plantations and slavery. Moreover, the United States would have been a decidedly different country had the war not occurred, had it been fought differently, or had it resulted in something other than a strategic draw.

Neither Victor nor Vanquished makes this case by investigating the ambiguity created by the war's two principal narratives. The narrative casting the war as "Mr. Madison's War" dominates the national memory of this conflict, emphasizing the indecisive military campaigns that repeatedly failed to conquer Canada or otherwise compel Britain to respect U.S. maritime rights. Conversely, the second narrative, with the war depicted as the "Second War of Independence," celebrates the defensive victories at Baltimore, Plattsburgh, and New Orleans that thwarted major British invasions in 1814 and 1815 and that led to the Treaty of Ghent in which American negotiators rebuffed London's harsh terms for peace. This book subjects these dominant interpretations to a series of "stress tests" and uses comparative and heuristic approaches to examine their central tenets to determine whether they are in conflict or are complementary. Overall, it concludes not only that these narratives are two sides of the same coin but also that they are individually and collectively inadequate to understanding the importance of the War of 1812.

Chapter 1 examines in detail Mr. Madison's War and the Second War of Independence before presenting two alternative narratives that go beyond this Janus-faced view of the conflict. The first of these alternatives focuses on the Jeffersonian Revolution that began before the war and suggests that the War of 1812 should be viewed as a Second Revolutionary War rather than as a Second War of Independence. The second views the War of 1812 as the first of a series of wars of expansion that led to the American Civil War. It depicts the rise of Andrew Jackson as a critical development brought about by the War of 1812 that had an immeasurable impact on the trajectory of the United States.

The second chapter assesses the alternative narratives through two classical perspectives on war offered by the Greek historian Thucydides and the Chinese master of statecraft Sun Tzu. Thucydides's three causes of war—fear, honor, and interest (wealth)—and Sun Tzu's major and minor factors for determining military capability are applied to both America and Britain. These perspectives shed light on the core military conclusions of the two dominant narratives of the War of 1812. They provide frameworks for understanding why and how "John Bull," with the world's foremost naval power and a credible professional army, and cousin "Jonathan"—an idealistic republic with commercial and agricultural aspirations that denied itself both an adequate army and navy as part of its national ideology—clashed and produced such a "strange" war.

Chapter 3, noting the concurrence of the War of 1812's bicentennial and the Civil War's sesquicentennial, similarly attempts to recalibrate the generally poor performance ascribed to U.S. forces by Mr. Madison's War. It directly compares Maj. Gen. Jacob Brown's 1814 invasion of Canada with Gen. Robert E. Lee's invasion of Maryland and Pennsylvania in 1863—arguably among the most ambitious campaigns of their respective conflicts. These summer campaigns resulted in key battles—Lundy's Lane and Gettysburg, respectively—which were completely different in scale but oddly similar in their conduct, tactics, and outcomes. Brown faired no worse, if not better, than Lee did. Yet, Brown is largely forgotten, and Lee remains lionized in the lost cause narrative of the Confederacy.

Chapter 4 looks at the republic and the men who governed the United States during the War of 1812—not the executives and legislators in Washington but those leaders in the state capitals. Most histories of the war pay scant attention to these governors, who in practical terms were as, if not more so, responsible for the general welfare and defense of the young republic than was the infant federal government. Its review of their roles and responsibilities as wartime leaders indicates that our views of the War of 1812 need to be adjusted to account for efforts and events that took place below the federal level.

The following chapter presents a detailed account of the numerous alternative historical paths that Henry Adams presented in his seminal account of the war written more than a century ago. As a critic of American military strategy and operations, Adams laid the framework for the largely negative interpretation we know as Mr. Madison's War. However, Adams used fictional constructs, often framed as "had only X done Y," to critique the poor political and military leadership that he found in his analysis of the American and British war efforts. Many of these what-ifs focus on the strategic turning points in the war and the diplomacy that brought it to a peaceful conclusion. By assessing key events in the War of 1812 from the standpoint not only of what happened—thereby legitimizing alternative history as a legitimate tool of inquiry—but also of what might have happened, Adams is probably the best lawyer for representing the arguments for both Mr. Madison's War and the Second War of Independence.

Chapter 6 adopts Adams's approach and takes a close look at the operational and tactical what-ifs specifically related to the Battle of Bladensburg in August 1814, the encounter that led to the British capture of Washington. This battle plays a prominent role in the Mr. Madison's War and Second War of Independence narratives both as a painful example of poor national, political, and military leadership and as a prelude to the British attack on Baltimore, where Key composed the lyrics for the national anthem. This chapter asks, could Washington have been saved? At first glance, this question may seem odd given how the battle is often described as a rout and how the American forces' hasty retreat quickly became known as the Bladensburg Races. Yet, these what-ifs suggest that the battle and its outcome were not preordained and that a British defeat might have altered the ultimate outcome and altered its place in our understanding of the war.

Chapter 7 takes the what-if approach to a higher level by exploring alternative strategic outcomes for the War of 1812 that would have decidedly changed the shape of the United States and its future. The discussion uses a more structured approach than the ad hoc what-if formulations that Adams and subsequent historians have presented. It creates and explores scenarios arising from differences in two key factors—the quality of generalship in the American and British armies and the direction of the European conflict that both caused and shaped the War of 1812. These scenarios intentionally depict more decisive American and British victories to make us think deeper about the importance of the war in terms of what did not happen and not only about what did occur. They also force us to consider whether our existing historical narratives could adequately accommodate such outcomes or whether their explanatory utility is narrowly confined to the peculiarities of the war as it unfolded.

Chapter 8 pursues this line of inquiry one final step further and imagines a worst-case scenario for the young republic in which the war takes a more pessimistic path than that presented even by Mr. Madison's War and has a radically different outcome from that of the Second Revolutionary War. This improbable, but still plausible, scenario suggests that history might have provided a different answer to Key's central question, "O! say does that star-spangled banner yet wave, / o'er the land of the free?" The importance of the War of 1812 to U.S. national history and traditions also becomes clearer in this outcome in which early America morphs into a less liberal republic.

The final chapter concludes the book by imagining how the United States might have evolved without the War of 1812, absent either the trauma of Mr.

Madison's War or the exhilaration that followed the Second War of Independence. It suggests how the young republic might have avoided a second war with Britain and how events and trends in our nation's formative years would have proceeded without the war's victories and defeats. It suggests that the country would have unfolded in a remarkably different fashion, underscoring the importance of the War of 1812 to the trajectory that the United States followed in the first half of the nineteenth century and beyond.

This book offers enough background information that raw recruits to the War of 1812 can familiarize themselves with the well-documented facts of the war and with the dominant themes (and a few fictions) that historical treatments have provided over the years. A chronology of the key events in North America at sea and in Europe is also provided. The book closes with a bibliographic essay that directs readers to standard histories of the war and more detailed volumes of particular campaigns and battles. For the truly curious and detail-oriented reader, four excellent reference works are John C. Fredriksen's *The United States Army in the War of 1812: Concise Biographies of Commanders and Operational Histories of Regiments, with Bibliographies of Published and Primary Resources* (2009); David S. Heidler and Jeanne T. Heidler's *Encyclopedia of the War of 1812* (1997); Donald R. Hickey's *Don't Give Up the Ship! Myths of the War of 1812* (2006); and Robert Malcomson's *The A to Z of the War of 1812* (2009).

— 1 —

THE NEED FOR
NEW NARRATIVES

S ocieties craft narratives that integrate wars into their cultures and histories.
These story lines explain why the war was fought, why it was just, and why
the cause or gains outweighed the costs. In the case of victory, the preferred historical account highlights the successes, minimizes the failures, and links the
war to the preservation, enhancement, and expansion of the nation. In the
case of defeat, the narrative scapegoats political and military leaders, highlights
the material and technical—but not the moral—superiority of the foreign victor, and emphasizes the honor of those who served and suffered, but it less often
leads to lessons learned or regrets. In either case, the enemy society is depicted
as having been responsible for the conflict, whether or not the enemy fired the
first shot.

The War of 1812 has two narratives in American culture. The first is a
triumphant account of a young nation defending its honor and territory in
what many have called the Second War of Independence. This account
focuses on the battlefield triumphs and the successful negotiations that denied
Britain its maximalist demands in 1814 and 1815. The second is presented as
"Mr. Madison's War," a tale of "amateurs to arms" in an unnecessary conflict
that is best forgotten or recalled only when a negative example of statecraft
and military strategy is required. It tells the story of a divided and unprepared
nation that embarked on a conflict ended only by a peace treaty that restored
the status quo antebellum but did not address the nation's grievances.
Although they appear to be in conflict, these narratives present perspectives
based on different sets of personalities and key events. Neither fully explains
the War of 1812, and they should be considered as complementary, rather
than as conflicting, story lines.

THE SECOND WAR OF INDEPENDENCE

Some Americans at the outset of the War of 1812 viewed it as a resumption of the Revolutionary War. Ohio governor Return J. Meigs stated, "The declaration of war is but a practical renewal of the Declaration of Independence; in which celebrated performance is contained a recital of many of those acts of injustice and oppression which caused its adoption."[1] While inspired by such sentiments, the Second War of Independence narrative that has developed over the past two hundred years rests on three broader propositions. First, British impressment of American sailors and interference with America's maritime trade were the principal causes of the war. Between 1803 and 1812, the British seized some six thousand seamen from U.S.-flagged merchantmen; some thirteen hundred were returned. Equally egregious was the frequent presence of British warships in U.S. territorial waters. In particular, the HMS *Leopard*'s 1807 attack on the USS *Chesapeake*, after the Americans denied the British permission to search the American warship's crew for deserters from the Royal Navy, foreshadowed the war. The imposition of the Orders in Council, or British decrees that regulated neutral trade with the European continent and impinged on American sovereignty, was another key factor leading to the conflict.

Second, American strength of arms at sea in 1812–1813 and on land in 1813–1815 won the war. Single ship victories on the high seas in 1812—for example, the USS *Constitution*'s ("Huzza, her sides are made of iron") sinking of HMS *Guerrière* and then HMS *Java*, as well as the capture of HMS *Macedonian* by the USS *United States*—begin this narrative. Commodore Oliver Hazard Perry's victory on Lake Erie and Maj. Gen. William Henry Harrison's rout of British Maj. Gen. Henry Procter at the Battle of the Thames in 1813, which undermined British power in the Old Northwest and shattered Tecumseh's confederacy, followed in close order. Sequential victories over the Duke of Wellington's veteran "Invincibles," who were released from their duties in Europe after Napoleon Bonaparte's abdication, occurred at the end of the war. These triumphs included the Battles of Chippewa ("Those are regulars, by God!"), Plattsburgh, Baltimore ("O! say does that star-spangled banner yet wave?"), and New Orleans. Maj. Gen. Andrew Jackson's victory at New Orleans was so surprising and lopsided—he suffered fewer than four hundred American casualties compared to more than two thousand for the British Army—that Americans in the first half of the nineteenth century celebrated its anniversary on January 8 as a second Independence Day.

Third, American negotiators at Ghent secured the victory when they successfully resisted British territorial demands that would have rolled back not only the Louisiana Purchase but also the original boundaries of the United States set by the Treaty of Paris in 1783. The peace negotiations, which lasted from August to December 1814, coincided with a series of British offensive amphibious operations: in Maine, aimed at clearing a land route to Quebec; in the Chesapeake, with substantial raids on Washington and Baltimore; and in the Gulf, focused on Mobile and New Orleans. These attacks were designed to relieve pressure on Canada, and from there the British planned a major attack through the historic invasion route via Lake Champlain in order to separate New England from the rest of the republic. For the Americans, the stout defense of Baltimore, which Francis Scott Key immortalized; the victory on Lake Champlain; and the resounding defeat of the British Army outside New Orleans quickly erased the British victory in Washington.

Anticipating success, British negotiators communicated with their American counterparts in notes that the latter described as "arrogant, overbearing and offensive," while one British newspaper summarized London's demands in a single word, "submission." The British insisted on a substantial Indian buffer territory in the Old Northwest, on boundary adjustments in Maine (a direct land route to Quebec) and what is now Minnesota (access to the Mississippi River), and on the U.S. demilitarization of the Great Lakes. They also declared that existing American fishing rights off Canada would not be renewed without a quid pro quo. These diplomatic demands coincided with American perceptions that Britain's fortunes had improved so much in Europe in 1814 that London might attempt to recolonize America or to pursue a military campaign that would lead to the dissolution of the United States.[2]

The members of the American delegation—John Quincy Adams, James Bayard, Henry Clay, Albert Gallatin, and Jonathan Russell—while often at odds with one another, outlasted their less capable counterparts. They rejected British demands, which President James Madison publicized by sending his envoys' dispatches to Congress. Members of the British opposition in Parliament criticized their government's terms, which were reduced in keeping with the principle of *uti possidetis*, whereby each country would retain the territory it occupied at the war's end. Again, the Americans refused these terms and arranged passage on a ship for home. London retreated in light of the lack of military progress in North America, the domestic protests over war taxes, and the specter of renewed hostilities in Europe. The British came to terms, and the Treaty of Ghent was signed on December 24, 1814.

The conclusion of the Second War of Independence saw an outpouring of patriotic pride and nationalism following the conflict. The war, in this version of the story, marked a turning point in the history of the young republic. People increasingly thought of themselves as "Americans," not simply as citizens of their individual states. A relatively brief but identifiable "Era of Good Feelings" ensued.

Mr. Madison's War

The story of Mr. Madison's War is decidedly different. In 1812, Federalist John Lowell, Jr., also known as the Boston Rebel, published a pamphlet titled "Mr. Madison's War: A Dispassionate Inquiry into the Reasons Alleged by Mr. Madison for Declaring an Offensive and Ruinous War against Great Britain." His tract criticized both Madison's justification for the war and its conduct. The narrative that carries this essay's name is a tale of inept statecraft compounded by a near total lack of military preparedness, poor strategy, and bad generalship. Madison, along with his dysfunctional cabinet and War Hawk allies in Congress, failed in his attempts to coerce the British by economic and then military means. And in the end, it was not so much special providence that saved the young republic as changes in European events that gave rise to the conflict with Britain (and very nearly France) in the first place.

The inept statecraft began with President Thomas Jefferson's decision to set aside the Monroe-Pinkney Treaty of 1806 whereby the British agreed to observe caution in the impressment of sailors and to not interfere with reexport trade in exchange for American benevolent neutrality. However, London's insistence on appending a note stating its intention to retaliate if the United States accepted the French "paper embargo" of Britain set forth in the Berlin Decree dissuaded Jefferson from submitting the treaty for ratification.[3] By refusing the accord, Jefferson chose commercial sanctions and war over peace and prosperity. In the run-up to hostilities in 1812, the Jefferson and Madison administrations embarked on a series of trade restrictions that failed to force Britain and France to respect American maritime rights.

As these economic measures failed, the Madison administration embarked on a "scarecrow strategy" intended to frighten London into concessions. At Madison's request, in late 1811 Congress passed measures that filled the ranks of the army, raised additional regulars and short-term volunteers, authorized the use of the militia, and increased the readiness of the navy. These measures were significant but failed to bring American forces to a level of preparedness required for a war and could not be completed in time for a spring offensive in 1812. Consequently, the country went to war before it was fully prepared, causing concern even among Republican legislators. Nevertheless, Madison's mentor and predecessor, President Jefferson, assured him that conquering Canada would be "a mere matter of marching."

Madison made two other missteps that reduced the chances of a diplomatic solution and increased the odds that, if war came, the country would enter it divided. First, he failed to replace the American minister in London who had returned to the United States in 1811 and consequently had no ranking diplomat present to report on declining support for the Orders in Council among the British political class. Second, in March 1812 Madison sent to Congress documents that he claimed constituted "proof of the Cooperation between the Eastern Junto [Federalists] & the Br[itish] Cabinet."[4] However, the administration, which had paid $50,000 to British agent John Henry for the papers, soon confessed that they could neither name any Americans involved in this purported plot nor produce Henry, who had fled the country after having been granted immunity. The net effect of the affair was Federalist outrage and Republican embarrassment. Not surprising, Madison failed to unite the Congress, or for that matter the country, behind the war effort. The votes in the House (79–49) and the Senate (19–13) for war were the closest ever in American history.

Madison's high command, moreover, was incompetent. Secretary of War William Eustis failed to execute his duties, the most important of which was competently directing his field generals. The latter included William Hull, who surrendered his army in Detroit in late 1812, and Henry Dearborn, who frittered away 1812 and saw his northern campaign the following year stall after capturing Fort George on the western bank of the Niagara River. The next secretary of war, John Armstrong, relieved Eustis of command and appointed Maj. Gen. James Wilkinson to head the next invasion. Like Dearborn, Wilkinson dallied in organizing a fall offensive down the St. Lawrence River, and it ended in the twin defeats at Crysler's Farm and Chateauguay.

What successes the Americans had in Canada under more competent generals—Henry Harrison's 1813 victory on the Thames and Jacob Brown's 1814 offensive across the Niagara River—never threatened Britain's hold on Canada. Indeed, after more than two years of campaigning with Canada as their central objective, American military leaders had achieved less than American forces had in the winter of 1775–1776, when they captured Montreal and laid siege to Quebec. Moreover, by the end of 1814 the British were on the offensive and in control of the American seaboard, launching amphibious invasions while blockading the coast.

While Britain's European affairs had originally pulled America into the war, they also ended it. British concerns about instability on the Continent—prescient given Napoleon's escape from Elba in early 1815—rather than the stubborn determination of American diplomats resulted in the Treaty of Ghent. The peace left unresolved the core issues that had led to the war. It devalued the importance of the Battle of New Orleans, which was fought while the signed treaty was making its way across the Atlantic for ratification, but Mr. Madison and his Republican-led Congress were all too happy to complete the document.

On the one hand, the Mr. Madison's War narrative is the tale of a "forgotten conflict" whose sacrifices and accomplishments pale in comparison to those of the Revolutionary War and the American Civil War. The strategic alliances that subsequent American and British statesmen fashioned in World Wars I and II and the even closer cooperation that evolved between London and Washington during and after the Cold War have also made the War of 1812 an inconvenient anachronism. As one historian noted in 1991, "Mr. Madison's war can never achieve the appeal of other wars in our history, such as the Revolution, the Civil War, and the two World Wars. This story of presidential ineptness, military incompetence, and internal party conflict has little of the epochal significant or dramatic appeal that attracted 15 million views to Ken Burns's marvelous documentary on the Civil War. Only a few determined specialists and history buffs will ever find the 1812 war of compelling interest."[5]

On the other hand, Mr. Madison's War has been recalled at key points in our nation's history as an object lesson on the dangers of inept diplomacy and defense planning. Nearly a century ago, John M. Stahl's *"The Invasion of the City of Washington": A Disagreeable Study in and of Military Unpreparedness* favorably compared President Woodrow Wilson's decision to strengthen the country's military forces in light of a major conflict in Europe with those of President Madison, who under similar circumstances did not. Similarly, Francis F. Beirne's *The War of 1812*, published shortly after the end of World War II, noted that "the War of 1812 teaches us that we should not neglect national defense to the point where a potential enemy will assume that we are so ill prepared we will not go to war under any circumstances. The enemy made that mistake in 1812 just as it did in 1917 and 1941."[6]

After two centuries, neither the Second War of Independence nor Mr. Madison's War has proven to be so compelling a narrative as to place the War of 1812 in a prominent position in American history. Both leave the War of 1812 in the shadow of other foundational conflicts: the American Revolutionary War that created the Union, the American Civil War that preserved it, and the world wars that turned the United States into a world power. By looking back to the Revolution, the idea of a Second War of Independence unavoidably minimizes the War of 1812 and the Treaty of Ghent, a document that is far less historically important than the Treaty of Paris in 1783. By focusing on the regrettable causes, conduct, and conclusion of the War of 1812, Mr. Madison's War fails to make a significant link to the larger and more successful national narrative that followed 1815.

However, two additional and alternative narratives can forge these links between the War of 1812 and subsequent national history. The first frames the War of 1812 as part of the Jeffersonian Revolution, or a "Second American Revolution" instead of a Second War of Independence. The other places the War of 1812 as the first in a series of wars of expansion that led up to the American Civil War. In this sense, the war should be called General Jackson's War, in recognition of its importance in the political era that bears his name, rather than as the object lesson in bad statecraft of Mr. Madison's War.

THE SECOND REVOLUTIONARY WAR

In this narrative, the War of 1812 is first and foremost a product of the Jefferson Revolution of 1800. President Thomas Jefferson described his election in 1800 "as real a revolution in the principles of our government as that of 1776 was in its form."[7] Similarly, President John Quincy Adams at his inauguration in 1825 captured the "revolutionary" character of the world when America broke away from Great Britain: "The revolutionary wars of Europe, commencing precisely at the moment when the government of the United States first went into operation under this Constitution, excited a collision of sentiments and of sympathies which kindled all the passions and embittered the conflict of parties till the nation was involved in war and the Union was shaken to its center."[8]

Jefferson's Republicans displaced the Federalists, who believed that they represented the natural aristocracy of society and doubted that ordinary people could play a direct role in governing the country. Jefferson's administration reversed the policies of his predecessor, John Adams, with regard to the National Bank, an oceangoing navy, and a professional army. Most important, the Republican Party gained majorities in the Senate and the House of Representatives that sustained Jefferson's and Madison's domestic and foreign policies, the latter being instrumental in the run-up to the first-ever declaration of war by the United States of America in 1812.

Like the Federalists, the Republicans believed that the United States should remain neutral in Europe's Napoleonic wars. However, they more firmly insisted on America's right to free trade with all belligerents and strenuously protested British impressment practices. The pursuit of these objectives in the absence of a national security strategy led to the War of 1812 after the Jefferson and Madison administrations exhausted efforts to defend American rights through diplomacy and embargoes. Both administrations wrongly believed that Britain was commercially dependent on the United States as a market for its manufactured goods and as a source of agricultural goods. When noncoercive measures failed, Madison and the Republican majorities in Congress had no choice but to declare war. As Gordon S. Wood notes, "They were compelled to go to war because their foreign policy left them no alternative."[9]

The conduct of the war was also revolutionary in the degree to which Madison held closely to Republican principles. He abstained from using executive privilege and resisted badgering Congress to obtain the resources needed to wage war. Madison also did not impose restrictions on political, civil, and religious rights. Faced with a real conflict, he did not resort to a Jacobin version of the Alien and Sedition Acts that were passed during the preceding Adams administration.

The run-up to the war and the conflict itself also paralleled and contributed to revolutionary changes in the character of the country. The population had doubled between the adoption of the Constitution and the end of the War of 1812. Within society, a new "middling" class had eclipsed the gentile aristocracy of the Enlightenment era. Economically, domestic manufacturing and trade increasingly displaced agriculture as the engine of growth, with one important exception: the proliferation of cotton mills combined with the acquisition of fertile land in the Southeast gave a second wind to the slavery-based agriculture that most observers at the time assumed would wither and eventually lead to emancipation. All of these changes forced Jeffersonian Republicans to rethink their basic concept of America as a yeoman society, free of the corrupting influences of commerce and large-scale manufacturing.

Thinking of the War of 1812 as a Second Revolutionary War is more than an exercise in semantics. The Second War of Independence narrative focuses on the political-military tensions that had existed between Britain and the United States since 1783. The Second Revolutionary War concept views the war as a product of the systemic economic and political changes that occurred in the United States during the first decade of the nineteenth century. In the Second War of Independence narrative, the critical origins of the war are external; in the Second Revolutionary War, they are internal. Rather than being a conflict over the imposition of British power on the fledgling republic, the War of 1812 can be seen as a conflict directly resulting from the emergence of Jeffersonian democracy.

THE WARS OF EXPANSION

As an alternative to the sad tale of Mr. Madison's War, the War of 1812 can instead be cast as the first of the American wars of expansion that were critical in transforming the original republic into Jefferson's continental "empire of liberty." The wars fought between the War of 1812 and the Civil War—the 1818 Florida War, the Texas rebellion, and the Mexican-American War—pushed America well beyond the territories that the 1783 Treaty of Paris had established and Jefferson's Louisiana Purchase supported. Concurrently, the Indian removal policies of the time consolidated those gains.

Perhaps because of its comparatively short national history, we prefer to think of America's wars as discrete affairs with definable beginnings and ends. However, now into the nation's third century, it is time to draw stronger connections between these conflicts. Such amalgamations of wars are not uncommon. Europe's Thirty Years' War bundled many wars fought between 1618 and 1648, the Napoleonic wars covered a number of separate conflicts punctuated by short-lived treaties, and later in the nineteenth century, the German Wars of Unification were three distinct conflicts between Prussia and Austria, Denmark, and France. Not too many years ago, President Richard Nixon also observed that the numerous wars and crises between the United States and the former Soviet Union from 1947 to 1989 constituted a "Third World War."

In a similar vein, viewing the wars of expansion that achieved the nineteenth-century goal of Manifest Destiny as a series of related wars highlights their individual and collective significance. As such, this narrative constitutes a more ambitious reconception of the War of 1812 and its place in American history. Those who characterize the first half of the century as the Age of Jackson might call these conflicts the Jacksonian wars. Indeed, in this telling, Mr. Madison's War becomes General Jackson's War for the future president's wartime exploits, the political capital they bestowed on him, and the impact of his presidency on the evolution of the United States.

To be sure, there is no consensus among historians regarding the War of 1812's place in American history as their recent books concerning the period illustrate. Sean Wilentz's *The Rise of American Democracy: Jefferson to Lincoln* focuses on the importance of political events, ideas, and leaders from 1800 to 1865, giving the war no particular prominence. Walter A. McDougall's *Freedom Just around the Corner: A New American History, 1585–1828* and *Throes of Democracy: The American Civil War Era, 1829–1877* use the election of Andrew Jackson, not the War of 1812, as a break point between the early republic and the run-up to the Civil War. In contrast, Daniel Walker Howe's *What Hath God Wrought: The Transformation of America, 1815–1848* begins with Andrew Jackson's victory at New Orleans and concludes with the Women's Rights Convention held at Seneca Falls, New York, surveying a period highlighted by the growth of the market economy, the awakened vigor of democratically organized Protestant churches and other voluntary associations, and the emergence of mass political parties. Similarly, George G. Herring's *From Colony to Superpower: U.S. Foreign Relations Since 1776* places the War of 1812 at the end of a fifteen-year period (1801–1815) where republicanism was "Purified, as by Fire."[10]

A few historians do argue for a broad chronology that begins with the War of 1812 and ends with the Mexican-American War. Robert Leckie's *From Sea to Shining Sea: From the War of 1812 to the Mexican War, the Saga of America's Expansion* provides a series of vignettes covering key events and personalities, but it neither tells a story nor provides a thesis. Walter R. Borneman's *1812: The War That Forged a Nation* makes this expansion a central theme:

> My chief goals here are to present a readable history of the War of 1812, place it in the context of America's development as a nation, and emphasize its importance as a foundation of America's westward expansion. Though frequently overlooked between the Revolution and the Civil War, the War of 1812 did indeed span half a continent—from Mackinac Island to New Orleans and Lake Champlain to Horseshoe Bend—and set the stage for the conquest of the continent's other half.[11]

The book concludes with a brief assessment of what the war accomplished, noting that the United States had become a force to be reckoned with in North America.

Other historical treatments also make this point. Kevin Phillips's *The Cousins' Wars: Religion, Politics, and the Triumph of Anglo-America* builds a continuum from the Great Revolution of 1666 to the American Revolution and the American Civil War by positing that they represented an ongoing struggle between two of the Anglo-American "cradle cultures"—the Puritans and the Cavaliers. Although he gives the War of 1812 and the other wars of expansion only passing treatment, Phillips notes that "west of the Appalachian Mountains an unmistakably new nation was taking shape" after the American Revolution and that "the 'War Hawks' tended to be from the South and West, from states like Kentucky, Tennessee, Georgia, and South Carolina." On that score, Robert Rutland's *The Presidency of James Madison* notes that while Manifest Destiny would be the rallying cry for the next generation, "as a political force it was first unleashed by the War Hawks of 1812."[12]

Walter Russell Mead's *Special Providence: American Foreign Policy and How It Changed the World* takes this assertion one step further by positing that Scots-Irish culture played a distinctive and major role in these conflicts. He, too, notes that the Scots-Irish who settled the backcountry of the Carolinas and Virginia went on to populate Alabama, West Virginia, Kentucky, Tennessee, Missouri, Texas, and Mississippi. The Scots-Irish, Mead writes, were a self-reliant and warlike people with a culture and outlook formed by centuries of conflict. Once in America, their descendants were dedicated to defending and expanding the frontier. Those who promoted the War of 1812 and the subsequent wars of expansion—Henry Clay, Andrew Jackson, Richard Johnson, Zachary Taylor, and James Polk—represented a distinct strain of American political culture. Recognizing these wars as a broad and continuous frontier conflict both sharpens and tightens Phillips's "Cousins' Wars" thesis and gives them equal prominence to the American Revolution and the Civil War. Along these lines, Frank Lawrence Owsley Jr.'s *Struggle for the Gulf Borderlands: The Creek War and the Battle of New Orleans, 1812–1815* observes, "The War of 1812 is usually considered to have ended in a draw, but the extraordinary luck and iron will of Andrew Jackson brought an American victory in one area. In the eyes of southerners and westerners, the conflict ended in a smashing victory for the United States."[13]

These works provide a foundation for a narrative of the War of 1812 as the first war of expansion that rests on three pillars. First, this interpretation recognizes that land was a factor (but not the key factor) that led the Madison administration and the War Hawks in Congress to attempt to resolve its disputes with London by invading Canada. Next, it notes that the War of 1812 was an important catalyst in the unintentional evolution of Jefferson's republic of limited means and ends into a national democracy replete with the military attributes of a normal state. Finally, it acknowledges that the war gave rise to historic personalities, primarily Andrew Jackson, who played leading roles in the expansion of the country. Jackson's campaigns in the War of 1812 and his victory at New Orleans set the stage for his Indian removal policies, his conquest of Florida, and his support for the annexation of Texas and the Mexican-American War that transformed the coastal republic into a continental empire.

The balance of evidence suggests that land was a contributing but not the foremost factor leading to the War of 1812. American rights on the high seas and the inept diplomacy on the part of the Madison administration were the primary causal factors.[14] Historian J. C. A. Stagg notes that Madison's focus on implementing economic diplomacy and depriving Britain of the fruits of trade with America were undermined once London developed triangular trade between the Britain, Canada, and the West Indies. The Royal Navy also increasingly relied on Canada for timber for its masts and spars once the wars in Europe threatened the Baltic trade. Moreover, Britain's preferred route through the Great Lakes and the St. Lawrence River for exports from the interior of the North American continent, bypassing the U.S. eastern seaports, added to Madison's concern. He came to believe that invading Canada, while Napoleon pursued his conquest of northern Europe, would compel London to yield to Washington's maritime demands.[15]

The argument that the War of 1812 was about the acquisition of Canada, for the land itself, rests in large part on an analysis of congressional behavior in 1811. Representatives of the Ohio Valley—from Indiana, Illinois, Kentucky, Ohio, and the western districts of Pennsylvania and Virginia—who met in the fall of 1811 at the Twelfth Congress, instigated the war. They represented an agricultural society without skill or resources where rudimentary farming and animal husbandry wasted the land and required settlers to move on, continuously bringing them into contact and conflict with Native Americans. With its abundant forests, which were not found on the plains of the Louisiana Purchase, and its rivers leading to the Atlantic, Canada was the logical next frontier.

Western congressmen did not hide their designs on Canada in debating the merits of war with Britain, whose maritime depredations on American sailors and ships did not give rise to support for war in the New England and Atlantic states, whose trade interests outweighed concerns about security or honor. Felix Grundy of Tennessee declared, "This war, if carried on successfully will have its advantages. We shall drive the British from our Continent. . . . I therefore feel anxious not only to add the Floridas to the South, but the Canadas to the North of this empire." The United States had taken control of West Florida in the spring of 1811 except for Mobile and was conspiring to seize East Florida (a scheme that Washington officially disavowed in early 1812). Richard Johnson of Kentucky added, "The waters of the St. Lawrence and the Mississippi interlock in a number of places and the Great Disposer of Human Events intended those two rivers should belong to the same people." The number of congressmen making such arguments prompted John Randolph of Virginia to observe, "Ever since the report of the committee on foreign relations [advocating war] came into the house, we have heard but one word—like the whip-poor-will, but one eternal monotonous tone—Canada, Canada, Canada!"[16]

Perceptions that the war would be short and successful aided the War Hawks' designs on Canada. Speaker of the House Henry Clay had boasted that "the militia of Kentucky are alone competent to place Montreal and Upper Canada at our feet," and Thomas Jefferson boasted that "the acquisition of Canada this year [1812] as far as the neighborhood of Quebec, will be a mere matter of marching; & will give us experience for the attack of Halifax the next, & the final expulsion of England from the American continent." Similarly, Senator John Calhoun assessed that Canada would be in the possession of American troops four weeks after the declaration of war. The press echoed these sentiments. One Ohio newspaper quoted another in Kentucky: "It would be a short campaign to expel the British from the Canadas and Nova Scotia."[17]

When Congress voted for war, it split along sectional and partisan lines. In the House, of the seventy-nine votes for war, forty-eight were from the South and West, fourteen from Pennsylvania, and only seventeen from other northern states. Of the forty-nine votes against the war, thirty-four were from the North, with only two from Pennsylvania and thirteen from the South. The Senate voted nineteen to thirteen for the war. In both houses of Congress, Republicans voted ninety-eight to twenty-three for the war, while all thirty-nine Federalists voted against it.

The prospective military liberators of Canada made high-minded proclamations to justify conquest by force of arms when they began their campaigns in late 1812. At the western end of Lake Erie, Gen. William Hull issued a declaration that read, "I tender you the invaluable blessings of civil, political, and religious liberty, and their necessary result, individual and general prosperity. . . ." At the eastern end, Brig. Gen. Alexander Smyth's proclamation told his troops that the Canadian people were not the enemy and they would soon be citizens. His proclamation read, "If we conquer, we will 'conquer but to save.'"[18]

Of course, the American invasions of 1812, 1813, and 1814 failed to liberate Canada. The attempts in 1812 were abject failures. The following year the Americans achieved tactical successes at York (Toronto) and along the Niagara frontier, as well as a strategic victory at the Battle of the Thames in Upper Canada, where Tecumseh's confederation fell along with Procter's command. But the only American thrust of strategic significance in Lower Canada during the three-year conflict failed miserably when Generals Wilkinson and Hampton quit their poorly coordinated efforts down the St. Lawrence. Major General Brown's summer campaign in 1814 again achieved tactical success at Chippewa, Lundy's Lane, and Fort Erie, but American forces retreated to U.S. territory at the end of the year.

Still, the desire to conquer parts if not all of Canada evidenced itself in American war plans and diplomatic efforts. Secretary of State James Monroe instructed the U.S. delegation at the peace talks in Europe to obtain, if possible, the cession of Canada. He also sent Col. Thomas Jessup, who commanded an army regiment in New Haven and knew many of Connecticut's leading Federalists, to Hartford in 1814 to suggest a plan to conquer Canada that first involved taking Nova Scotia. Monroe hoped to sway New England oppositionists with the prospect of an expansive maritime domain.[19]

Although the War of 1812 failed to gain territory for the United States to the north, it secured the Louisiana Purchase and the Northwest Territory won during the Revolutionary War. Wilentz notes that many Americans viewed the Louisiana Purchase as a Second Declaration of Independence. In this context, the War of 1812 was a Second War of Independence insofar as it secured the fruits of that second declaration. The war also expanded the amount of U.S.-held land available to European Americans. Tennessee governor Willie Blount in October 1813 argued that the removal of the Creek Nation would spur farming and commerce in the Southeast, noting that "each southern and western inhabitant will cultivate his own garden of Eden, and will, through the natural channels placed by a wise and just Creator, convenient for his use, export his own produce, and import such comforts . . . by the shortest routes of communication with the ocean."[20]

In support of this goal, Andrew Jackson followed his January 1814 victory at Tohopeka (Horseshoe Bend) with what he called a capitulation of surrender the following August with the Fort Jackson Treaty. The Creek Nation lost half of its land, or 23 million acres; the Cherokee Nation lost 4 million acres. As historian Robert Remini notes, Jackson had "converted the Creek civil war into an enormous land grab and ensured the ultimate destruction of the entire Creek Nation."[21] Just as Harrison's success on the Thames secured the Northwest, Jackson's triumphs in the Creek War and at New Orleans secured the Southwest. Both victories set the stage for continued migration in the 1830s and 1840s into the northern areas of Mexico, including Texas and California.

These conquests were made possible in large part because the U.S. military instituted reforms and efforts at professionalization that began during the War of 1812. As historian Donald E. Graves has observed, "The birthplace of the regular army is not at Valley Forge, but along the Niagara in 1814."[22] Between the Revolutionary War and the War of 1812, the government allowed the size and strength of the U.S. military to diminish and deteriorate. The Jefferson administration opposed a large standing military on both ideological and financial grounds. Having struggled to raise and maintain adequate forces during the war, President Madison broke with Jefferson's preference for a military based on militias and coastal gunboats. He noted in his 1815 message to Congress, "Experience has taught us that a certain degree of preparation for war is not only indispensable to avert disasters in the onset, but affords also the best security for the continuance of peace."[23] After the ratification of the Treaty of Ghent, acting secretary of war Monroe responded cautiously to a congressional request for his views on reducing the size of the military: "By the war we have acquired a character and rank among other nations which we did not enjoy before. . . . We cannot go back."[24] Monroe recommended a peacetime army of twenty thousand men, as well as maintaining the existing Corps of Engineers, and implicitly suggested leaving the bloated officer cadre at its then current strength. Congress agreed to a little more than twelve thousand men, or five thousand more than the U.S. Army had at the beginning of 1812.

When Monroe became president, Secretary of War John C. Calhoun reorganized the department; with congressional support he created positions for a surgeon general, quartermaster, and commissary general in the army staff located in Washington. Calhoun also regularized internal policies and procedures. He accepted Gen. Winfield Scott's offer to craft standard regulations for the army that were enacted in 1820, and he assigned the U.S. Army Corps of Engineers the task of supporting road and canal improvements and of constructing coastal forts.

The navy also made changes to its organization and fleet. The success of the few American frigates against their British counterparts early in the war made it clear that the country had seriously underinvested in naval power. In their wartime exchange of letters, former presidents Adams—a proponent of a large navy—and Jefferson, an opponent, noted the navy's success and the need for more ships. Jefferson wrote, "I sincerely congratulate you on the success of our little navy, which must be more gratifying to you than to most men, as having been the early and constant advocate of wooden walls." If only a few more such ships had been built, the war might have ended differently. Further, as Adams observed, "Without this [navy] our Union will be a brittle china vase."[25]

In early 1815, Congress established a Board of Navy Commissioners to prepare rules and regulations necessary for securing uniform vessels, equipment, and repairs. The board members, who carried the rank of commodore, had control over the navy yards and their associated contractors and agents. The creation of the board freed the navy secretary to focus his attention on strategy, personnel assignments, and vessel movements. In April 1816, Congress undertook a plan for the gradual and broad expansion of the navy that included nine ships of the line, twelve heavy frigates, and ten sloops.

Two of the nine "liners" served in the Mexican-American War. Returning from an unsuccessful diplomatic mission to Tokyo, the USS *Columbus* arrived off Monterey, California, on March 2, 1847, to support blockade operations against Mexico. The USS *Ohio* joined the bombarding fleet off Veracruz in March 1847. Some of its seamen and marines landed to man shore artillery in cooperation with the army assault that led to the city's surrender. Three hundred of its sailors and marines, led by fifteen officers, were transferred to the steam frigate USS *Mississippi* to participate in the successful expedition against Tuxpan. Later that year after rounding Cape Horn, the USS *Ohio* became the flagship of the commodore who was in charge of naval operations on the western coast of Mexico.

The war also produced military and national leaders who extended the boundaries of the United States. By far, the most important of these men was Andrew Jackson. When skirmishing began in late 1817 between Creeks and the U.S. Army on the Georgia-Florida border, President Monroe summoned Jackson to take command of the situation. Operating under vague (and possibly deniable) orders that he interpreted as presidential authorization to conquer Spanish Florida, Jackson began his campaign in March and forced the surrender of Pensacola, the capital of Spanish West Florida, in May. He sent the

Spanish governor and his garrison to Cuba, appointed a U.S. territorial governor, and returned to Tennessee. Jackson's execution of two British subjects and two Indian chiefs inflamed the congressional investigation of the "undeclared war" that followed. Henry Clay compared Jackson to Alexander the Great, Julius Caesar, Oliver Cromwell, and Napoleon in an act that Jackson never forgave. However, all of the congressional motions to criticize Jackson were defeated, and the people greeted the general as a national hero when he arrived in Washington.

Jackson continued his program of national expansion by championing the removal of Native Americans from their ancestral lands east of the Mississippi. Late in the Monroe administration, he supported the state of Georgia in its defense of the Indian Springs Treaty with the Creeks whereby the latter agreed to sell all of their Georgia lands and move west of the Mississippi. Federal commissioners and the tribe discovered that the head of the Creek delegation who had negotiated the treaty had been bribed; thus, the incoming Adams administration annulled the treaty. Although the crisis was defused when the Creeks signed a more favorable treaty, Jackson's political capital in the South was enhanced.

As president, Jackson supported Indian removal more vigorously. When a faction of the Cherokee Nation signed the Treaty of New Echota in 1835, exchanging their lands in Georgia for $5 million and land in Oklahoma, most Cherokees did not abandon their homes voluntarily. The U.S. Army rounded them up, placed them in detention camps, and then moved them west in a poorly planned and executed mass evacuation in the fall and winter of 1838–1839 that became known as the Trail of Tears. Earlier similar removals of Creek and Chickasaw tribes in Alabama and Mississippi had also featured fraudulent deals and army-organized removals, and had seen resistance in the 1836 Second Creek War. The Jackson administration's Indian removal policies also led to the Second Seminole War in Florida in 1835 and to the 1832 Black Hawk War in Illinois.

Howe highlights Jackson's personal involvement in Indian removal: "The treaty-making process was notorious for coercion and corruption, as Jackson knew from firsthand experience, and the new treaties concluded under his administration carried on these practices. . . . During the Removal process the president personally intervened frequently, always on behalf of haste, sometimes on behalf of economy, but never on behalf of humanity, honesty, or careful planning."[26] Howe also places Jackson's stand on this issue in a larger analysis equally applicable to U.S. designs on Canada in the War of 1812:

Indian Removal reveals much more about Jacksonian politics than just its racism. In the first place it illustrates imperialism, that is, a determination to expand geographically and economically, imposing an alien will upon subject peoples and commandeering their resources. Imperialism needs not be confined to cases of overseas expansion, such as the western European powers carried on in the nineteenth century; it can just as appropriately apply to expansion into geographically contiguous areas, as in the case of the United States and tsarist Russia. *Imperialism* is a more accurate and fruitful category for understanding the relations between the United States and the Native Americans than the metaphor of *paternalism* so often invoked by both historians and contemporaries (as in treaty references to the "Great White Father" and his "Indian children").[27]

Howe concludes, "Indian Removal set a pattern and precedent for geographic expansion and white supremacy that would be invoked in years to come by advocates of America's imperial 'manifest destiny.'"[28]

Jackson's territorial expansion later focused on Texas, which he saw as an opportunity to expand the slave-cotton plantation industry and to secure the southwestern frontier. In 1829, he made an unsuccessful effort to obtain Texas through diplomatic subterfuge. In 1836, Jackson offered to buy it from the discredited Mexican dictator Gen. Antonio Lopez de Santa Anna for $3.5 million, but authorities in Mexico City refused. Although he maintained formal U.S. neutrality in the war between Texas and Mexico, Jackson allowed American financial and matériel support to the American-led Texan rebellion. On his last day in office in March 1837, Jackson formally recognized the government of President Sam Houston and lobbied for the annexation of the Lone Star Republic after he left office.

Yet, Texas remained an independent republic for a decade after Houston imposed the Velasco agreement on the defeated Santa Anna following the Battle of San Jacinto in April 1836. Mexican forces withdrew only six months after Texans declared themselves to be independent of Mexico and less than two months after Stephen Austin and a Texas Convention proclaimed independence while Santa Anna besieged the Alamo. President Martin Van Buren's administration, which followed a conciliatory policy toward British Canada and Mexico, was also sensitive to the issue of adding Texas—a territory that might be divided into several states—to the Union, fearing it might disrupt the balance between slave and non-slave states.

The Texas government, meanwhile, played a double game with Washington and London. Its leaders pursued a goal of annexation that offered security and capital to resolve their national debt and offset the effects of the twin economic panics of 1837 and 1839. They also held out hope that the Lone Star Republic would expand to the Pacific and absorb other unstable Mexican states. Britain's financial and military support would be crucial for this more ambitious future. President John Tyler adroitly moved to check British influence and concluded the Webster-Ashburton Treaty of 1842, which resolved border issues with Canada west to the Oregon Territory and improved relations with London. His administration subsequently hyped British abolitionist designs in Texas and publicly argued for the annexation of Texas to secure southwestern slavery, promising Texans that Washington would send troops to defend the citizens against Mexico once a treaty of annexation was signed. The government of Texas agreed in April 1844. However, when the treaty went to the Senate, a letter declaring that the United States acquired Texas in order to protect slavery there from British interference accompanied it. This revelation sank the treaty in a 35–16 Senate vote in June.

The ensuing turmoil in the Republican Party over the slavery issue resulted in the candidacy of James Polk, nicknamed "Young Hickory" since he was a protégé of "Old Hickory" Jackson's. Polk's aggressive position on annexation was favorable in an election in which expansion was the dominant issue. The party's platform called for the "re-annexation" of Texas at the earliest opportunity, implying that Texas had been included in the Louisiana Purchase. Jackson publicly endorsed his friend Polk, adding that the United States must obtain Texas peaceably or forcefully. Northern Democrats also supported annexation, arguing that Texas would provide both a larger market and, in the long run, a venue for slaves to migrate south after cotton production had exhausted the soil of the Southeast. Henry Clay, the Whig candidate, warned that annexation would lead to war with Mexico and proposed amicable relations with British Canada and a sovereign Texas. Polk won the Electoral College handily but only a plurality of the popular vote, underscoring that the nation was as divided on the question of expansion as it had been on the War of 1812. Nevertheless, the new Congress narrowly passed an annexation treaty prior to Polk's inauguration, with the House voting 120 to 98 in favor and the Senate, 27–25. Outgoing President Tyler signed it into law.

With Texas a fait accompli in his mind, Polk continued the Jacksonian policy of expansion and set acquiring California as a key goal of his administration.

He worked toward a compromise with Britain on the Oregon Territory so that London would not come to Mexico's aid in any future conflict. Faced with an overzealous British envoy and some naval posturing, Polk threatened to terminate the joint occupation agreement. Congress endorsed his response, adding an amendment that urged an "amicable settlement." In May 1846 the British proposed extending the border on the forty-ninth parallel to the Pacific, excluding the southern tip of Vancouver Island. Within a month, Polk had a draft treaty ratified and on its way to London.

Polk simultaneously took military and diplomatic steps toward provoking a war with Mexico. In April 1845 he sent a naval squadron under Commodore Robert Stockton to Galveston, where Stockton began organizing an expedition of Texans into the disputed territory between the Nueces River and Rio Grande. He also ordered Brig. Gen. Zachary Taylor to cross into Texas in June with orders to treat a Mexican army's crossing of the Rio Grande as an act of war against the United States. That same month, Capt. John C. Fremont began a military expedition from St. Louis to California and arrived in December.

In the fall, Polk sent Louisiana congressman John Slidell to Mexico to declare that the annexation of Texas was nonnegotiable, to collect some $2 million in debts that Mexico owed to U.S. citizens, and to negotiate the purchase of California and/or New Mexico. Slidell was given the rank of minister plenipotentiary, making it difficult for the Mexican government to receive him. Doing so would resume diplomatic relations, which Mexico City refused to do so long as U.S. military forces still occupied what it considered to be Mexican territory. Slidell arrived in Mexico City in December 1845, only to be confronted with a change in government. He sailed home when the new regime refused to receive him. Polk sent Stockton around the Cape of Good Hope to California to encourage a revolution against Mexico, while U.S. naval squadrons prepared to blockade key ports on both sides of Mexico.

Ultimately, Taylor's demonstrations in the disputed territory provoked hostilities in April 1846. News of the fighting reached Washington as Polk was preparing a message to Congress urging it to declare war on Mexico based on its refusal to receive Slidell and pay its debts. On May 12 a combined war declaration and military appropriations bill passed the Senate 40–2, with its margin masking significant opposition. Eighteen Whigs and two senators from South Carolina, including John C. Calhoun, had opposed the war in procedural votes. The next day, Polk announced that the United States was at war with Mexico. The Mexican government did not issue a proclamation of resist-ance, or a de facto declaration of war, until July.

As in the War of 1812, American expectations of an early and easy victory were disappointed. Polk's strategy called for rapidly seizing Alta California and Neuvo Mexico and drawing up a treaty giving the United States legal title to the territory it had conquered.

Fremont assisted a U.S. emigrant rebellion that declared California inde-pendent on June 14, 1846, but Commodore John D. Sloat (USN) seized Monterey, California, on July 7 and proclaimed the annexation of California. In August, Gen. Stephen Watts Kearny's Army of the West captured Santa Fe unopposed.

Taylor's forces, however, did not take Monterey, Mexico, until September, after a hard fought battle. With his forces depleted and poorly supplied, he arranged an eight-week armistice that cost him Polk's confidence. Realizing that only a decisive campaign would compel the Mexican government to accept huge territorial losses, the administration abandoned hopes for a short, inexpensive campaign and backed an ambitious invasion from Veracruz on the Gulf of Mexico to Mexico City. Reluctantly, Polk put the army's senior general, Winfield Scott, a Whig, in command. After a brilliant and grueling campaign that foreshadowed the combat of the American Civil War and was, as Howe notes, "one of the monumental military victories of the nineteenth century," Scott raised the Stars and Stripes over the Zocalo grand plaza on September 14, 1847.[29]

It was Nicholas Trist, however, who secured the peace. Attached to Scott's headquarters, he presented a draft treaty to the Mexicans in August. Negotiations stalled in September when the Mexicans refused to accept Polk's minimal demands: California, New Mexico, and the Rio Grande as the border of Texas. Polk then added Baja California, a canal route across the Isthmus of Tehuantepec, and possibly territory as far south as Tampico to the U.S. list of demands. Some in his administration were also sympathetic to the bifurcated "All Mexico" movement that comprised a majority arguing for the total absorp-tion of Mexico and a minority of antislavery advocates whose plan would offer admission to all of Mexico's nineteen states where slavery had already been abolished. These new and presumably free states would send senators and rep-resentatives to Washington.

Polk recalled Trist in October, but the notification did not reach Trist in Mexico until November. He disobeyed Polk's instructions and offered the

Mexican government a peace based on the original set of U.S. territorial demands, reducing the amount paid for these territories from $20 million to $15 million. Faced with the prospect of harsher demands, the government accepted his terms and signed the Treaty of Guadalupe Hidalgo on February 2, 1848. Polk received word of the agreement in January and, although dismayed by Trist's actions, submitted the draft treaty to the Senate, which ratified it on March 10.

Polk added more territory to the United States than any other president had. Historians concur on the scope of his achievement. Howe writes, "His war against Mexico did more to define the nation's continental scope than any conflict since the Seven Years War eliminated French power between the Appalachians and the Mississippi." Similarly, McDougall writes of the Mexican conflict, "Most obviously, the war displayed an impatient expansionism."[30]

Both statements equally apply to the War of 1812. That war defined America's northern border just as Polk's war did its southern border. The War of 1812 was the last major conflict between the United States and Britain (albeit for London, it was a sideshow of the titanic struggle between Britain and France in Europe), and it led to a long-lasting security agreement to limit warships on the Great Lakes and fortifications along the Canada-U.S. border. The historic invasion route along Lake Champlain from Quebec to New York that British generals James Wolfe, John Burgoyne, and George Prévost traversed was never used again. The characterization of "impatient expansionism" also readily applies to the War of 1812. The War Hawks' designs on Canada in 1812, occurring less than a decade after President Jefferson's Louisiana Purchase, and Harrison's and Jackson's efforts to acquire Indian lands show a blatant lack of patience on the part of a growing nation that lacked an adequate or competent military establishment.

In conclusion, casting the War of 1812 as the first link in a chain of conflicts raises rather than diminishes its importance. Commemorations of the war's bicentennial remind people of the specific issues, battles, and negotiations that shaped the war's beginning and end. However, by placing those events in this broader context, the War of 1812 can be viewed as leading an expansion that was more durable and important than either the false steps and failures of Mr. Madison's War or the perceived triumph over British forces that contributed to a Second War of Independence. This territorial expansion created by the War of 1812 and its associated conflicts is as significant as the Revolution, the Constitutional Convention, and the combined impact of the

Civil War, emancipation, and the subsequent return of local rule to the former states of the Confederacy.

It should be noted that this narrative of expansion is not a restatement of Frederick Jackson Turner's "frontier thesis."[31] Turner cast the frontier as he defined it—that is, as an area of free land that served as the key variable in America's movement to the West. Geography, in his analysis, triggered a demographic advance whose political, economic, and social results began at the end of the seventeenth century. The wars of expansion thesis covers a much shorter period and notes that land was a secondary causal factor in the origins of the war that transformed Jefferson's republic and elevated leading personalities, particularly Jackson, to national prominence. It places these individuals and their strategic-political interests and calculations—particularly American concerns about British and Spanish interests—as the significant drivers of the expansion. It also notes that the expulsion of the Native Americans was not preordained. Without the War of 1812 and its legacy, American history would have blazed a different path.

---◆ 2 ◆---

A CLASSICAL VIEW OF
THE MILITARY BALANCE
IN THE WAR OF 1812

Thucydides noted in his history of the Peloponnesian War that conflicts are fought for three core reasons: fear (security), interest (wealth), and honor (prestige, sovereignty). For the United States, honor—more specifically, London's acknowledgment of its rights as a sovereign state—trumped interest and fear. The slogan "Free Trade and Sailors Rights" provided an ideological justification to declare war to protect the nation's honor. The War Hawks' interest in conquering Canada was primarily a means to an end, although American legislators and generals said more about the benefits of additional territory than did President James Madison's government. However, the New England maritime states, whose shipping industry suffered more from the British and French "paper" blockades, preferred the resumption of commerce and diplomatic settlement with London to a costly war that disrupted the immense trade they had come to enjoy during the Napoleonic wars in Europe.

U.S. leaders did not fear a British attack given London's preoccupation with its campaign in Spain and wavering allies on the Continent. Politicians and military officers from the western states expressed concerns over British-inspired and enabled Indian attacks on the frontier, concerns that were substantiated in November 1811 when British-made arms allegedly were discovered at Prophetstown in the Indiana Territory after the Battle of Tippecanoe. However, this issue was a comparatively minor item on the list of American grievances against Britain, whose officials in Canada urged restraint on their Indian allies because they wished to avoid war with the United States while their army was preoccupied in Europe.

For the British, the War of 1812 was an offshoot of their global war against Napoleon's French Empire. London feared that Paris would not only establish and maintain control over the European continent but also invade the British Isles and seize its overseas territories. The British viewed their antagonistic relationship with the United States through this prism. Washington's efforts to assert its rights on the high seas interfered with British maritime supremacy, which was its main strategic advantage over France. Maritime supremacy was also tied to maintaining Britain's effort to finance and support its military operations and key allies through international trade; thus, it became an important secondary reason London risked war with Washington. Once hostilities began in 1812, British honor came into play, particularly after the U.S. Navy scored surprising ship-to-ship victories in 1812 and after American attacks on Upper Canada resulted in the burning of public buildings in York (Toronto) and the town of Newark (Niagara on the Lake) in 1813.

American and British offensive and defensive operations alternated throughout the war. The centerpiece of the Madison administration's strategy in 1812 was to launch a three-pronged attack into Canada from Detroit, Buffalo, and northern New York State. This tactic was not so much a coherent plan as an amalgam of political imperatives originating with provincial Republican leaders, including Speaker of the House Henry Clay, New York governor Daniel D. Tompkins, and Buffalo congressman Peter B. Porter.[1] Conversely, Governor-General Sir George Prévost adopted a defensive strategy that husbanded Canada's limited men at arms to defending Lower Canada, specifically Montreal and Quebec. He ordered Maj. Gen. Isaac Brock in Upper Canada to maintain a defensive posture and retreat if necessary since reinforcements were out of the question. The Americans' plans failed miserably in 1812. William Hull, as well as Stephen Van Rensselaer and Alexander Smyth, respectively, launched attacks on the left at Detroit and in the center across the Niagara River while Maj. Gen. Henry Dearborn made a late and purely demonstrative thrust on the right and north of Albany.

With John Armstrong replacing William Eustis as secretary of war, American operations in 1813 could be summed up as, "If at first you first do not succeed, try, try again." On the left, Maj. Gen. William Harrison wisely deferred winter efforts to retake Detroit and remained largely on the defensive until Commodore Oliver H. Perry's flotilla on Lake Erie engaged and defeated its British counterpart in September. Harrison then pursued Gen. Henry Procter and Tecumseh's forces, defeating them at the Battle of the Thames in October. In the center, Dearborn attacked York in May and sailed to capture Fort George on the Niagara River. The British counterattack at Beaver Dams and the seesaw race for supremacy on Lake Ontario between British commodore James Yeo and American commodore Isaac Chauncey foiled American plans to advance around Lake Erie to Burlington. On the right, Armstrong brought Maj. Gen. James Wilkinson and Maj. Gen. Wade Hampton up from their southern military districts to command the two wings of an October assault down the St. Lawrence River to Montreal. This campaign, the only American effort in the War of 1812 to cut the central line of communication between Lower and Upper Canada, failed. Before the campaign Armstrong selected northern New York as the winter quarters for the army, suggesting that he had little faith that the offensive would succeed. He continued the strategic ineptitude of the preceding year.

British strategy in 1813 remained focused on defending Upper Canada, which Prévost fulfilled by defeating Wilkinson and Hampton. However, the British also aimed to take advantage of American battlefield failures and bring the fight to U.S. soil in the form of limited offensives aimed at American weak points. In the West, Procter and Tecumseh took advantage of Hull's defeat to invade Ohio. While successful against the tactically careless Brig. Gen. James Winchester in January at the Battle of the River Raisin, their attacks against Forts Meigs and Stephenson proved unsuccessful. British efforts to defend Upper Canada achieved mixed results, losing western Ontario to Harrison but regaining Fort George and capturing Fort Niagara in December. In the North, the British failed in their attacks on the U.S. naval base at Sackets Harbor, New York. Rear Adm. George Cockburn's invasion of the Chesapeake Bay in April spread panic, but Vice Adm. Sir John Borlase Warren's attack in June on Norfolk (Carney Island), Virginia, failed. In the Southeast, the British and their Spanish allies in Florida supported the Red Sticks faction under William Weatherford in the Creek civil war. The opening Battle of Burnt Corn Creek in July and the subsequent attack on Fort Mims in August gave way to a wider conflict across Alabama that culminated in the Battle of Tohopeka (Horseshoe Bend) in March 1814. Historian Francis Beirne summed up the strategic importance of the campaign for the British by noting, "At the cost of a small quantity of powder and shot dealt out to the Indians at Pensacola by their Spanish allies they had succeeded in distracting the attention of 15,000 troops that could have been put to more effective use elsewhere."[2]

In 1814, the roles of strategic offense and defense reversed. After two years of war, American leaders had reprioritized Thucydides's trilogy of concerns. Their fear of a British invasion from Canada or the Royal Navy's gaining control of the sea had replaced concerns over honor and interest. With troops freed up by Napoleon's abdication in the spring of 1814, the British launched major offensive operations in North America. In July, the British seized a hundred miles of the Maine coast, giving them a direct land route to Quebec. In late August, Prévost invaded northern New York State with ten thousand men and reached Plattsburgh, where he hurried a newly formed flotilla on Lake Champlain into battle. The American victory, echoing the Battle of Saratoga in the Revolutionary War, left Prévost worried about his supply line from Canada, and he ordered a retreat.

Concurrently, Vice Adm. Alexander Cochrane led the British invasion fleet that entered the Chesapeake Bay in August 1814 and landed some four thousand troops at Benedict, Maryland. Under Adm. George Cockburn and Maj. Gen. Robert Ross, the British troops destroyed a trapped gunboat flotilla; fought a brief battle at Bladensburg against a composite force of seven thousand militiamen, sailors, marines, and soldiers; and proceeded to capture Washington in four days before marching back to Benedict.

The British next attacked Baltimore. Senator Samuel Smith, a major general in the Maryland militia, organized a well-prepared defense anchored on Fort McHenry that rebuffed the British and killed Ross. After being refitted and reinforced in Jamaica, in December this British force landed near New Orleans, where Andrew Jackson had cobbled together a mixed force of regulars, militiamen, volunteers, and pirates. Jackson's immediate counterattack and successful defense against two British assaults in early January 1815 proved to be the last major ground combat of the war, albeit after the Treaty of Ghent had been signed on the preceding Christmas Eve.

American offensive operations in 1814 consisted of an invasion across the Niagara River in July aimed, once again, at forcing the British back to Burlington or possibly farther. Maj. Gen. Jacob Brown's army achieved notable tactical successes at the Battles of Chippewa and Lundy's Lane and mounted a spirited defense at Fort Erie against British units that had fought in Wellington's Iberian campaign. But when the fighting stopped in November, the Americans retreated across the Niagara, having achieved nothing of strategic value.

In addition to targeting each other's military forces and territories, both sides conducted attacks on civilian populations and economic targets throughout the war. Some occurred when military discipline failed: American soldiers burned public buildings in York, and British troops (Chasseurs Britanniques, recruited from captured French soldiers) sacked Hampton, Virginia. However, the worst of these attacks were deliberate and took place along the Niagara frontier in late 1813 and early 1814, beginning with the Americans' burning of the town of Newark in conjunction with the troops' retreat from Fort George. The British responded by sacking Lewiston, Black Rock, and Buffalo on the other side of the river. That attack, in turn, led the Americans to burn the town of Dover on Lake Erie's northern shore in May 1814. In October and November 1814, Gen. Duncan MacArthur launched a raid from Detroit up the Thames River, south to Dover, and back to Detroit. He laid waste to homes, barns, and mills, making it impossible for any large British force to sustain itself in the area.

Although the British used the American attacks in Canada to justify their own attacks in the Chesapeake Bay, Admiral Cockburn's campaigns there in 1813–1814 were a deliberate effort to intimidate the American populace as he punished any community that showed the slightest resistance. As he told the citizens of Havre de Grace, Maryland, "You shall now feel the effects of the war."[3] In contrast, Cockburn's and Ross's burning of public buildings in Washington in August 1814 was not accompanied by widespread attacks on civilians or looting.

Former president Thomas Jefferson proposed both retaliation and escalation in suggesting that the Americans sponsor attacks on civilian targets in Britain: "Perhaps the British fleet will burn New York or Boston. If they do, we must burn the City of London, not by expensive fleets or Congreve rockets, but by employing an hundred or two Jack-the-painters, whom nakedness, famine, desperation and hardened vice, will abundantly furnish from among themselves."[4] "Jack-the-painter" was a reference to James Hill, alias John Aitkin, who sympathized with the colonial rebels during the American Revolutionary War. With financial assistance from the American minister in Paris, Hill had gained employment at the British naval yard at Portsmouth, where he then set fire to a warehouse in 1776. He was captured the following year and hanged.

MAJOR FACTORS

The key factors that determined which goals were attained and which strategies succeeded also differed on the American and British sides of the ledger. Sun Tzu's five major and five minor factors for gauging relative military strength serve as a useful framework for taking stock of these relative advantages and disadvantages.[5] The major factors consist of national leadership, geography, weather, generalship, and rules (doctrine). The five minor factors include quantity of troops, quality of troops, discipline (punishment and rewards), administration, and training.

The British held a decided advantage in the first of Sun Tzu's major factors, leadership. The contrast between the two nations was stark. Robert Banks Jenkinson, Second Earl of Liverpool, became prime minister after the assassination of his predecessor, Spencer Perceval, on June 8, 1812, days before the U.S. Congress declared war on Great Britain. Serving as prime minister for fourteen years, Liverpool guided Britain through the end of the Napoleonic Wars and the Congress of Vienna, which established the basis for a century of relative peace in Europe. Liverpool used his considerable political skill to manage the liberal and reactionary wings of the Tory Party, which included highly capable ministers. In particular, Lord Castlereagh, who served as foreign secretary for ten years, pursued a successful policy of engagement on the Continent and helped bring about the Treaty of Ghent. That said, the British ministerial system left considerable room for competition between the foreign secretary, the home secretary (internal defense), and the war secretary over strategy and the disposition of forces.

In contrast, President Madison led a divided and unprepared country into a war of choice. Madison, father of the Constitution, is generally considered to have been a relatively weak president who did not effectively manage his cabinet. He chose many of his cabinet secretaries because they represented key states or factions in his party. Many of these men were incompetent or frequently at odds with one another. Madison's first secretary of war, William Eustis, resigned in January 1813 after America's early battlefield losses. His successor, John Armstrong, then resigned in August 1814 after the British captured Washington, whose defense Armstrong neglected because it would have diverted forces from the Canadian front. Similarly, Madison's first secretary of the navy, Paul Hamilton, resigned in 1813. Finally, as commander in chief, Madison in his first term largely perpetuated Jefferson's preference for a small standing army and navy. His meager efforts to step up war preparations in November 1811 left the country dependent on poorly trained militiamen and volunteers for the first two years of the war.

Geography, the second factor, operationally favored the defense—that is, Britain in 1812–1813 and the United States in 1814. Strategically, however, geography favored the United States with its interior lines of communication. Moving and provisioning large numbers of troops across the continent had bedeviled armies in the French and Indian War and the American Revolutionary War. British historian John Keegan observed that armies fighting in North America "could rarely achieve preponderance at a decisive point, and they were often too weak absolutely to exercise power over the enormous distances at which the sheer scale of North America required them to operate."[6] The British were also handicapped regarding their geographic knowledge of Europe and North America. Their only repository for maps was in the Drawing Room in the Tower of London, which proved unhelpful even for British forces on the European continent.[7]

U.S. forces used inland waterways and roads to reach the frontiers and as necessary, particularly in Ohio and Alabama, built new roads and supply depots. Unfortunately for the British, an ocean separated Canada from the British Isles, and east–west transport in Canada depended on waterways, principally the St. Lawrence River and the Great Lakes, which lay perilously close to the American frontier. The distance between Detroit, the site of the first major battle of the war, and London was sixty-five hundred miles. Supplies generally took four to six months to arrive, and Canadian subsistence agriculture could barely support the population much less thousands of additional British troops. In particular, the distance from the manufacturing base in the home islands made achieving and maintaining naval superiority on the Great Lakes exceedingly difficult for the Royal Navy. The Duke of Wellington noted this key factor in his devastating assessment of British prospects in late 1814 when he was offered command of British forces in Canada, observing that his presence in North America would only prove that Prevost was right in retreating from Plattsburgh, and delay negotiating a peace agreement:

> Till that superiority is acquired, it is impossible . . . to keep the enemy out of the whole frontier, much less to make any conquest of the enemy. . . . The question is, whether we can acquire this naval superiority on the Lakes. If we can't I shall do you little good in America; and I shall go there only to prove the truth of Prévost's defence, and to sign a peace that might as well be signed now.[8]

Weather, perhaps the most important of what Sun Tzu referred to as "cyclic natural occurrences," also favored the defense given that winter (and the lack of ample supplies on both sides) shortened the campaign season along the American-Canadian border. Washington amplified this disadvantage in 1812 and 1813 by launching key offensive operations relatively late in the season. Hull's advance on Fort Malden occurred late in the summer, and winter storms marred Van Rensselaer's and Smyth's attacks across the Niagara River in

October and November 1812. Storms also hit in late 1813 when Wilkinson advanced down the St. Lawrence. Although Brown's summer offensive the following year began in July, the retreat to Fort Erie and the subsequent unsuccessful British siege lasted into November when conditions caused the Americans to demolish the fort and retreat across the river to Buffalo.

Harsh field conditions combined with the climate to reduce the effectiveness and longevity of soldiers. The Canadian historian Donald Graves notes that deaths from illness were twice as high as deaths from combat in the American Army. With regard to specific conditions in the area that was the cockpit of the war, he writes, "Given the unsanitary conditions of the time, the Niagara area, with its hot, humid summers, and cold wet winters was an unhealthy place."[9]

Weather also confronted British offensives in 1814. When General Ross's troops disembarked at Benedict and began their advance in Maryland, the hot, humid summer gave them more trouble than the enemy did. These veterans of the Iberian campaign confessed that they had never felt anything equal to southern Maryland on an afternoon in August. Their retreat from Washington was also accelerated by a severe summer storm that knocked men from their horses and tore roofs off buildings. Walter Lord writes of the severity of the storm, "Nobody could remember anything else that came near it—the crashing thunder, blinding rain, the howling lashing wind." These same units and the reinforcements that joined them later that fall in Jamaica experienced unusually extreme winter weather during the expedition to New Orleans. One officer described the rain as "such as an inhabitant of England cannot dream of, and against which, no cloak could furnish protection" and the cold as having deadly effect on West India regiments. The men "to whom frost and cold were altogether new fell fast asleep and perished before morning."[10]

Canadian historian Wesley B. Turner provides a useful framework for assessing the strengths and weaknesses of generalship on both sides of the conflict. Turner notes that the characteristics of good generalship during the Napoleonic period included martial qualities (e.g., courage) and professional skills, knowledge of the "art of war," and the ability to exercise civil leadership.[11] These faculties are roughly comparable to Sun Tzu's list of key traits of wisdom, credibility, benevolence, courage, and discipline. Based on his criteria, Turner ranks the five British generals who commanded Upper or Lower Canada and assigns each a dominant attribute. In descending order they are:

Audacity, Maj. Gen. Isaac Brock: As the civil and military commander of Upper Canada, Brock brought combat experience and an ability to "lead from the front," both of which were critical in defeating the American attacks from Detroit and the Niagara frontier in 1812. Brock also exercised competent civil administration through his understanding of the class-based political system of Upper Canada. However, his death at Queenston Heights less than six months after the beginning of the war leaves an open question as to how he would have coped against a more competent American adversary in 1813 and 1814.

Persistence, Lt. Gen. Gordon Drummond: Having assumed command of Upper Canada in December 1813, Drummond faced the improved American forces. He, too, demonstrated aggressiveness by capturing Fort Niagara and making plans to reconquer Detroit. In the following summer of 1814, Drummond ordered his forces to counterattack General Brown's men and showed determination in holding the high ground at Lundy's Lane, where he was seriously wounded. His pursuit of the American retreat was methodical and prudent, but he did not anticipate that the Americans would make a stand at Fort Erie.

Prudence, Maj. Gen. Roger Hale Sheaffe: His victory at Queenston was his first and only victory in the war. Although he proved to be a competent civil and military administrator after taking command of Upper Canada following Brock's death, he resisted taking any offensive operations across the Niagara River. His unsuccessful defense of York in April 1813 irrevocably tarnished his reputation.

Disappointment, Lt. Gen. George Prévost: Governor-general of Canada and military commander of Lower Canada, Prévost lacked combat experience and was inflexible in responding to operational contingencies. His decision to retreat from Plattsburgh, which led to his removal as governor and to his court-martial, detracted from his overall successful defense of Lower Canada. He also failed to inspire either his soldiers or citizens, although he was a competent administrator.

Detachment, Maj. Gen. Francis de Rottenburg: Replacing Sheaffe as the civil and military commander of Upper Canada, General de Rottenburg served for seven months until Drummond arrived in December 1813. On his watch, the British lost the Battle of Lake Erie and the Battle of the Thames, and U.S. military forces unsuccessfully attempted to attack Montreal by moving down the St. Lawrence. His principal concern was to preserve the army rather than taking aggressive action, and he provided his subordinates with little guidance.

Vice Adm. Alexander Cochrane, who assumed the position of commander in chief of the Halifax and West Indies naval stations in March 1814, should be added to the bottom of this list as "ambitious." He extended the British naval blockade to include New England and oversaw the amphibious operations against Washington, Baltimore, and New Orleans. Cochrane regarded the Americans as a "whining, canting race" and argued that attacks on these cities would halt American operations against Canada. That prediction proved false. Moreover, the assaults on Baltimore and New Orleans were rebuffed with the loss of both field commanders—Maj. Gen. Robert Ross and Maj. Gen. Edward Pakenham. British historian Jon Latimer judges that the Battle of New Orleans was an unmitigated disaster brought on by Cochrane's desire to sack the city. He quotes J. W. Fortescue's *History of the British Army*: "The callous manner in which he deliberately placed the troops in a most dangerous situation and then worked his faithful blue-jackets to death to keep them there—all with the principal object of filling his own pockets—cannot be too strongly condemned."[12] Pakenham also contributed to the defeat by underestimating the cohesion of the American forces opposing him and believing, as was the case at Bladensburg, their ranks would break in the face of a determined attack.

In a ranking of senior American generals similar to Turner's listing of British general, it is striking that the three most capable—Brown, Harrison, and Jackson—began the war as militia generals, whereas the less impressive Dearborn and Wilkinson were experienced but aging Revolutionary War veterans. This situation is not surprising given the low opinion observers of the time had about senior officers in the U.S. Army. The *Boston Gazette* complained during the Jefferson administration that "beardless boys who belch beer and democracy" had replaced experienced veterans. Similarly, Winfield Scott recalled, "Many of the appointments were positively bad, and a majority of the remainder indifferent."[13]

Performance, Maj. Gen. Jacob Brown: Undoubtedly the best senior American commander in the War of 1812, General Brown exhibited a performance that was consistently above that of other American generals and of his British opponents as well. As a New York State militia general at the beginning of the war, he successfully defended Sackets Harbor against an attack that Prévost led in May 1813 and earned the rank of brigadier in the regular army. Later that year, during the Battle of Crysler's Farm, he launched a successful attack that drove the British forces from their strongpoint below the rapids on the St. Lawrence. In 1814, he led the invasion across the Niagara River and bested British regulars in three consecutive engagements: Chippewa, Lundy's Lane, and Fort Erie. Though wounded in the second engagement, he returned to his besieged army at Fort Erie and orchestrated a surprise attack on the British artillery batteries, after which Drummond withdrew. Although the campaign achieved little of strategic importance, it proved that the U.S. Army could go toe-to-toe with Britain's best and helped offset the psychological impact of the British capture of Washington, D.C.

Patience, Governor William Henry Harrison: As governor of the Indiana Territory, Harrison won the Battle of Tippecanoe only seven months before Congress declared war in June 1812. He was a natural candidate to replace Hull as the Northwest commander, and when Kentucky selected him as a major general for the state militia, it sealed his federal appointment. Harrison showed patience in preparing his offensive to retake Detroit and to invade the Ontario peninsula between Lakes Michigan and Erie. He built and defended a series of forts in Ohio and consulted with Commodore Oliver Hazard Perry, whose victory in September 1813 quickly led to Harrison's advance into Canada. In less than a month he caught and defeated Gen. Henry Procter's and Tecumseh's combined forces at the Battle of the Thames. To be sure, many Republicans in the East regarded Harrison's patience as timidity in not striking quickly to regain Detroit in 1813. A Virginia newspaper, for example, likened him to an incompetent watchmaker, "always winding up, but . . . never striking."[14] Harrison's victory at the Battle of the Thames secured the Northwest and proved to be the only conquest of Canadian soil to last through the war. Harrison's efforts all but decided the question of the Northwest's boundary and rendered moot British demands for an Indian buffer state. Harrison resigned when Secretary of War John Armstrong passed him over in favor of Maj. Gen. James Wilkinson for command of the northern expedition against Montreal later that year.

Pluck, Andrew Jackson: Jackson began the war as a major general in the militia of his home state, Tennessee. By force of personality and without any previous military experience, he led more than a thousand volunteers to Natchez and back to Nashville in the winter of 1812–1813, earning him the nickname Old Hickory. After the massacre at Fort Mims, Jackson again led the Tennessee militia to Alabama and mounted a campaign that led to the defeat of the poorly armed Red Sticks at the Battle of Tohopeka (Horseshoe Bend). Jackson was then awarded both a regular commission in the U.S. Army as a major general and command of the Seventh Military District. His subsequent efforts to repulse the first-line British forces at New Orleans with a composite force of regulars, pirates, volunteers, and militiamen made him a national hero and legend. However, some historians, such as Henry Adams, assert that

Jackson's decision to divide his forces between Mobile, where he thought the British would land and then march west, and the Crescent City marred his defense of the city. This lack of focus on New Orleans angered Madison, Monroe, and Louisiana governor William Claiborne. Even after shifting his attention back to New Orleans, Jackson found his defenses nearly undone because he failed to post adequate numbers of sentries along the bayous, one of which the British used to advance within a few miles of the city. Jackson was fortunate that the British commander did not immediately march on New Orleans. Concurrently, his heavy-handed imposition of martial law on New Orleans was the most extreme measure infringing on state authority that a federal officer adopted during the conflict and provoked considerable resentment.

Disappointment, Maj. Gen. Henry Dearborn: Based on his experience as a Revolutionary War officer and as secretary of war in the Jefferson administration, Dearborn was given the senior-most command in the U.S. Army for the Northeast at the beginning of the war. Dearborn's missteps in 1812 eliminated any chance that U.S. forces would fulfill Jefferson's prediction that Montreal would be taken that year. When he heard that the British had repealed the Orders in Council, Dearborn concluded an armistice with Prévost on August 9 that only lasted for less than one month before President Madison terminated it. Combined with his delay in assembling a force capable of offensive operations—a task for which he received little help from New England's governors even while he tread lightly to avoid provoking anti-Republican reactions—Dearborn ensured that the 1812 strategic plan for concurrent offensive operations from Detroit, Buffalo, and New England was stillborn. He was also hazy about whether his command extended to the Niagara frontier, where Gen. Stephen Van Rensselaer and Brig. Gen. Alexander Smyth launched independent sequential and unsuccessful attacks. Although he offered to resign at the end of the year, Madison refused, and now under the guidance of Secretary of War John Armstrong, Dearborn commanded the attacks on York and Fort George in the spring of 1813. The success of those operations belonged to his subordinates—Brig. Gen. Zebulon Pike, Jr., and Col. Winfield Scott—but were marred, respectively, by the burning of the public buildings in York and by Dearborn's order to stop pursuing the British retreating from Fort George. Dearborn was relieved of command in July. Stagg offers an additional insight into Dearborn's disappointing performance: "He had failed not so much because he was a bad soldier—indeed, his fighting skills, whatever they were, we never really tested—but because he was an ineffective politician who could not serve his two constituencies in Washington and in Massachusetts. In trying to help his fellow New Englanders too much, he helped his country not at all."[15]

Dereliction, Maj. Gen. James Wilkinson: Commander of the Seventh Military District, headquartered at New Orleans, at the beginning of the war, Wilkinson had participated in a series of scandals: the Revolutionary War Conway Cabal to remove George Washington as commander of the Continental Army, the (Aaron) Burr Conspiracy to create an independent republic in the Mississippi River Valley, and misconduct in 1809 and 1811 that was investigated. He immediately quarreled with Andrew Jackson but did succeed in quickly occupying Mobile and West Florida. However, when Armstrong tapped Wilkinson to take command of the Northeastern Command in May 1813, he traveled slowly and did not arrive at Sackets Harbor until August. After two more months of poor planning and fractious behavior toward his erstwhile subordinate, Maj. Gen. Wade Hampton, he finally launched the invasion down the St. Lawrence in October. Wilkinson sedated himself with whiskey and laudanum in the face of illness and poor weather, although biographer Andro Linklater judges that "the frustration of seeing the last chances of success being relentlessly chipped away must have done more damage to his temper than any drug."[16] The campaign proved to be a complete failure when the American forces suffered defeats at the Battles of Chateauguay and Crysler's Farm. Wilkinson made one more attempt to invade Canada in March 1814 but was rebuffed at La Colle Mills. He was removed from command and traveled to Washington to answer charges of conduct unbecoming an officer, drunkenness, encouraging disobedience of orders, and neglect of duty. As an appropriate exclamation point on his career, Wilkinson offered the administration his services when British troops approached the capital in August, but Madison kept a relative novice, Brig. Gen. William Winder, in charge of the city's defenses. Wilkinson was acquitted of all charges in March 1815.

How the British and American officers fared against each other suggests that generalship favored the United States over the course of the war. Brock, Britain's best, was victorious over Hull, America's worst in 1812. Similarly, middle-ranked Prévost successfully defended against Wilkinson, America's worst in 1813. However, Dearborn and Winchester defeated Sheaffe and Rottenburg in 1813, and Brown's offensive in 1814 succeeded against Drummond. Finally, Jackson in New Orleans defeated the invading Cochrane and Pakenham in 1815.

The rules or doctrines that the American and British forces followed during the war were essentially Napoleonic age improvements on the linear tactics of the seventeenth century. In most cases, the battle plan involved massing and moving lines of musket-armed infantry, supported by artillery and cavalry. Effective tactics consisted of organizing troops on the battlefield (formations), moving them to an advantageous terrain or position relative to the enemy, massing weapons fire, and reacting to or anticipating situations on the battlefield. By combining these elements—the Napoleonic wars being a laboratory for constant innovation and assessment—military officers attempted to achieve a local advantage over the enemy in combat. In part because of their numerical inferiority early in the war, British commanders were more innovative and successful in their tactics than their American counterparts were. However, they made costly errors at Baltimore and New Orleans, where they underestimated the American forces based on the poor showings of U.S. regulars and militias elsewhere. On balance, though, the British had an edge on this score.

Given the frontier terrain that most of the war was fought on in the west, south, and north, battles often took place along rivers and near fortifications that served as strongpoints and depots. Flanking movements were commonly used to unhinge the enemy's linear formations and avoid frontal assaults, such as Hampton's unsuccessful maneuvers at Chateauguay, Scott's movements at Chippewa, and Ross's rout of American forces at Bladensburg. Also effective were surprise night attacks: the British attacks at Stoney Creek, Canada, and River Raisin in Michigan Territory and their capture of Fort Niagara, as well as Jackson's preemptive strike on the initial British landing force outside New Orleans. Adequately manned fortifications held out against determined assaults on most occasions, with the capture of Forts George and Niagara being rare exceptions.

That both British and American land forces during the War of 1812 consisted of regular forces, militias, and Native Americans is worth noting. The latter combined their approach to war with European technology. Traditionally, the Indians balanced military objectives with their desire to minimize casualties and to provide warriors with an opportunity to demonstrate their skill and bravery. Often used as light infantry, they excelled, having learned to hunt, stalk, and shoot from an early age. Historian Carl Benn's *The Iroquois in the War of 1812* captures this difference in European and Native American approaches to war by quoting Black Hawk, a Sauk veteran of the war:

I explained to them the manner the British and Americans fought. Instead of stealing upon each other, and taking every advantage to kill the enemy and save their own people, as we do (which, with us is considered good policy in a war chief), they march out, in open daylight, and fight, regardless of the number of warriors they may lose! After the battle is over, they retire to feast, and drink wine, as if nothing had happened.[17]

The British used their Indian allies' established reputation as ferocious warriors who were unwilling to adhere to European conventions in ruses that led to the surrender of numerically superior American forces at Detroit and Beaver Dams. The presence of Senecas at Queenston Heights also caused hundreds of American soldiers to desert. Indian attacks on Fort Dearborn, Fort Mims, and Frenchtown not only added to their reputation but also later contributed to political support for harsh Indian removal policies.

MINOR FACTORS

Sun Tzu's five minor factors—quantity of troops, quality of troops, rewards and punishments, administration, and training—provide a more tangible, and in some cases quantifiable, measure of British and American military forces during the War of 1812. The quantity of troops favored the British throughout the war. In 1812, the British Army had a little less than 10,000 troops in North America compared to almost 12,000 for the United States, of which 5,000 were recruits. Native Americans allied with the British numbered around 10,000 troops compared to 2,000 troops for the Americans. Militias in Canada consisted on paper of some 60,000 soldiers in Upper Canada, 11,000 in Lower Canada, and some 15,000 in the Maritime Provinces for a total of 68,000 "boots on the ground," but many were "ill-armed and without discipline."[18] Some 50,000 American militiamen were called to duty in 1812, usually for six-month periods and often with restrictions on fighting outside the United States. The continuous competition between state and federal authorities for available manpower, enshrined in the Constitution's division of responsibilities for the defense of the country, constantly imperiled the American war effort. By the end of the war, several states enacted legislation to create state armies in light of Washington's inability to provide for an adequate defense. Given that the British strategy was largely defensive through 1813 and the American strategy largely offensive, the force ratio favored the British. By the end of 1814, the British Army had approximately 48,000 troops in North America compared to some 46,000 in the U.S. Army, including 3,000 rangers and 10,000 volunteers.

The quality of troops in terms of combat experience also favored London. The British Army was well into its reform and rebuilding effort when Washington declared war. It had grown from almost 40,000 men in 1793 to more than 250,000 at the end of 1812, with 65,000 combat veterans under Wellington in Spain, or more soldiers than the U.S. Army had at any point during the war. Unlike American soldiers, who served for fixed enlistment periods, British soldiers normally enlisted for life. And even though approximately 10 percent of that force needed to be replaced each year, the British Army did not experience the high turnover that the U.S. Army did. Desertion was so common that President Madison issued a proclamation in October 1812 pardoning those who returned within four months.

Rewards and punishments were much the same in both armies. Neither side resorted to conscription despite their significant security threats, making inducements or rewards for enlistment a critical tool in recruiting soldiers. Congress offered a $31 bounty and 160 acres of land to encourage enlistments at the beginning of the war, eventually raising them to $124 and 320 acres. Peer pressure and corporal punishment—and when necessary, executions in peace and war—enforced military discipline. For example, Sheaffe and Brock executed seven deserters in 1803 while Jackson executed six ringleaders of a Tennessee militia mutiny in September 1814. Although severe by today's standards, such measures were not uncommon, but better commanders used them with moderation. Wellington noted, "From the time I entered the army it was the desire of every commanding officer I have ever seen, and who knew his duty, to diminish corporal punishment as much as possible."[19]

Administration, or the organization of the army to maintain itself and support its operations, was more developed in Britain than in the United States but was by no means satisfactory in either country. Several British ministries shared responsibilities in this regard: the secretary of war and colonies; the master general of ordnance; a Transportation Board and a commissary general, both responsible to the first lord of the Treasury; and a commander in chief responsible to the king rather than to Parliament. A key shortcoming was the lack of any coherent organization for sustaining troops in the field. The British Army never developed an efficient logistics system for maintaining armies in the field during the war. Indeed, the Royal Army Service Corps was not established until 1855.

American military administration, in contrast, was in its infancy and sorely neglected, leaving the states to act as local quartermasters when the war began. Throughout the conflict, federal and state officials often assumed each others' responsibilities in making ad hoc arrangements to feed, clothe, and arm their troops. The War Department was poorly organized and understaffed with only eleven clerks, all of whom had less than a year's experience. The secretary of war oversaw the provision of the army's subsistence by soliciting competitive bids for rations, leaving the department dependent on the integrity of contractors and their employees. The purveyor of public supplies in Philadelphia, who relied on handbills and newspaper advertisements to draw bids from manufacturers, purchased equipment. Congress in March 1812 created a redundant Commissary General's Office with little positive effect. Callender Irvine, who accepted the post, described the supply system as "totally inefficient and so rotten in all its parts as not to admit to being patched."[20] Congress also created a Quartermaster's Department and an Ordnance Department in the run-up to the war, but neither functioned well, leaving the army without adequate support.

As for the last minor factor, British historian Richard Glover notes, "It is likely that no one reform . . . did more to make the British army an effective force than this steadily applied system of training."[21] The British had a key advantage in this area, ironically by virtue of their experience in the American Revolutionary War, where the need for light infantry and skirmishers followed a number of tactical experiments that took place in Europe during the first half of the eighteenth century.[22] In 1788, Col. (later field marshal sir) David Dundas published *Principles of Military Movements* based on his own experiences. However, in 1792, King George III decreed that an abridgement of the book, *Rules and Regulations for the Formations, Field Exercises, and Movements of His Majesty's Forces*, should be the standard drill manual for all infantry battalions in the British Army. In comparison, the U.S. military entered the war with three doctrinal manuals. The most widely used manual after the Revolutionary War was Gen. Friedrich von Steuben's *Blue Book*, which had been adopted in 1799. Early in 1812, the War Department, however, required the regular army to use General Smyth's *Regulations for the Field Exercises, Manoeuvres, and Conduct of the Infantry of the United States*, an abridged translation of the French 1791 regulations. Also available was William Duane's *Handbook for Infantry*, a more truncated version of the French regulations that the U.S. Army formally adopted in 1813. The militias, however, were not as well trained or led in many cases, and their employment of European military doctrine was uneven.

Figure 1 summarizes the comparative advantages of the American and British land forces in the War of 1812 and shows a major net advantage for Britain. Once the American strategy of quickly conquering Canada failed in 1812, the impact of these advantages steadily accrued to the British. Nevertheless, the conflict ended in a draw, underscoring how fortunate the young American republic was in this "strange" conflict.

FIGURE 1. KEY FACTORS: COMPARATIVE ADVANTAGES		
AMERICAN	**MAJOR FACTORS**	**BRITISH**
	Leadership	X
X	Geography	
	Weather	X
X	Generalship	
	Rules (Doctrine)	X
	MINOR FACTORS	
	Quantity of Troops	X
	Quality of Troops	X
X	Rewards & Punishments	X
	Administration	X
	Training	X

NAVAL FORCES

American and British operations on the high seas were quite different. The Royal Navy had a decided advantage in numbers with 607 active naval vessels, plus auxiliaries, against the U.S. Navy's 16 ships, which were augmented by several dozen coastal gunboats. U.S. warships were few in number (thanks to Jefferson's preference for small coastal gunboats) and achieved remarkable success early in the war, but by 1814 the increasingly effective British blockade left them largely confined to port. U.S. frigates, brigs, and sloops did considerable damage to British commercial shipping though not enough to be a major factor in the outcome of the conflict. However, the U.S. Navy allocated sufficient men and matériel to support naval operations on Lakes Ontario and Erie, leading to the capture of York and Fort George and to the defeat of Procter and Tecumseh after Perry's victory on Lake Erie.

As Wade G. Dudley points out in *Splintering the Wooden Wall: The British Blockade of the United States, 1812–1815*, the British did not use their numerical superiority effectively.[23] Because of the war in Europe, the Admiralty chose to position few ships in the western Atlantic and gave its commands at Halifax and Bermuda low priority for supplies and manpower. London compounded this error by insisting on its terms in diplomatic exchanges with Washington but not backing its demands with military power. Subsequently, the mistakes in force allocation, the blockade's gradual expansion, the competing objectives, and the command conflicts systematically undermined the blockade. British warships blockaded the U.S. coast at first in the south and then extended their operations to encompass New England by 1814. In addition to supporting amphibious operations along the coast, they also convoyed merchant shipping from the Indies to Europe and attempted to hunt down American warships and privateers.

Tactical combat proficiency was a critical issue in 1812 when British warships opted to engage in one-on-one combat with the U.S. Navy's Humphreys frigates. The frigates enjoyed advantages in overall size, firepower, crew size, and sea worthiness. Dudley observes that the British risked going up against the frigates because they had a low opinion of the U.S. Navy and because their operational code accepted combat, even on disadvantageous terms, to avoid the taint of cowardice and court-martial associated with running from an engagement. Strategically, the early U.S. ship-to-ship victories over HMS *Guerrière*, *Java*, and *Macedonian* provided a public rallying point and boosted support for the war in the wake of the disastrous invasions of Canada at Detroit and Niagara.

Admiral Warren's replacement by Admiral Cochrane in 1814 further strained the blockade, which had been extended to cover New England as larger raids were planned in the Chesapeake Bay and the Gulf of Mexico. Although the British easily bottled up most of the U.S. Navy's warships, those that escaped were more often than not successful in taking prizes and destroying British shipping. Resources spent on containing American warships in American ports could not be used to protect merchant shipping, which fell prey to American privateers and merchantmen carrying letters of marque. U.S. Navy and other vessels took nearly seventeen hundred prizes during the war, totaling some $45 million in losses to British vessels and cargoes.

NARRATIVES

The narratives of Mr. Madison's War and the Second War of Independence address the factors identified by Thucydides and Sun Tzu, but each gives greater emphasis to particular factors. However, when combined, their complementary assessments provide a more holistic military analysis of the war. Regarding Thucydides's causes of war, Mr. Madison's War asserts that the administration and the War Hawks in Congress weighed the country's "interest" in seizing Canada to deprive Britain of a critical market and source of naval stores. They placed this interest above that of preserving U.S. maritime trade with Europe by negotiating or acceding to British terms on impressment and London's blockade of France and its allies because doing so would have sacrificed the country's "honor." This narrative also suggests that Madison saw the need to defend the national honor on this issue after giving London sufficient time to lift its Orders in Council and to stop seizing American seamen for service in the Royal Navy. The Second War of Independence narrative shares this point of honor but emphasizes the Americans' "fear" of British-inspired attacks by Native Americans along the frontier and British designs on New Orleans, East and West Florida, and the inland areas of the sparsely populated Southeast.

The balance of American advantages and disadvantages in military capability is also different in these narratives. Mr. Madison's War's criticisms of American war planning and execution reflect the overall balance favoring Britain across Sun Tzu's major and minor factors for gauging relative military strength. This interpretation places greater emphasis on the poor leadership that Madison and his cabinet demonstrated, the U.S. military's general lack of understanding of the rules of warfare, and the weak generalship that American field commanders such as Dearborn, Hull, Wilkinson, and Winder exhibited. American shortcomings across Sun Tzu's list of minor factors also underscores this narrative's critique of American military competence. Finally, Mr. Madison's War credits geography—specifically, Britain's distance from its possessions in North America and its involvement in Europe—for London's decision to accept the terms that American negotiators proffered in Ghent.

The Second War of Independence thesis rests largely on American advantages in generalship as embodied by Brown at Sackets Harbor; Harrison at the Thames; George Izard at Lake Champlain; Jackson at New Orleans; and Smith at Baltimore. These victories also showed how American commanders had instilled a greater appreciation of the rules of war among their subordinates and troops. Scott's training of his troops prior to the 1814 campaign across the Niagara River and Jackson's use of spoiling attacks and a well-fortified line supported by artillery to defeat the British at New Orleans stand in marked contrast to Smyth's futile attempts to invade Canada in 1812 and Winchester's defeat at Frenchtown in 1813. The importance of generalship also foreshadows the key roles that many of these officers—particularly, Brown, Harrison, Jackson, and Scott—played in subsequent decades as the country continued to expand and consolidate its newly won territories.

3

INVASIONS OF 1814 AND 1863

The concurrent bicentennial of the War of 1812 and sesquicentennial of the American Civil War provide a unique opportunity to compare two prominent campaigns—Maj. Gen. Jacob Brown's invasion of Upper Canada in 1814 and Gen. Robert E. Lee's invasion of Pennsylvania in 1863. These campaigns were the final attempts of the James Madison and Jefferson Davis administrations, respectively, to invade their neighboring opponent and set the stage for peace negotiations on favorable terms. The American Left Division and the Army of Northern Virginia (ANV) faced parallel challenges as they made their way across enemy territory with the aim of creating the military conditions for a negotiated settlement. Brown's division, numbering twenty-three hundred soldiers, crossed the Niagara River on July 3, 1814, and withdrew from Canada on November 5 after a four-month campaign. Lee's army of eighty thousand men left its positions along the Rappahannock River in Virginia on June 3, 1863, and retreated across the Potomac River on July 19, concluding a six-week campaign.

These campaigns emerged from the grand strategies pursued by the United States and the Confederate States of America, whose military and political leaders expected them to have a decided impact on the prospects for a diplomatic solution to their conflicts. Brown's and Lee's plans reflected the overall military strategies of their presidents' administrations and the critical failures regarding unity of command, respectively, between General Brown and Commodore Chauncey and between General Lee and Maj. Gen. James Ewell Brown (Jeb) Stuart. Their initial engagements (Chippewa and Brandy Station), their flanking maneuvers and direct assaults at the main engagements (Lundy's Lane and Gettysburg), and their retreats and pursuits (Fort Erie and Williamsport) provide a framework for comparing the inception, execution, and conclusion of these campaigns.[1] Moreover, their levels of success and places in their wars' respective narratives—Mr. Madison's War and the Second War of Independence for General Brown and the Confederacy's Lost Cause for General Lee—offer additional points of comparison.

WAR AND PEACE

When Brown crossed into Upper Canada and Lee into Maryland, their governments hoped that military success would bolster their chances for a negotiated settlement. Neither the Madison administration nor the Davis administration thought force of arms alone could attain their key war objectives. In 1814, for instance, America's and Britain's long-standing flirtation with a negotiated settlement served as a backdrop to Brown's invasion as the United States had been largely unsuccessful in its efforts to conquer Canada during the preceding two years.

In 1812, the British repealed their Orders in Council soon after the U.S. Congress narrowly passed its declaration of war. Negotiations for a cease-fire failed later that year when the British refused to end the practice of impressment. Madison subsequently sent a delegation to St. Petersburg in March 1813 in response to a Russian offer to mediate the dispute. London privately rejected its ally's offer. British foreign minister Lord Castlereagh ostensibly signaled Britain's peaceful intentions in a letter offering direct negotiations to Secretary of State James Monroe in November 1813. Gothenburg, Sweden, was to be the venue for these talks, but the end of the war in Europe the following spring made talks in Ghent more convenient. By the time the American and British delegations met on August 8, 1814, Brown's campaign had peaked, and British forces were en route from Europe to North America with great expectations of success.[2]

In contrast, in what would prove to be yet another of the Confederacy's sporadic and unsuccessful efforts, Davis sent Lee into Maryland and Pennsylvania with a plan for initiating peace talks. In February 1861, members of the Peace Convention called by Virginia attempted to reach a compromise on the issues threatening disunion before Congress adjourned in March. They met with President-elect Abraham Lincoln the day he arrived in Washington, but they could not produce a proposal that would command a majority in Congress. Now, Davis thought that a military victory would strengthen the peace movement in the North and might impress European powers into intervening or at least mediating the conflict.[3]

Lee on June 10 warned Davis that the South could not afford to neglect, and to the extent possible should shape, "the rising peace party of the North." Davis concurred, having received a wire from Confederate vice president Alexander H. Stephens offering to initiate talks over prisoner exchanges and hoping for wider discussions with the Lincoln administration. Davis ordered Stephens to Richmond with the aim of attaching him to Lee's army as a peace commissioner who could readily capitalize on the general's anticipated battlefield successes. Stephens balked at the idea of joining Lee, moving the potential venue for talks to the Virginia Peninsula. However, by the time the Confederate vice president requested a meeting with the Lincoln administration on July 4, Lee's prospects for a successful campaign had disappeared.[4]

MILITARY STRATEGY

Washington and Richmond designed their respective 1814 and 1863 campaigns to avoid enemy positions of strength in the east and to attack to the west. The Madison administration ordered Brown to cross the Niagara River, to march around the eastern end of Lake Ontario from Burlington to York, and then head to Kingston, the center of British military and naval power in Upper Canada. The Davis administration accepted Lee's stratagem to break contact with the Army of the Potomac on the Rappahannock, march up the Shenandoah Valley, cross into Pennsylvania, and engage Union forces in a series of decisive battles that would relieve pressure on Richmond and threaten Washington. Both plans critically depended on the cooperation of a detached force: Brown needed Commodore Chauncey's fleet to control Lake Ontario and to provide logistic support, while Lee depended on Major General Stuart's cavalry to supply information on the strength, location, and movements of the Union army.

When Madison's cabinet met on June 7, 1814, the men rejected the notion of a direct assault on British and Canadian defenses around Montreal. They had no desire to repeat Maj. Gen. James Wilkinson's unsuccessful invasion down the St. Lawrence in late 1813. The cabinet agreed on a four-part offensive. Commodore Arthur Sinclair, commanding U.S. naval forces on Lake Erie, would sail to Lake Huron and destroy a shipyard the British were building on Georgian Bay. Brown would invade Upper Canada at Long Point on Lake Erie (with Sinclair providing transport), march on Burlington Heights, and recapture the Niagara Peninsula before advancing to York. Concurrently, new gunboats built at Sackets Harbor at the eastern end of Lake Ontario would harass the British supply line on the upper St. Lawrence River, and Maj. Gen. George

Izard's Right Division at Plattsburgh, New York, would make a demonstration toward Montreal to dissuade the British from reinforcing units opposing Brown's advance. Izard, however, disliked Secretary of War John Armstrong and expressed this view to Monroe while threatening to resign, thus creating a division in the American high command similar to what had occurred between Major General Hampton and Major General Wilkinson in 1813.[5]

Brown's success ultimately depended on whether Chauncey's fleet at Sackets Harbor on Lake Ontario could defeat or blockade British commodore James Yeo's fleet based at Kingston. In addition to needing Chauncey's ships to protect his lines of communication, Brown also required them to transport his siege cannons and supplies. Brown conveyed his expectations to Chauncey, saying, "I shall consider the Lake as yours, the moment you have your new vessels in condition to appear on it." Brown also asked, "When will you be out and if I may expect you in the neighborhood of Fort George by the 10th of July? on what day?"

Chauncey, however, replied that he had no intention of immediately supporting Brown's invasion:

> I shall proceed in quest of [British Cdre.] Sir James [Yeo] and offer him battle if he accepts the invitation. I shall either go to Kingston [as prisoner if defeated] or be at leisure to cooperate with you upon any enterprize [sic] against the enemy. But if Sir James pursues the policy that he did last Year of avoiding a general action I should be obliged to watch his movements to prevent his doing mischief. I shall therefore be governed by circumstances if he visits the head of the lake with his fleet you may expect to see me there also if he returns to Kingston I shall remain in this vicinity to watch his movements.[6]

Subsequently, Secretary of War Armstrong informed Brown that Sinclair would not be providing transport to Long Point, putting the effort against Burlington on hold. Armstrong recommended an attack on lightly defended Fort Erie as an alternative. Brown's two senior subordinates—Brigadier Generals Winfield Scott and Eleazer W. Ripley, respectively commanding the First and Second Brigades—had opposing views of this option. Scott, an aggressive commander, urged Brown to begin the invasion before Chauncey's arrival. Ripley, a more cautious officer, urged him to wait until the fleet arrived. Brown weighed their advice and decided not to wait for Chauncey, believing that the invasion, even if not totally successful, would "restore the tarnished military character of the United States."[7] Brown's decision to begin the operation with only Chauncey's conditional support, and the conflicting styles of Scott and Ripley, would have an enormous and detrimental impact on the campaign.

President Jefferson Davis, Secretary of War James Seddon, and General Lee attended the meeting in which the ANV hammered out its strategy for the invasion of Maryland and Pennsylvania on May 15, 1863. In the preceding days, Lee had summoned his trusted corps commander, Lt. Gen. James Longstreet, to the army's headquarters at Fredericksburg. Longstreet had been advocating taking two divisions or more from the ANV west to join forces with Gen. Braxton Bragg's army in central Tennessee. He envisioned engaging Maj. Gen. William Rosencrans's Union forces that were threatening Chattanooga and then breaking Maj. Gen. Ulysses S. Grant's siege of Vicksburg. Lee argued that splitting the ANV would force him to retire to Richmond and that supporting such a westward march would be a logistical nightmare. Even under optimum circumstances, Longstreet and Bragg would not reach Vicksburg in time.

Lee wanted to keep his army intact, maneuver around the Union's Army of the Potomac, and strike northward. He noted that the ANV had fought five "fruitless" major engagements—on the Virginia Peninsula and at Second Manassas, Sharpsburg, Fredericksburg, and Chancellorsville—where it had suffered heavy losses, gained no ground, and watch defeated Union forces slip away to fight again. He argued that a northern campaign was an opportunity to take the strategic initiative, engage the enemy at a time and place of his choosing, and as Longstreet later wrote, "either destroy the Yankees or bring them to terms."[8]

Lee saw this campaign as the ANV's only option since the Confederate army would never gain parity in numbers or matériel with the Union army. His intelligence sources reported that Maj. Gen. Joseph Hooker was being reinforced, and Lee judged that his current location on the Rappahannock River was not a good position for another battle. However, if he could move to more favorable ground and engage the enemy, Lee was confident of success based on his assessment that Hooker was demoralized after his defeat at Chancellorsville and that the Union army was likely to be weakened by the infusion of newly conscripted soldiers. Lee also reckoned that an invasion would give the army an opportunity to replenish its food stocks by living off the rich farmlands in western Maryland and Pennsylvania.

Lee's march began by deceptively disengaging from Hooker's army and swinging northeast through the Shenandoah Valley, across the Potomac River, through Maryland's panhandle, and into Pennsylvania. The river between the opposing armies and the forested wilderness to the west of Fredericksburg helped conceal the ANV's initial movements. Lee chose as his assembly point the village of Culpepper, twelve miles south of the Rappahannock and to the right of the Army of the Potomac. Lee moved Longstreet's I Corps (each corps had three divisions) and then Lt. Gen. Richard S. Ewell's II Corps, while temporarily holding Lt. Gen. A. P. Hill's III Corps entrenched along the river to keep Hooker's army fixed and to protect Richmond. Lee was confident that once his army had moved north enough to threaten Washington, Hooker would pull back, leaving Hill free to rejoin the invading force.

Lee planned to use Stuart's cavalry division—with five cavalry brigades and six batteries of horse artillery, the largest Confederate cavalry force ever assembled—to screen his army's northward march, which began on June 3. After the initial disengagement from the Union forces was complete, this mission changed after Lee and Stuart met on June 18 at Paris, Virginia, east of Ashby's Gap. Lee instructed Stuart that if the enemy moved north in pursuit, the cavalry should move into Maryland to guard Ewell's right flank and to gather intelligence. Stuart was also ordered to "collect all the supplies you can for the use of the army." This directive came through Longstreet, who—with Lee's approval—also suggested to Stuart that his division "pass by the enemy's rear if he thinks he may get through."

Lee then sent an order to Stuart to leave two brigades to watch the Blue Ridge passes and take the remaining three brigades if Hooker "remains inactive" but to pull back through the passes and cross the Potomac with the rest of the army should Hooker "not appear to be moving northward." Stuart ignored this ambiguity and followed the concluding language in Lee's order: "You will, however, be able to judge whether you can pass around their army without hindrance, doing them all the damage you can, and cross the river east of the mountains. In either case, after crossing the river, you must move on and feel the right of Ewell's troops, collecting information, provisions, &c." On June 25, Stuart took three of his brigades and set off for Pennsylvania, riding around Hooker's army. He did not contact Lee for eight critical days. His failure to communicate with Lee on the Union forces' movements undermined the central premise of Lee's strategy—that is, that he would engage the Army of the Potomac at a time and place of his choosing.[9]

First Contact

In the initial battles of these two campaigns, the defending British and federal forces attacked without sufficiently massing their forces because they were unaware of the strength of the approaching American and Confederate invaders, who were victorious at Chippewa and Brandy Station, respectively. However, while the invading American Left Division's morale rose after defeating an equally matched British force in 1814, in 1863 the defending federal cavalry forces' morale improved after they proved their mettle against Stuart's renowned mounted troopers.

On July 3, 1814, the Left Division cast off from the eastern shore of the Niagara River at 2 a.m. and by noon had invested its initial objective, Fort Erie. The British commandant of the fort sent word of the American landing to his superior, Maj. Gen. Phineas Riall, at Chippewa. Then, despite the willingness of his officers to fight "to the last extremity," he surrendered his 137 men and the fort. This response was "rather too soon perhaps to satisfy the claims of military etiquette," according to Brig. Gen. Peter B. Porter of the New York militia, commanding Brown's Third Brigade.[10]

Riall, unaware of the fort's surrender, was surprised the following day at sunset when Scott's brigade approached his position on the north bank of the Chippewa River where it emptied into the Niagara. Riall ordered his engineers to drop the bridge across the Chippewa, and his artillery fired at the approaching Americans. Scott withdrew a few miles south to make camp and was joined by the rest of the Left Division. Riall sent out his Indian and militia scouts to reconnoiter the American camp the next morning, and they set off several hours of prolonged sniping and skirmishing. Convinced that his force of nearly two thousand British regulars, Canadian militias, and Indians was qualitatively superior to the equal number of Americans to his front, Riall ordered the bridge repaired and his troops readied for a sortie at 3 p.m. As they formed their battle line on the south bank of the Chippewa, the British encountered Porter's Third Brigade, which had successfully driven the Canadian and militia skirmishers from the woods to the west of the American encampment and the plain to its front. The ensuing firefight delayed Riall's deployment but pushed Porter's force back. By 4:30 p.m., Riall's force was drawn up on the plain and marching toward the American position.

The intense skirmishing in the wood prompted Brown to order Scott's brigade forward, and Riall, upon seeing the advancing gray-clad column, judged them to be poorly trained militiamen who would not stand and fight. Riall deployed his three infantry battalions in line for attack; this force was anchored on the left by his artillery, which had opened fire on the advancing American brigade. As Scott's First Brigade marched forward in a steady and disciplined fashion, with the Ninth, Eleventh, and Twenty-Second Infantry Regiments heading straight forward as well and the Twenty-Fifth angled toward the woods, Riall recognized his error and famously declared, "Why, those are regulars." As the opposing lines closed to a hundred yards, Scott ordered the U.S. artillery-men to turn their attention away from the British artillery and toward the infantry. He also ordered his infantry to fire. Shortly thereafter, the commander of the Twenty-Fifth shifted away from the skirmishers in the woods and toward the right flank of the main British line. At this close range, the Americans tar-geted British officers with individual fire. Slowly, the British advance halted and then fell back in good order. Brown, meanwhile, ordered Ripley to take his best unit, the Twenty-First Infantry Regiment, into the woods and fall on the British rear. Also in the woods, Porter regrouped his Third Brigade and pressed toward the Chippewa River. However, little daylight was left as the British pulled back, and Brown ordered the division back to camp rather than con-tinue an attack against the fortified British position.

The battle had lasted ninety minutes. Riall counted some 450 casualties and Brown nearly 300. Riall's official report to Lt. Gen. Gordon Drummond, British commander in Upper Canada, noted that the Americans had "deployed with the greatest regularity" under fire. Riall also acknowledged that the bat-tle did not go as planned. A Canadian officer who had been present later observed that Riall had acted hastily and did not "employ all the means in his power and should have waited for more reinforcements before attacking." Drummond echoed these sentiments to Lt. Gen. Sir George Prévost, governor-general of Canada and British commander in chief of North America. Prévost in turn recognized Riall's errors, commenting that "in the Sortie at Chippewa, neither the Union of Science, organization or force will give the affair any eclat."[11]

On June 6, 1863, Lee instructed Stuart to lead his cavalry division toward the Rappahannock. Stuart dispersed his brigades so that they could cross the river in parallel columns on June 9 and made his headquarters on Fleetwood Hill, overlooking the town of Brandy Station. Unknown to Stuart, the Union cav-alry was massing across the river and preparing to carry out a spoiling attack on the Confederate cavalry that Major General Hooker knew to be assembling in the vicinity of Culpepper. Maj. Gen. Alfred Pleasonton, commanding this force, planned a two-pronged attack. The right wing—a cavalry division, a reserve cavalry brigade, and an infantry brigade—under Brig. Gen. John Buford would cross at Beverly Ford, four miles from Brandy Station. The left wing—two cavalry divisions and an infantry brigade—under Brig. Gen. David Gregg would attack across Kelly's Ford, six miles downstream and eight miles from Brandy Station. There, the two planned to join and move six miles to Culpepper.

The operation was supposed to begin at 4:30 a.m., but only half of Gregg's force arrived on schedule and the left wing did not complete its crossing until 9 a.m. The right wing crossed on time and caught the Confederate pickets off guard, but the Union troopers were, in turn, surprised to find enemy forces deployed so close to the river. An intense battle immediately ensued about a mile south of the crossing with repeated charges and countercharges. The left wing made more progress, bypassing a rebel cavalry brigade posted near Kelly's Ford. One of Gregg's divisions shortly threatened Stuart's headquarters at Brandy Hill in a battle for the high ground. The other, however, swung south and made only a weak attempt to dislodge a small Confederate force guarding that approach. By midday Pleasonton saw that his two wings would not unite and ordered his subordinates to withdraw. Stuart, under orders not to expose the strength of his forces, did not pursue them, and the Union cavalry pulled back across the Rappahannock by 9 p.m.

The Battle of Brandy Station was inconclusive. Pleasonton neither severely damaged Stuart's forces nor discovered the size and direction of Lee's campaign. However, the battle gave his commanders and troopers confidence that they could engage and hold their own in a pitched battle with their renowned opponents. "The Cavalry begins to hold its head up," one trooper reported. The opposite was true of Stuart, who received private and public criticism for allowing Pleasonton to catch him unawares. Southern newspapers described the battle as an "ugly surprise" and concluded that Stuart's generalship was characterized by "negligence and bad management." These negative remarks may have weighed on Stuart's decision to make the bold sweep around the Union army in Maryland and Pennsylvania. His operation contributed to Lee's failure to engage the enemy on his terms.[12]

MEETING ENGAGEMENTS

The Battles of Lundy's Lane and Gettysburg were meeting engagements where advancing forces, incompletely deployed for battle, engaged enemy forces at unexpected times and places. In the case of Brown's Left Division, his First Brigade under

Winfield Scott advanced toward Fort George and encountered the British-Canadian "Right" Division, which had been hastily deployed in a defensive position across the road that lent its name to the major battle of the campaign and the most bitterly fought engagement of the war. In the case of Lee's Army of Northern Virginia, Lieutenant General Hill's "reconnaissance in force" to determine the strength of enemy forces around that Pennsylvanian town provoked a fight with Union cavalry that both sides fed with corps-level reinforcements, culminating in the largest and costliest battle of the Civil War. In both cases, key subordinate commanders made critical errors that unraveled larger strategic plans. Further, the invading armies' efforts to gain a critical tactical advantage by turning the enemy's left flank also proved unsuccessful.

Following the July 4 Battle of Chippewa, Brown was eager to reach Lake Ontario, where he hoped to see Chauncey's fleet on July 10. With the British forces withdrawing toward Fort George, Brown made camp at Queenston Heights, south of the fort. Queenston, ironically, was the site of the British victory in October 1812 where the British commander of Upper Canada, Maj. Gen. Isaac Brock, was killed and where Col. Winfield Scott was captured along with most of the American invasion force. Brown began aggressive patrolling while receiving reinforcements and supplies via Lewiston on the opposite bank of the Niagara River. Brown waited three days past what he believed was the rendezvous date before writing to Chauncey, "For God's sake let me see you . . . we have between us the command of sufficient means to conquer Upper Canada within two months if there is prompt and zealous co-operation, and a vigorous application of those means."[13] Brown complained to Armstrong, who took up the matter with Madison, and he in turn went to Secretary of the Navy William Jones. Jones first defended Chauncey, and when the latter's poor health came to his attention, Jones replaced him with Capt. Stephen Decatur. Jones's orders to Decatur, however, placed primacy on maintaining control of Lake Ontario and not on supporting the army.[14]

The British concluded that Brown was waiting for Chauncey. Riall moved the bulk of his two brigades of regulars, now augmented by two brigades of Canadian sedentary militia, to the west to avoid being trapped by the American fleet and Brown's forces. Riall's superior, Lieutenant General Drummond, decided that he needed to engage Brown while the British controlled the lake. He sped to the Niagara Peninsula to assume command of the situation.

Brown waited for Chauncey until July 20 before deciding to invest Fort George, hoping to provoke either the garrison or Riall's forces. Riall made tentative moves toward the American forces but did not engage, explaining to

Drummond, "Should any reverse occur, I look upon it as fraught with the greatest danger to the province."[15] While the Left Division retraced its steps to Queenston two days later, Drummond arrived, determined to drive Brown from the peninsula. But he first wanted to disrupt reported American efforts to build new siege batteries near Fort George. To that end, he ordered Riall to make a demonstration toward Queenston.

Concurrently, Brown received word that Chauncey was ill at Sackets Harbor and his fleet would not arrive. Brown again changed his plans, informing Secretary of War Armstrong that he intended "to march into the interior of the country as far as I can carry or find subsistence in hopes of finding Riall and forcing him into action."[16] However, Brown did not take up Armstrong's suggestion that he advance inland to attack Burlington, probably because he would have needed the same siege cannons Chauncey was unable or unwilling to transport across Lake Ontario for an attack on Fort George.[17]

Brown remained firm in his plans even when he was informed on the afternoon of July 24 that the British were advancing south from Fort Niagara to attack the American artillery battery at Lewiston and might continue their advance, threatening his supply base at Fort Schlosser. Believing that the best defense against such an attack was to advance on Fort George, Brown ordered Scott to take the First Brigade, a company of artillery, and a cavalry detachment north to Queenston. Scott was to report whether he encountered enemy units and to call for assistance, if necessary.

Scott moved forward at 5 p.m. and learned from a tavern keeper at the falls that Riall was nearby with a thousand men. He sent this information to Brown along with his decision to engage what appeared to be a small force detached from the British thrust advancing down the other side of the river. When Scott's patrols discovered that a larger-than-expected British force was drawing up along Lundy's Lane, he still decided to advance. Shortly after 7 p.m., three of the First Brigade's four regiments—the Ninth, Eleventh, and Twenty-Second—emerged from the woods into a clearing below the fifty-foot-high hill that the bulk of Drummond's forces had recently occupied. The British artillery opened fire as soon as Scott's gray-clad troops came into view.

Leading two militia brigades, Drummond had intercepted Riall's force, which was withdrawing from Queenston in light of Scott's advance. He instead quickly decided to make a stand at Lundy's Lane. Drummond judged that it was an ideal defensive position from which he could make a "killing ground" of the open fields. The British drew up along the road running east to west above an open field to the south, the direction from which the American Army was approaching. To the left of the British position was the Portage Road, running north–south along the woods and brush. To the west was a parallel track running from the Green homestead north of the hill to the Skinner farm to the south.

Upon finding a large force to his front, Scott may have believed that the British were in even greater strength and elected not to advance up the hill until reinforcements arrived. He also considered retreating but opted to remain, explaining in his memoirs that by "standing fast, the salutary impression was made upon the enemy that the whole American reserve was on hand and would soon assault his flanks." He had high confidence in the discipline of his troops to make such a stand, "for an extravagant opinion generally prevailed throughout the army in respect to the prowess—nay the invincibility of Scott's brigade."[18] After forty-five minutes of deadly bombardment, he ordered his troops to advance 150 yards as a feint. They never came within effective musket range of the British and took horrendous casualties of 60 percent killed or wounded before dusk. Following Brown's order to have the First Brigade stand in clear view and range of British artillery resulted in a slaughter that essentially deprived Brown of his most effective unit and precluded any possibility of his marching on Burlington, much less on York and Kingston.

Drummond did not attack because he did not wish to lose his superior defensive position and was convinced that the brigade to his front represented only part of an American Army that outnumbered his two-thousand-man force by two to one. Moreover, fighting on his left flank concerned him. Scott had sent his reserve, Maj. Thomas Jesup's Twenty-Fifth Regiment, through the woods and to the right of the hill to create the impression of a flanking movement. Concealed by the forest and brush, Jesup's regiment attacked and overran two militia companies on Drummond's eastern flank. Jesup's force also captured individuals and small groups moving in the dark right behind the British line. These prisoners included Riall. Receiving word that the rest of the First Brigade was no longer an effective force, Jesup retreated while Brown arrived in force.

After the Battle of Brandy Station, Stuart's cavalry prevented Pleasonton from accomplishing his primary mission of determining the location of Lee's main force; however, while on the defensive, Stuart's cavalry could not keep tabs on the Army of the Potomac. Ignorant of his opponent's whereabouts, Lee ordered a concerted attack across the Susquehanna River aimed at the Pennsylvania capital, Harrisburg. He directed Ewell's II Corps to capture the city and destroy the railroad network connecting the rest of the North to Washington and the Army of the Potomac. Upon learning that the federal army was massing east of Frederick, Maryland, Lee recalled Ewell, who was at Carlisle and, absent any sense of urgency, countermarched at a normal pace. The bulk of the ANV proceeded to march east from Chambersburg to Cashtown, beyond which lay Gettysburg.

Hill's III Corps led this movement, and on June 30 he sent a foraging party to Gettysburg. Under orders not to "precipitate a fight," the unit returned when it observed Union cavalry approaching the town. The following day, Hill ordered a reconnaissance in force to discern the enemy's strength in that town, confident that the Union army was in Middleburg, twenty miles to the south. Lee approved but still had no word from Stuart and only a general idea of the disposition of the federal army. Meanwhile, Maj. Gen. George Meade, who had replaced Hooker soon after Lee began his campaign, knew the deployment and direction of Lee's major components and was moving his army toward Gettysburg. He hoped to draw the Confederate army toward Pipe Creek, a small tributary of the Monocacy River, where the Union army could occupy a high ridge and fight a defensive battle. This plan mirrored Lee's intentions, but the sequence of events prevented both generals from engaging the enemy at a time and place of their choosing.

On July 1, Hill's lead elements engaged Union cavalry on the northwest outskirts of Gettysburg. In keeping with Lee's orders to avoid a major engagement, Maj. Gen. Henry "Harry" Heth, commanding the expedition, should have withdrawn to Cashtown or at least stopped on high ground and requested instructions from Hill. But contrary to Lee's standing orders, he attempted to occupy the town. Heth's effort prompted Union Maj. Gen. John F. Reynolds to commit his I Corps to the fight, certain that Hill's entire corps was advancing. By late afternoon, these opposing corps had been reinforced, respectively, with Ewell's corps arriving from the north and Union Maj. Gen. Oliver Howard's XI Corps arriving from the southeast.

Toward the end of the day, Confederate troops had pushed Union forces off McPherson's Ridge and Seminary Ridge and had occupied Gettysburg. Lee, however, had missed two opportunities to end the Battle of Gettysburg in what historian Stephen Sears terms "a tale of misapprehension and misjudgment on the part of the high command of the Army of Northern Virginia." Hill had

three brigades available to block the southern exits from the town and to capture thousands of Yankee troops and numerous artillery pieces, but Hill was
cautious after the day's fierce fighting. He reported, "My own two divisions
exhausted by some six hours' hard fighting, prudence led me to be content with
what had been gained, and not push forward troops exhausted and necessarily
disordered, probably to encounter fresh troops of the enemy." Ewell's division
commanders, meanwhile, urged him to attack Cemetery Hill south of
Gettysburg. Shortly after sending riders to gain Lee's permission and support
from Hill's troops, Ewell received orders from Lee "to carry the hill occupied by
the enemy, if he found it practicable, but to avoid a general engagement until
the arrival of other divisions of the army." Ewell decided against an attack after
receiving an unconfirmed report that Union troops were approaching from the
northeast to his rear, where he dispatched some of the troops he could have
used to assault the hill. He then received Lee's response to his initial request.
Lee regretted that the other corps were not positioned to support him, but he
"wished him to take the Cemetery Hill if it were possible," indicating Lee's
continued unease over this unplanned battle with an unknown portion of
Meade's army. Ewell decided against attacking Cemetery Hill and shifted his
attention to nearby Culp's Hill, which he planned to advance against the following day to support the main effort against the Union's left flank.[19]

Lee determined that the main effort on July 2 would be a flanking attack
by Longstreet's I Corps through the Peach Orchard, Rose Woods, and what
became known as the Devil's Den toward what he believed to be the southern
edge of the Union line on Cemetery Ridge. One division from Hill's III Corps
would begin the attack at the center of the Union line with Longstreet's forces
attacking in echelon, preventing General Meade from reinforcing his left flank.
The division had to delay the attack, however, while waiting for one brigade
to get into proper position. Then because Lee lacked adequate cavalry, his
troops did not detect that Maj. Gen. Daniel Sickles's III Corps had unilaterally
moved to higher ground directly in Longstreet's line of march, but they foiled
the attack. Sickles's corps was decimated in the ensuing fight, but Meade moved
twenty thousand men to reinforce his left flank and thwarted Lee's plan.
Meanwhile, Ewell's efforts around Culp's Hill were only partially successful and
never developed into a full-scale attack. There, too, interior lines allowed the
Union to shift troops and block Confederate advances.

In making this flanking attack, Lee effectively abandoned his strategy of
fighting at a time and place of his own choosing. He rejected Longstreet's

advice to march around Meade's left and secure high ground between the Union army and Washington. Such a position would have threatened not only Washington but also Meade's supply lines, forcing him to attack. Longstreet believed this plan was in keeping with their agreement to combine offensive strategy with defensive tactics in this campaign. Instead, the Confederate army was attempting to do what the Union army had failed to accomplish at Fredericksburg: conduct a mass attack against a similarly sized force occupying the heights above the city.

Lee omitted mentioning Longstreet's option in his memoirs, arguing that his only alternatives to the flanking attack were to pull back to or through the mountain passes to the west or to wait for the Union army to attack. Lee believed it was important to retain the initiative and to attack an enemy that he held in low regard with what he considered as his superior troops. Lee also probably took Longstreet's suggestion as doubting his generalship and, in an approach Lee had not taken in the past, proceeded to provide his corps commanders with tactical plans that they should follow. The result was an operational failure. Sears summarizes the day's fighting: "Lacking unified command, the Confederate attacks had been raggedly executed, grinding down the defenders, certainly, but failing so far to dislodge them." He also quotes Lee's aide as concluding, "The whole affair was disjointed. There was an utter absence of accord in the movements of the several commands, and no decisive result attended the operations. . . ."[20]

Taking the Heights

The Left Division's assault against the British artillery and infantry positions on the hilltop at Lundy's Lane and "Pickett's Charge" against the center of the Union army on Cemetery Ridge are usually depicted as the climactic engagements of their respective battles. Poor planning and flawed execution doomed both, though, as neither side had on hand the necessary reinforcements to hold those positions. Moreover, these attacks eliminated any chance of accomplishing the two campaigns' central objectives of engaging the enemy at an advantageous time and place.

General Brown reached the battlefield at 8:30 p.m. and immediately advanced Ripley's brigade toward the enemy while disengaging Scott's brigade and holding it in reserve. Seeing the British pickets withdrawing toward Lundy's Lane, Brown assumed the British were retreating. Ripley's troops marched in column with the Twenty-First Infantry to the left of Portage Road and the Twenty-Third Infantry to the right. To Ripley's left was the First

Infantry, which had recently arrived from garrison duty on the east bank of the Niagara. Brown intended for that regiment to mount a demonstration, but its commander advanced on the British artillery. As the unit came under intense fire, it countermarched to the base of the hill. Distracted by this attack and having failed to post pickets to the front of their position, the British neither saw nor heard Ripley's regiments approach. The Twenty-First fired and rushed the British artillery, driving off the gunners. The British quickly made successive efforts to recover their artillery but failed. Both sides took heavy casualties. Soon after the British withdrew, the Twenty-Third and Twenty-Fifth Infantry Regiments formed up on the right, and Porter's brigade arrived to secure the Americans' left flank.

General Drummond was determined to launch a counterattack and recover his guns. Over the next half hour, he organized his forces into two wings west of the hill at the juncture of Lundy's Lane and the track leading to the Skinner farm; however, Drummond again failed to deploy skirmishers to feel out the American positions. Coincidentally, Brown and Ripley made the same mistake. Thus, the battle's second phase began with a sudden rupture of fire between the two forces at 10 p.m. The first volley of the British line did not shake the Americans, so Drummond's troops did not advance but continued firing, often aiming too high while firing up the hill. After twenty-five minutes, Drummond ordered a withdrawal that the men executed without confusion.

The British advanced again at 10:45 p.m. and launched a second attack. This exchange was "more severe, and . . . longer continued than the last," and some of the American units gave way.[21] On the American left, the Canadian volunteers in Porter's brigade retreated, prompting other units to take flight down the hill until their officers halted them and reestablished order. In the center, Ripley's regiments also edged back until he rallied them. At this point, Scott took his reformed brigade—down to only 240 men—into the center of the fight and attempted to attack in column. Rather than moving north toward the British, Scott's column marched west between the two armies, receiving devastating fire from both sides before retreating in disorder down the track to Skinner's farm. Firing along the line soon sputtered out, with the British failing to recapture their artillery.

Still determined, Drummond launched a third assault shortly before 11:30 p.m. and again at the center of the American line. It is not clear why, after having failed twice to crack the American center, he did not maneuver to launch an attack on either of Brown's flanks. Marching directly toward the

American line, the British stopped and fired in volleys. This time, the Americans counterattacked. First, Scott's re-formed brigade—down to a hundred men—attempted to turn the British right flank but marched in front of it, took heavy casualties, and broke. Then, Porter's brigade moved forward with the same objective and succeeded in driving the enemy back and in taking prisoners as well. On the Americans' right flank, superior firepower compelled the British to retire. However, in the center, the British closed with Ripley's brigade and engaged in a vicious melee among the captured artillery. After the British flanks gave way, Drummond pulled his troops back.

Casualties on both sides were high. Drummond reported that the British and Canadians had lost 878 killed, wounded, captured, and missing—or a quarter of his force—although other accounts put the number at around 800 men. Brown reported a comparable 860 casualties of all types. Among the high-ranking wounded, Brown recovered at a friend's home in Buffalo, and Scott and the captured Riall both received care from the same surgeon in nearby Batavia, New York. Most of the British wounded were cared for at Fort Erie, and American soldiers were sent to a hospital in the village of Williamsville, northeast of Buffalo.

One of Brown's brigadiers accurately summarized the cause of this butchery: "We should not have wasted our forces by detachments when no advantages could have been gained nor have fought by accident when we might have planned an attack." Another commentator cites Scott's character and poor decision making as contributing to the butcher's bill and noted that he was "utterly regardless of human life and willing to make any sacrifice for his own personal renown."[22]

Two developments shortly after the battle also suggest that Scott's and Brown's haste in engaging the British doomed their attainment of the campaign's strategic objectives. First, more than a thousand troops recently arrived from eastern New York were found at Chippewa after the battle. Had these soldiers been properly organized and added to the ranks of the Left Division, they could have reinforced the army and consolidated their position at Lundy's Lane, probably forcing the British to withdraw toward Fort George or Burlington. Second, Chauncey's fleet arrived off the mouth on the Niagara only a few days after the battle. Had better communication existed between Brown and Chauncey, the movement north from Chippewa could have compelled the British to vacate Forts Niagara and Erie and to retreat toward Burlington. In that scenario, the reinforcements added to Brown's army would have given him considerable options in confronting the British-Canadian forces on his own terms.

General Meade met with his corps commanders and staff at 8 p.m. on July 2. His intelligence reports told him that Lee had engaged his entire army, except for Maj. Gen. George Pickett's division, and had been repulsed at every point. Looking ahead, the Union generals discussed (a) whether they should remain or pull back to a position closer to their supply base in Maryland; (b) if they stayed, whether they should remain on defense or attack; and (c) how long they would wait for another Confederate attack. They unanimously agreed that the Army of the Potomac would remain at Gettysburg in a defensive posture, unless the Confederates threatened their lines of communication to Washington. The officers present did not agree on when or where Lee would attack, but Meade judged that if Lee attacked, he would direct his forces at the center of the Union line on Cemetery Ridge.

His judgment was prescient. Lee had simultaneously concluded without consulting his corps commanders that infantry, attacking in columns with proper artillery support, could collapse the Union forces' left flank. Lee did not share his lieutenants' more sober assessment of the previous days' fighting. With little knowledge of the strength of Meade's troops, he planned a direct assault instead of repeating the previous days' flanking movement, which had unexpectedly met up with Brig. Gen. Alfred Scales's brigade. Lee wanted Ewell to resume his attacks on the Union right, while Longstreet's corps—spearheaded by Pickett's fresh division—and elements of Hill's corps attacked Cemetery Ridge with the Confederate artillery's support. Lee believed that with a massive artillery bombardment, nearly eighteen thousand of his infantry would break through the center of the Union line. Stuart's recently arrived cavalry would also make a diversionary attack on the Union rear.

When Lee arrived at his headquarters before sunrise on July 3, Longstreet again proposed a turning movement to threaten the Union flank and its supply lines. He wanted to swing Ewell's corps around his position to seize a strong point in the Union rear area and force Meade to attack. Referring to the Union positions on the ridge, he pointedly told Lee, "No fifteen thousand men ever arrayed for battle can take that position." In response, Lee simply ordered Longstreet to prepare his corps for the attack. In historian Sears's words, "Lee was taking a military decision utterly divorced from reality."[23]

As on July 2, Lee's attack on July 3 was not properly synchronized. Ewell attacked too soon and Longstreet too late. Although more than 150 guns bombarded Cemetery Hill, the artillery attack fell short of expectations, in part, because defective fuses led to duds and premature explosions. The infantry also failed to act in concert. The advancing regiments were forced to make constant adjustments in their lines of march, owing to the terrain and their initial dispositions, all the while under Union artillery fire. Although they outnumbered the Union defenders and briefly seized the Union artillery pieces when they reached the point of attack at that famous low stone wall, Lee's men had suffered so many casualties from the Union's final artillery rounds that Union reinforcements quickly drove them back from their high-water mark. Meanwhile, Union forces put up a stronger-than-expected resistance and disrupted Jeb Stuart's diversionary attack.

RETREAT AND PURSUIT

Assessments of the Battles of Lundy's Lane and Gettysburg often cite the British and Union armies for their tardy pursuit of their retreating opponents. Fatigue and prudence are noted in both cases, but the two situations differed significantly. Whereas the Left Division refused to retreat from Canada and was later unsuccessfully besieged at Fort Erie, the Army of Northern Virginia disengaged and safely crossed the Potomac. The successful defense of Fort Erie suggests some of the problems Meade might have encountered had he overruled his generals and attacked Lee's retreating army while it was in a strong defensive position on the Potomac River's northern bank and waiting to cross into Virginia.

Before dawn on July 26, command of the Left Division devolved to Ripley as Brown and Scott headed across the Niagara River to tend to their wounds. Ripley judged the army was too weak to withstand another British attack and ordered it to retire and take up a defensive position on the southern bank of the Chippewa. Owing to a lack of horses and to confusing orders, they left the captured British artillery pieces and two American guns scattered on the battlefield until the British discovered them later the following morning. From Chippewa, Ripley wanted to withdraw across the Niagara, but Brown, who had lost confidence in his subordinate, ordered him to Fort Erie. Meanwhile, Secretary of War Armstrong ordered Major General Izard to take the Right Division to Sackets Harbor for either an attack on Kingston or a rendezvous with the Left Division for an assault on Burlington, but neither came to pass.

Drummond's caution in reengaging the American Army aided Ripley's retreat to Fort Erie. Suffering from high casualties as well, Drummond also lacked the means for a siege of Fort Erie. He initially opted to launch a raid across the river to attack Buffalo and thereby compel the Americans to withdraw from Canada. The Americans, however, repulsed the poorly executed raid in less than three hours. Meanwhile, the Americans had strengthened the bastion at Fort Erie and built a fortified line eight hundred yards south to Snake Hill, where they placed an artillery battery. American artillery across the river at Black Rock and American schooners offshore also supported Fort Erie.

The British constructed an artillery battery north of the fort to reduce the American defenses, but it was poorly positioned and did little damage until it created a small secondary explosion on August 14. They followed up this minor success with a multipronged attack on the night of August 15. The new American commander, Brig. Gen. Edmund P. Gaines, however, anticipated this action. From the outset, the attack went wrong, with a tardy demonstration toward the center of the American line and with the infantry leading an equally late bayonet charge on Snake Hill after having removed the flints from their muskets to prevent any intentional or accidental firing that might alert the garrison. The Americans routed this attack. At the fort itself, two British spearheads made some progress until an accidental explosion of a powder magazine created significant casualties and confusion, prompting the British to withdraw. British losses amounted to nearly nine hundred out of twenty-five hundred men, or higher casualties than the British had suffered at Lundy's Lane; and this rate would only be surpassed by casualties at the Battle of New Orleans a few months later. In contrast, Gaines reported sixty-two American casualties.

Drummond continued the siege by building two additional batteries, but Gaines's improvements to his fortifications offset Drummond's efforts. Poor weather and a spoiling attack by Porter's brigade in early September did not improve matters. Brown, who had recovered from his wounds and returned to command the Left Division, led a large American sortie from the fort on September 17 that resulted in five hundred more casualties on both sides. Drummond, who decided prior to this attack to pull his force away from the fort, did so on September 21. Concurrently, Izard's Right Division arrived and positioned itself south of Chippewa, but Drummond refused to take the bait. With winter approaching and his naval support retiring to Sackets Harbor, Izard reported, "I can discern no object which can be achieved at this point worthy of the risk which attend its attempt."[24] On November 5, he ordered Fort Erie destroyed and led the American Army back across the Niagara, 125 days after its summer campaign had begun.

In contrast to the debate Brown and his subordinates had over whether to pull back from Lundy's Lane, after Pickett's Charge, Lee immediately ordered his army to march back to Virginia. His principal concern was that Meade would quickly cut off his escape route across the Potomac; consequently, he had little time to spare in getting the army moving. In the words of a civilian observer, "Hurry was the order of the day."[25] Lee organized a convoy to take the wounded to the Williamsport, Maryland, bridge and cross the Potomac. He then ordered Ewell's II Corps to fall back west to Cashtown and position itself as a rear guard. Hill's and Longstreet's corps followed, turning south toward Williamsport and the Confederate pontoon bridge six miles to the east at Falling Waters, West Virginia. By the morning of July 4, the Confederates had completely evacuated the town of Gettysburg; coincidentally, Vicksburg surrendered to Grant that day as well. By the next evening, Lee's army had abandoned its positions in the surrounding area.

Meade, assuming that another attack on his position was imminent, busied himself with more urgent tasks than contemplating his next moves. He telegraphed Washington that he was moving supplies forward and resting his troops, and planned to order a reconnaissance of enemy positions. He also issued a congratulatory message to his troops, noting that he "looks to the army for greater efforts to drive from our soil every vestige of the presence of the invader." This phrase drew a rebuke from President Lincoln as efforts "to get the enemy across the river again without further collision, and they do not appear connected with a purpose to prevent his crossing and to destroy him."[26] Yet, as Sears notes, on July 4, Meade had been in command of the Army of the Potomac for barely one week, and to switch quickly from defense to offense was asking a great deal of him. He would have had to anticipate Lee's retreat and positioned the army to pursue immediately. At a conference that evening, Meade and his lieutenants decided to remain at Gettysburg until they had determined the direction of the enemy's movements and not to attack any enemy formations remaining on Seminary Ridge. However, if Lee was retreating, they also agreed to move toward Williamsport and to pursue him with a show of force.

The Confederate retreat was repeatedly threatened, first with two Union attacks on the leading column of wounded and prisoners. Upon reaching Williamsport, the lead element discovered that while the bridge under light guard remained intact, a Union cavalry force from Harper's Ferry had destroyed the pontoon bridge at Falling Waters. On July 6, Confederate forces narrowly won a pitched battle at Williamsport, while on the same day Jeb

Stuart's screening force successfully warded off another attack about half a dozen miles to the northeast at Hagerstown, Maryland.

Meanwhile, the Army of the Potomac was closing on Lee's position, and Meade expected another battle before his quarry escaped across the Potomac. A Union officer noted that their respective positions at Gettysburg were now reversed, with Lee dug in and Meade expected to attack. However, the Union forces moved too slowly, and Lee had time to erect his defenses and complete a new pontoon bridge by July 13. Meade could have engaged Lee with two of his corps a day or two beforehand, but he knew that an unsuccessful attack would have given the South a victory, offsetting its defeat at Gettysburg. Meade held another conference with his generals on July 12, and five of his seven corps commanders recommended against an attack. In a final episode of confusion, Stuart's cavalry failed to cover the final retreating elements, which Union cavalry attacked on the morning of July 14. The Confederates rallied, however, fending off the Union's final effort to harry their retreat.

CONCLUSION

Neither Brown's nor Lee's campaign achieved its strategic objective. Brown failed to take and hold territory in Upper Canada that could have been used as a bargaining chip in peace negotiations with London. Lee failed to inflict a decisive defeat on the Union that would have encouraged antiwar radicals in the North to push for peace; would have enticed European powers to intervene politically, if not militarily; and would have prompted Washington to open negotiations with Richmond.

Both campaigns also failed to achieve their military objectives. Brown was unable by battle or maneuver to clear British forces from the Niagara frontier. His lack of rapport with Chauncey made an advance against Burlington problematic, and his decision to engage Drummond at Lundy's Lane resulted in high casualties that eliminated any hope of advancing farther into Canada. Both of these situations reflected fundamental flaws in the American command structure, not only between Brown and Chauncey, but also among Armstrong, Jones, Monroe, and Madison. In the Civil War, Lee also failed to engage his opponent Meade at a time and place of his choosing. Stuart's absence deprived him of intelligence on the location of Meade's corps, and he stumbled into a battle at Gettysburg that left him advancing against a similarly sized force in a strong defensive position, or exactly the opposite of what he had intended when he crossed the Potomac.

Tactical mistakes were also evident on both sides in these battles. Scott's handling of the First Brigade left it exposed to British artillery, which effectively destroyed its combat capabilities. Brown's decision to continue the attack well into the night against a comparable force in a well-defended position compounded this error. Heth's precipitation of the battle at Gettysburg, Ewell's hesitancy to attack Cemetery Hill on July 1, and Longstreet's subsequent unsuccessful flanking maneuver on July 2 all set the stage for Lee's disastrous decision to launch Pickett's Charge on July 3. Both Brown and Lee mistakenly believed that the élan of their infantry would be the key to victory.

The tactical victories after the main battles at Lundy's Lane and Gettysburg hardly offset these losses. Gaines's defense of Fort Erie inflicted the costliest defeat of British forces in Canada during the war, yet his role in the campaign did not achieve the notoriety that Scott had gained at Chippewa. Despite Gaines's defensive success, weather and logistic concerns compelled Izard to pull U.S. forces back into New York and blow up the fort. Lee's successful and speedy retreat across the Potomac was better executed than was his advance on Gettysburg. Had Meade followed Lincoln's pleas to destroy the invaders and not simply to drive them out, Lee might have fought the battle he had hoped for at the end of his campaign. Both the Left Division and the Army of Northern Virginia benefited from opponents who had been shaken by their own losses and were unwilling to launch an immediate, full-scale, and determined pursuit of their adversaries.

The similarities of these critical campaigns have been obscured, however, not so much by the nearly half a century separating them as by the immense differences ascribed to their character and consequences. Brown's invasion was the last major unsuccessful American offensive in Mr. Madison's War. Aside from Winfield Scott's skilled handling of his regiments at the Battle of Chippewa—an event woven into the fabric of the Second War of Independence narrative—the American Army's efforts along the Niagara River that summer and fall provided no victories of lasting importance. None of the battles stood out, in contrast to those at Baltimore and Plattsburgh and more crucially at New Orleans, where Andrew Jackson emerged as a national hero. Collectively, those battles—not Brown's campaign—set the stage for a peace agreement.

Most generally view Lee's storied sortie into Pennsylvania, meanwhile, as a heroic last attempt to take the war to the Union and bring the Civil War to an end on terms favorable to Richmond. Lee, unlike Brown, became the

revered icon of heroic defeat in the Confederacy's effort to secede from the
union. Those who consider Lee to be the hero of the Lost Cause narrative of
the Confederacy and who thus view Gettysburg as a calamitous national defeat
blame Longstreet for his unsuccessful flanking attack on July 2. Moreover, Lee
did not have any officers comparable to Andrew Jackson who could rebuff an
invasion of the Mississippi River Valley. Ironically, Lee assessed that he could
do nothing further to rescue Vicksburg and the western theater, and that the
Army of Northern Virginia should remain intact and march north. Although
Lee's gamble did not succeed, he earned his lasting place in history at
Appomattox more than a year and a half after his strategic gamble failed.[27]

Brown's campaign, the last major American offensive of the War of 1812,
presents important insights into the complementary nature of the Mr. Madison's
War and Second War of Independence narratives. Most important, it stands in
the Second War of Independence narrative as a dramatic counterpoint to the
assertion that poor execution marred U.S. military operations, such as those at
Bladensburg, Crysler's Farm, and Queenston. Brown's effort to prepare and engage
his forces in Canada compared favorably to Lee's effort in Pennsylvania. Brown's
investment in training prior to the invasion paid handsome dividends throughout the campaign. His regulars fought Britain's finest to a draw for several months.
Moreover, they did so under the command of several successive officers: Brown,
Ripley, and Gaines. Finally, the Americans withdrew to New York as winter
approached because of the problem of sending supplies across the frozen Niagara
River and Lake Erie and not because of a British counteroffensive.

That said, the U.S. invasion of Canada in 1813 was frustrated by three
higher-level operational failures that support the more dour narrative of Mr.
Madison's War. First, Armstrong and Brown did not settle on the specific objectives of the campaign. Second, Brown's lack of communication with and support from Chauncey doomed the invasion's general objective of seizing and
holding territory, perhaps as far as York on the northern shore of Lake Ontario.
Third, Armstrong's order committing Izard's Right Division to support Brown's
Left Division removed a key blocking force that would have stopped Prévost's
invasion from Montreal toward Albany. This move was among the most ill-
conceived American deployments of the war. Had the British prevailed at the
Battle of Lake Champlain or had Prévost attacked that city afterward as his
subordinates had urged, where British Gen. John Burgoyne had failed in 1777
the British might have succeeded in gaining control of the upper Hudson River
Valley and in cutting New England off from the rest of the country. The British

would have had an important bargaining chip, enabling them to force the Americans to accept a peace treaty on the basis of *uti possidetis*, or to trade land they occupied for control of the Niagara River and the establishment of an Indian buffer state in the Old Northwest. In this strategic context, Brown's invasion, with Izard marching away from Plattsburgh, could have changed the terms of the peace agreement and, literally, the shape of the country.

—— 4 ——

THE MEN WHO GOVERNED
AMERICA DURING THE
WAR OF 1812

Histories addressing the politics of the War of 1812 have focused primarily on the personalities, policies, and plans of the Madison administration, as well as its congressional supporters and opponents. Less attention has
been paid to the governors of the states and territories.[1] Their performance and
accomplishments are generally ignored even though the federal government
at this time in the history of the republic was far weaker given the "limited
government" philosophy of the founders and of President Jefferson, in particular. Although not military commanders or cabinet officers, they were a key
part of the country's "leadership" in a broader sense than Sun Tzu's definition,
as outlined in chapter 3.

State governors were both closer to the people and, with the notable
exception of the British capture of Washington, closer to the action than
members of Madison's government were. Indeed, having placed great weight
on the efficacy of militia forces over a standing army and navy, which were
viewed as threats to democracy and peace, Madison relied heavily on the
state governors to man and fund an offensive strategy aimed at seizing Canada
in order to compel Britain to cease its maritime policies of blockade and
impressment.

More than thirty men served as governors during the War of 1812, and
Republicans outnumbered Federalist governors by two to one. Their average
age in 1812 was forty-eight years old, with half having been born before the
French and Indian War ended in 1763 and only two born after 1776. Five had
served in the Revolutionary War. One attempted to arrange a separate peace
with the British during the War of 1812, another went on to become vice president of the United States, and a third became the secretary of war.

The experiences and abilities of the men who governed the six most populous states, which accounted for half of the U.S. population at the time, provide yet another basis for examining Mr. Madison's War and the Second War of Independence narratives. In alphabetical order, they were James Barbour (Republican, Virginia), William Hawkins (Republican, North Carolina), Simon Snyder (Republican, Pennsylvania), Caleb Strong (Federalist, Massachusetts), Daniel Tompkins (Republican, New York), and Levin Winder (Federalist, Maryland). Each struggled to recruit, equip, and pay militia forces. They were simultaneously responsible for the defense of their states while both supporting the Madison administration's offensive operations against Canada and responding to the demands of the federal district military commanders who had responsibilities for multiple states. These governors also worked with their legislatures to address local problems and budgetary challenges with little, if any, assistance from Washington. They were, to borrow a modern colloquialism, "where the rubber meets the road" and almost certainly as critical to the nation's success as were the leaders in Washington and the generals in the field.

FRONTLINE STATES
Virginia

> Debarred from manufactures, possessed of no shipping, and enjoying no domestic market, Virginian energies necessarily knew no other resource than agriculture. Without church, university, schools, or literature in any form that required or fostered intellectual life, the Virginians concentrated their thoughts almost exclusively on politics; and this concentration produced a result so distinct and lasting, and in character so respectable, that American history would lose no small part of its interest in losing the Virginia school.[2]

James Barbour (1775–1842) became governor of Virginia in January 1812 after newly elected governor George Smith was killed in a theater fire in Richmond. Barbour, a lifelong friend of James Madison's and a staunch Republican, was an ardent supporter of the war. After the HMS *Leopard* attacked the USS *Chesapeake* in 1807, he privately favored war, believing that the United States had suffered too many insults and encroachments on its sovereignty at the hands of Great Britain. He made his views public as bilateral relations with

Britain waned. In March 1812, he told the Virginia Assembly, "It seems no alternative is left but an appeal to arms or ignominious submission."[3]

Barbour tirelessly worked to prepare the state for conflict in the months leading up to the declaration of war and to execute his responsibilities as a wartime governor. Barbour was guided in these efforts by experience. As an officer in the Orange County militia, he was acquainted with the inherent limitations of the young republic's reliance on citizen soldiers who were often poorly organized, trained, provisioned, and led. As a legislator and later as the speaker in the Virginia Assembly, he was aware of that institution's wariness of executive power. In fact, the governor of Virginia was checked not only by the legislative branch but also by a Council of State from which he was required to obtain a majority vote to approve any action on his part. Fortunately, Barbour was on good terms with these men, who, being generally less experienced than the governor, followed his lead.

Barbour also benefited from muted opposition to the war from the Virginian Federalists and Republican Tertium Quids who did not want war with Britain. Some have cited Virginian Republicans' "fundamental nationalism" as a reason why they did not oppose the war to the extent that similarly minded Federalists did in New England. Supporters of the war also harshly criticized John Randolph and Federalist newspapers that questioned the decision to declare war. Jefferson remarked, "A barrel of tar to each state South of the Potomac will keep all in order, & that will be freely contributed without troubling government." Madison, however, earned 75 percent of the votes in Virginia for his reelection in late 1812, suggesting that Barbour faced only a modest antiwar sentiment.[4]

In January 1812, Barbour requested a special grant of emergency powers from the assembly that included authority over the state militia and power to act as military necessity demanded. He also asked the assembly to overhaul the antiquated militia system and to replenish military stores. The assembly dismissed his concerns and only empowered him to purchase eight tons of lead and two tons of gunpowder. Nevertheless, the governor placed the militia of the Tidewater communities on a war footing in March, ordered up 12,000 militiamen to meet Virginia's quota of the 100,000-man force Madison called for, toured and inspected specific locations in the Jamestown-Williamsburg-Yorktown and Norfolk areas, and drew up defense plans for key harbors. In May, he addressed and presided over a large public meeting in Richmond that adopted resolutions calling for war. The subsequent congressional declaration of war in June necessitated no significant changes in Barbour's plans although he did send detachments to the western frontier and renewed standing pleas to Secretary of War William Eustis to repair various federal fortifications in the state. Barbour also repeatedly wrote to Madison, asking what federal resources would be committed to Virginia's defense. After not receiving a reply, he relied heavily on state funds without counting on reimbursement from Washington. He also complained to Secretary of War Eustis about the removal of nearly all regular troops from the state in the early months of the war.[5]

Barbour won reelection to a second term as governor in November 1812 and the legislature praised him for "the ability with which you have heretofore discharged the duties of this office. . . ."[6] The appearance of a British squadron in the Chesapeake Bay in early February 1813 provided Virginia with its first clear and present danger. The Virginia Assembly responded by moving on some of Barbour's requests but in a parsimonious fashion, allocating $350,000 for defense purposes and refusing to approve his plan to reform the militia. The assembly also consented to the creation of a small state army with one regiment of infantry, one troop of cavalry, one company of riflemen, and two companies of artillery. The Madison administration objected to this law but agreed to pay for a draft of the militia; Virginia repealed the law in May 1813.

Barbour was continuously active in the second year of the war, largely in response to British raids. Shortly after the British entered the Chesapeake Bay in 1813, Barbour called out three thousand additional militiamen and ordered them to Norfolk, where he reviewed the units and encouraged them with a stirring speech. After activating another two thousand militiamen, he also called the assembly into session. The members gathered in May and passed several specific measures that gave the governor greater powers and allocated funds for military preparations. When the British attacked Craney Island, which guarded the approaches to Norfolk, seven hundred Virginia militiamen under Brig. Gen. Robert Taylor's command defeated them. The British then proceeded to sack the nearby town of Hampton, prompting Barbour to write British Vice Adm. George Cockburn and to protest his troops' barbaric conduct.

After a British flotilla subsequently proceeded up the mouth of the James River, Virginians believed Richmond was the likely target. Barbour met with the Richmond Vigilance Committee to take additional defensive measures, including more thoroughly drilling the local militia and putting the city under martial law. When the British retreated to the bay and up the Potomac, Barbour dispatched militia to respond to British raids. As the year drew to a close, Barbour pressed Washington to approve and fund a permanent state defense plan, including making improvements to fortifications and creating a state army of seventy-six thousand men in Norfolk and "flying camps" (quick response forces) of cavalry, artillery, and mounted riflemen elsewhere. The administration reduced the size of the proposed army in Norfolk to five thousand men and disallowed the flying camps, instead promising—but never delivering—additional forces to counter future British incursions. Barbour funded these measures by having the state banks borrow the necessary funds, and when that effort proved insufficient, he borrowed an additional $200,000 on his own signature. He also exhorted the state legislature to pay the state's quota of a direct tax passed by Congress. The legislators did so and reelected him to a third term on a vote of 133–53, albeit a disgruntled faction had accused him of recklessly spending state funds for unnecessary defensive preparations.

When British forces returned to the bay in 1814 and burned Washington, Barbour called out an additional ten thousand men for the defense of Richmond. He also issued a proclamation calling for all able-bodied men to defend the state capital. The response was so overwhelming that he had to issue a second proclamation and turn away unnecessary volunteers. He ordered fortifications erected along the York River, a likely route of advance for the British, and in October called the assembly into a special session to consider creating a "permanent force," completely reorganizing the militia, establishing regional arsenals, and appropriating other improvements. The assembly took months to consider these measures and in early 1815 passed a law calling for a standing army of ten thousand men contingent upon federal funding to equip, train, and pay for these troops. A month later, news of the Treaty of Ghent and its immediate ratification overtook these plans.[7]

By then, Barbour had been elected to the Senate, where he served until 1825, when he accepted the position of secretary of war in the administration of John Quincy Adams. Barbour subsequently served as a minister to England before returning for a brief time as a delegate in Virginia's General Assembly. Biographer Charles D. Lowery sums up Barbour's service in the War of 1812: "No one in Virginia acted more responsibly than Barbour in waging that war. Upon assuming office in 1812, he took a more realistic view of the approaching conflict than most leaders and wisely set out at once to prepare the state. Consequently, when the war did come, Virginia was better prepared, psychologically if not otherwise, than the rest of the country."[8]

New York

New York cared but little for the metaphysical subtleties of Massachusetts and Virginia, which convulsed the nation with spasms almost as violent as those that, fourteen centuries before, distracted the Eastern Empire in the effort to establish the double or single nature of Christ. New York was indifferent whether the nature of the United States was single or multiple, whether they were a nation or a league. Leaving this class of questions to other States which were deeply interested in them, New York remained constant to no political theory. There society, in spite of its aristocratic mixture, was democratic by instinct; and in abandoning its alliance with New England in order to join Virginia and elect Jefferson to the Presidency, it pledged itself to principles of no kind, least of all to Virginia doctrines.[9]

Daniel D. Tompkins (1774–1825) was elected governor of New York in April 1807 and inaugurated on July 1, coincidentally the same day that news reached Albany of HMS *Leopard*'s attack on the USS *Chesapeake*. Towns along the Canadian frontier immediately established committees of safety that appealed to the governor for arms, ammunition, and other forms of assistance. Tompkins offered a measured response, providing what the law and the treasury allowed while explaining the need of local militia officers to be accountable for these arms and to ensure their eventual return to the state. Tompkins also had to deal with immediate and broad opposition in the state to the embargo proposed by the Jefferson administration and approved by Congress. He firmly supported Madison in his first message to the state legislature in January 1808, arguing that the embargo was better than a declaration of war: "What patriotic citizen will murmur at the temporary privations and inconveniences resulting from this measure, when he reflects on the vast expenditure of national treasure, the sacrifices of lives and of our countrymen, and misery consequent upon our being in the war between the nations of Europe."[10]

Responding to the administration's directive to mobilize the militia to help enforce the embargo on Canada, Tompkins raised 12,700 men to fulfill New York's quota of the nationwide call for federal service. These forces were held at the ready until March 1808. Subsequently, in November 1808 and April 1812, New York fielded militia units at Washington's request. Each call required Tompkins to issue orders and direct activities with a multitude of militia and local officials. He also raised and improved fortifications and arsenals, obtained land for federal forces, assigned officers, reviewed units, and allocated arms and supplies. At times he used his own funds and waited for Washington to reimburse him. Tompkins looked to the defense both of the frontier settlements and of New York City. Although he did not approve Tompkins's request for federal arms in state arsenals, Secretary of War Eustis praised the New York governor's efforts in 1809: "The prompt and patriotic disposition manifested by your Excellency to co-operate with the General Government, in such measures as the public defense and safety may require, is highly favorable to the character of the first magistrate of a powerful State."[11]

Tompkins's desire to support the administration and win the praise of the "Virginia dynasty" overlapped with his duties as governor. He moved to take control of the militia and regular forces along the frontier to enforce the embargo, defend customs officials, maintain the peace, and make necessary preparations for war should the embargo fail. However, Secretary Eustis did not share with him the administration's national war strategy or even plans for New York's role in the coming conflict. Tompkins learned of his state's central role as the staging area for an invasion of Canada when he read the November 29, 1811, House Committee on Foreign Affairs report, authored by his close friend New York congressman Peter Porter, in the *National Intelligencer*. He framed his January 1812 speech to the state legislature in terms of his recommendations for protecting New York City and the northern frontier and for revising the militia law. The legislature turned down his request for funds to improve the defenses of New York's harbor, but he went as far as the law would allow in preparing the militia and dispatching troops to critical areas.

General Dearborn reported to Eustis that Tompkins "is doing everything in his power and will not fail in performing his duty with the greatest promptitude. I wish all our Gov⁵ would do as well."[12] For the most part, Tompkins's relationship with Dearborn was cordial and cooperative. Tompkins agreed to federal command of the activated state militia, but initially he insisted that as governor he should directly command the militia when it comprised the main force.[13]

When Congress voted for war in June 1812, seven of New York's ten Republican representatives in the House and one of its senators voted against the declaration largely because of the state's exposed position. Few of the state's ninety-five thousand militiamen were properly trained, equipped, or led. The details of appointing officers, requisitioning supplies, and locating armaments absorbed much of the governor's time and energy. Tompkins also argued for the establishment of a naval force on the Great Lakes to protect his state's northern and western frontiers. He traveled in September to Sackets Harbor with Commodore Isaac Chauncey, newly appointed commander of the U.S. naval forces on Lakes Ontario and Erie. Tompkins was still there in October when Maj. Gen. Stephen Van Rensselaer of the New York militia launched an unsuccessful attack across the Niagara River at Queenston, followed by U.S. Army Brig. Gen. Alexander Smyth's equally unsuccessful efforts to mount an offensive across the river.

The war along New York's frontiers went from bad to worse in 1813. Multiple American defeats along the Niagara River—including the retreat from Fort George, the capture of Fort Niagara, and the burning of Buffalo—and the St. Lawrence River, where General Wilkinson's and General Hampton's campaigns fizzled, understandably left Tompkins dismayed. He complained to Secretary of War Armstrong that these setbacks created "apprehension and dissatisfaction in the public mind."[14] Nevertheless, he lobbied for a winter campaign to take the Canadian town of Prescott along the St. Lawrence, offering to lead the attack and then suggesting that Dearborn take command. Armstrong opposed both the plan and the appointment. David Parish, a wealthy landowner and investor in the town of Ogdensburg on the New York side of the river opposite Prescott, had loaned the Madison administration millions of dollars with a tacit understanding that U.S. military operations and troops would be kept far away from his business interests, which depended on Montreal as a market.[15]

Tompkins's political clout and wartime effectiveness improved in the spring of 1814 with the election of a Republican-dominated state legislature that approved several of the governor's requests for increasing the militia's pay, creating a privateering association, and raising a force of Sea Fencibles, or naval militia, to defend New York City. He also ordered Maj. Gen. Amos Hall of the militia to call up all available militia to defend against a potential attack on the city. As these measures were being enacted, U.S. forces won a decisive victory at Plattsburgh.[16]

Shortly thereafter, Madison asked Tompkins to take over the State Department, which James Monroe had vacated to succeed Armstrong as secretary of war. Tompkins declined, citing his duties as governor at this crucial point in the war. The president gave him command of the Third Military District covering New York and New Jersey, and Tompkins replaced Maj. Gen.

Morgan Lewis, with whom he had clashed over federal supplies to the New York State militia. This appointment did not come with an explicit military rank, but as Monroe explained to Governor William Pennington of New Jersey, who was upset that his state militia had been subordinated to another state governor, all governors called into federal service automatically possessed one rank higher than a major general. Although the immediate threat to the city had dissipated by the time Tompkins arrived in October, Monroe thought the governor's presence could be useful in securing loans for the cash-strapped federal government. Tompkins managed to find a total of $600,000.[17]

Some suspect that Tompkins's interest in running for president influenced his decision to remain in New York, but others observe that two years in Washington would have improved his chances in the election of 1816. In any event, as the commander of the Third Military District, Tompkins was headquartered in New York City. The governor spent the final months of the war focused on defending the city in light of the proven threat of British amphibious operations against New England and the cities of Washington and Baltimore. He also spent more time on financing the war effort; having already personally vouched for loans in the summer of 1814, he did so again in December. He relinquished his command in February following news of the Treaty of Ghent and its quick ratification. Historian Julius Pratt summed up Tompkins's performance as a war governor by noting that "he devoted his great energy and very considerable ability to the conduct of the war, risking both health and fortune for the cause. The importance of Tompkins' loyalty was proportionate to the part in the war which geography assigned to his state."[18]

The considerable political and antiwar opposition Tompkins faced in New York made his wartime accomplishments even more impressive. His support for the prewar embargo contrasted with the Federalists' position and brought him into conflict with New York State senator and Republican Party leader DeWitt Clinton, who had nominated and supported Tompkins for election. Clinton denounced the embargo and wanted the New York State's presidential electors to vote as a bloc for his uncle the former New York governor and then vice president George Clinton in the election of 1808. Tompkins opposed this move, believing that it would divide the Republican Party and weaken the state's influence in the new administration. DeWitt Clinton relented, and Madison was elected. When Tompkins explicitly gave a lower priority to the defense of New York City in 1812, Clinton, who had opposed the war and was running for president as a peace candidate, embellished his credentials when the state's Federalist-controlled Council of Appointments commissioned him as a major general in the militia. Clinton engaged in constructive efforts to improve the defenses of the city, where Federalist Party leaders convened in September and agreed to support Clinton for president. The resulting Federalist-Clintonian Republican alliance captured the state's legislature and electoral votes in 1812. The New York State Senate consisted of nineteen Clintonians and nine Federalists compared to four Madison Republicans, and the Assembly comprised twenty-nine Clintonians and fifty-eight Federalists versus twenty-two Madison Republicans. Clinton thus easily carried the state but lost to Madison in the Electoral College by an 89–128 vote. Tompkins, however, narrowly won reelection the following spring over the Federalist candidate, General Rensselaer, by a margin of less than 5 percent of the votes cast.

After the war ended, Tompkins continued to stress the need for military preparedness. His address to the New York legislature in 1816 was more focused on the continuing British threat than on the building of canals, including the proposal to build what became known as the Erie Canal, which DeWitt Clinton championed. In response to his opposition, Tompkins remarked, "England will never forgive us for our victories on land, and on the ocean and the lakes; and my word for it, we shall have another war with her within two years."[19] Later that year, the state Republican Party nominated Tompkins for president, while he concurrently and reluctantly ran for governor against the popular Federalist U.S. senator Rufus King. Tompkins beat King by a comfortable margin and, then as Monroe's running mate, handily beat the Federalists later that year in the Electoral College. In 1817, Tompkins resigned as governor and served as vice president until 1825, dying shortly after leaving office. During his time in office, his inaccurate prophecy regarding war with Britain, his wrongheaded opposition to the Erie Canal, and his tenuous personal finances led to alcoholism. He sometimes presided over the Senate while inebriated. Curiously, he ran again for governor in 1820, narrowly losing to Clinton (probably because of the latter's support for the canal) but serving as president of the New York State Constitutional Convention in 1821.

Maryland

Between Pennsylvania and Virginia stretched no barrier of mountain or deserts. Nature seemed to mean that the northern State should reach toward the Chesapeake, and embrace its wide system of coasts and rivers.

The Susquehanna, crossing Pennsylvania from north to south, rolled down wealth which in a few years built the city of Baltimore by the surplus of Pennsylvania's resources. Any part of the Chesapeake Bay, or of the streams which flowed into it, was more easily accessible to Baltimore than any part of Massachusetts or Pennsylvania or New York.[20]

Levin Winder (1756–1819) became governor of Maryland in November 1812 in an election that gave not only the governor's mansion but also the state House of Representatives (54–26) to the Federalist Party. A wave of anti-Republican sentiment swept the elections following attacks on the offices of the Federalist newspaper that had resulted in casualties to its staff and several prominent supporters. The state Senate, consisting of fifteen Republican senators, had been elected the previous year and left Winder with a strongly divided legislature.

Entering office well after the declaration of war, Winder inherited a situation where his predecessor, Robert Bowie, had made key decisions that left him little latitude. In June, Bowie had convened the General Assembly to solicit appropriations for six thousand militiamen, which was Maryland's quota that President Madison had called into federal service. Most of these troops marched to New York, where they subsequently participated in campaigns in Canada in late 1812 and early 1813. Brig. Gen. William Winder, the governor's nephew, participated in the attacks on York and Fort George before being captured at the Battle of Stoney Creek. He remained a prisoner until he was exchanged in 1814.

The absence of Maryland's militia forces was keenly felt in 1813 when Admiral Cockburn began a campaign of raids against towns and individual farms around the Chesapeake Bay. Governor Winder, as early as March of that year, appealed to Secretary of War John Armstrong for assistance, arguing that Maryland had fulfilled its constitutional requirement to provide for the common defense by raising its militia forces and now required the federal government to hold up its end of the constitutional bargain by supporting Maryland's defense with men and matériel. Armstrong promised, but did not deliver, a battalion of troops to protect the state capital, Annapolis. Maryland's newspapers pointed out that Virginia, the president's home state, and New York—both with Republican governors—had received assistance. In May, Winder convened the legislature for a special session and provided his correspondence with Armstrong. The legislature established a committee that recommended measures of self-defense and appropriations of $100,000. The only tangible federal assistance that the state received at this time was Secretary of the Navy William Jones's deployment of a gunboat flotilla commanded by Capt. (and Marylander) Joshua Barney for the defense of the bay.

More important to Maryland were the efforts of Baltimore's political leadership to strengthen the city's defenses. These measures suggest that Winder's performance as a wartime governor and chief executive fell short of expectations and that while the state found the federal government's effort inadequate, the city also determined the state's effort was unsatisfactory. Winder inspected the city's defenses in March 1813 and authorized U.S. senator and Maj. Gen. Samuel Smith, commanding Maryland's third militia division, to "take the earliest opportunity of making the necessary arrangement of the militia for the defenses of the Port of Baltimore."[21] Smith, already recognized by the city's officials as the senior officer in charge, interpreted Winder's vague order in the broadest possible manner and strengthened the forces and fortifications in and around the city. He also used his considerable power and influence in Washington to obtain what meager assistance he could coax from Armstrong and Jones. Perhaps Smith's greatest accomplishment in this regard was eventually persuading Armstrong to replace Maj. Lloyd Beall with Maj. George Armistead as the commander of Fort McHenry.

In the spring of 1813, however, Armstrong complicated matters when he responded to a plea from Smith with a letter to Winder authorizing Smith to call up two thousand troops from his militia division for the defense of Baltimore until a newly drafted militia could replace them. The letter, however, left unclear who would command these forces and determine when they were adequately trained. Smith assumed these responsibilities and convinced the newly formed Committee of Public Supply, consisting of many of his friends and associates in Baltimore, to provision these soldiers in the expectation that Washington would reimburse them. Winder cooperated by allowing Smith to purchase arms at the state's expense but nominated fellow Federalist and state militia Brig. Gen. Henry Miller as their commander. Miller tried to convince the city elders to recognize his appointment, but they declared their loyalty to Smith. Armstrong backed Miller unless Smith could prove that Winder had called him into active service. Smith cited the governor's March order, and Winder waited a day before sending notification confirming Smith's interpretation of this order. It is not clear whether this delay suggested that Winder was considering replacing Smith with Miller or, having unintentionally created the appearance of a conflict, the governor was being cautious in resolving it with the least possible damage to himself and the generals. In any event, Winder's decision to confirm Smith's command allowed the city's defenses to be strengthened, ultimately leading to a successful outcome when the British attacked in the summer of 1814.

The same cannot be said of Winder's involvement in appointing his nephew, General Winder, the commander of Madison's newly created Tenth Military District, which encompassed Annapolis, Baltimore, and Washington, in July 1814. To fill the post, Armstrong recommended Brig. Gen. Moses Porter, the commander of the Ninth Military District, which had included these cities and the state of Virginia. Secretary of State Monroe is rumored to have recommended William Winder, ostensibly because his uncle would be more likely to provide the militia required to defend against the anticipated British campaign. Monroe may also have been looking beyond the impending emergency to his 1816 presidential campaign and hoping that the recently appointed general would yield command to him in the field. When the invasion did come, Monroe himself led the cavalry reconnaissance of the British forces that had landed in Benedict, Maryland, and then altered the deployment of the Maryland militia at Bladensburg, albeit with disastrous effect. Monroe's subsequent appointment as Armstrong's replacement as secretary of war after the capture of Washington also supports the notion that he participated in the war effort to burnish his military credentials. In any case, Governor Winder's involvement in the Miller-Smith and Winder-Porter appointments points to his tendency to view these assignments in political as opposed to military terms.

In the short term, his nephew's appointment served the governor's interests. Governor Winder had refused to call out the militia at the state's expense that summer, drawing angry denouncements in the press. General Winder's appointment relieved him of that responsibility. Late in the year, however, the federal government's inability to defend itself, much less Annapolis and Baltimore, as well as its inability to pay for militia deployments elsewhere, prompted the governor to call for the creation of a state army purely for the defense of Maryland. The legislature agreed to this request in January, passing a bill to raise an army of five thousand men for five years to serve within the boundaries of the state, southeastern Pennsylvania, and northern Virginia. Further, the federal government would have to pay Maryland's troops if they were called into federal service.[22]

Levin Winder, who served until January 1816 and died in 1819, played a far less activist role as a wartime governor than Barbour or Tompkins had. He did not take the field when the British invaded or become personally involved in tactical deployments or the construction of fortifications. Whether his party affiliation precluded him from doing so or he was simply content to leave the responsibility (and potential blame) for outcomes to Republican officials at the federal, state, and local level is not clear. Certainly in terms of Maryland's role in the War of 1812, his contributions pale beside those of other native sons, particularly General Smith and Captain Barney.

REAR AREA STATES
Massachusetts

> Society in Massachusetts was sharply divided by politics. In 1800 one half the population, represented under property qualifications by only some twenty thousands voters, was Republican. The other half, which cast about twenty-five thousand votes, included nearly every one in the professional and mercantile classes, and represented the wealth, social position, and education of the Commonwealth; but its strength lay in the clergy, the magistracy, the bench and bar, and respectable society throughout the State. This union created what was unknown beyond New England—an organized social system, capable of acting at command either for offence or defence, and admirably adapted for the uses of the eighteenth century.[23]

Caleb Strong (1745–1819) was narrowly elected governor, by a margin of only 1,200 out of more than 100,000 votes, in 1812 as part of wave of Federalist opposition to the Madison administration and the looming war with Britain. Massachusetts Federalists had selected him based on both his deep political experience—he had been a member of the Constitutional Convention in 1780, was a member of the U.S. Senate (1789–1796), and had served as governor before (1800–1807)—and his reputation for moderation, or what one contemporary described as his "unostentatious, republican simplicity."[24] Strong shared the prevailing view of his party, which was articulated in a resolution that the Federalist-dominated House of Representatives passed at the end of June: the war resulted from Madison's mistaken judgment that France had repealed its embargo, a Republican determination to place southern and western interests over those of the eastern states, and a strategic miscalculation that Britain would eventually yield to France.

As one of his first acts as governor, Strong designated July 23 as a statewide day of fasting and for clergy to proclaim opposition to the war. Backed by his governor's council, Strong also refused General Dearborn's request for forty-one militia companies from Massachusetts, because only some of them would be used to relieve regular units manning coastal fortifications and other Massachusetts troops and militiamen would participate in operations against Canada. At the same time, Strong ordered the militia to "repel any invasion," arguing that if such a danger existed, the federal government should not call on his state's militia to serve elsewhere. Dearborn took this recalcitrance as a sign that the governor did not recognize his authority under federal law over the state's militia. Strong sought and received the approval of the state's Supreme Court in refusing to provide these troops or to put them under federal command. He did show some flexibility, however, in sending three companies to Passamaquoddy on the coast in Maine (then part of the commonwealth of Massachusetts) because it faced "a peculiar danger of invasion." Like his fellow Federalist governors, Strong also did not interfere with exclusively federal matters within his state.[25]

In 1813, Strong's position was strengthened when he was reelected and his party retained control of the state's House and Senate. He directed his attention, albeit unsuccessfully, to securing federal armaments for the state's militia as provided for by an 1808 congressional appropriations act. Washington had provided none, and Secretary of War Armstrong had explained the frontier states and militias in the service of the country needed the arms more. Strong also urged the state legislature to investigate the causes of the war and efforts to promote a reconciliation with Great Britain. The legislature passed a "memorial" (a declaration) blaming France for the current state of affairs and against the federal government's plans to add additional states to the Union without the consent of the original thirteen members.

The passage of the Embargo Act of 1813, designed to reduce trade with the enemy—particularly trade conducted in New England, where the British did not extend their maritime embargo until 1814—prompted Strong to question the act's constitutionality. Neutral trade had made Massachusetts and other New England states both the principal supplier of foreign goods in the United States and the recipient of specie and out-of-state bank bills used to pay for these goods. The latter gave Boston banks considerable potential leverage for draining specie from the rest of the country if they chose to redeem those notes. When a New York customs officer used the embargo to prevent the transfer of

a consignment of specie to the Bank of New England in Boston, Strong had little trouble securing its release after the Massachusetts Senate published a study
of this local advantage in liquidity.

Strong easily won reelection in early 1814, this time by twelve thousand
votes as the Federalists gained additional strength in the legislature. The British
extension of their naval blockade to New England prompted the legislature to
pass a million-dollar defense appropriations bill, leaving Strong to spend the
money at his discretion. Despite the increased threat, Strong refused to seek
assistance or cooperation from Dearborn, who then commanded the First
Military District responsible for defending New England. When the British
landed forces in Maine in July, Strong sent a thousand militiamen but not under
the command of a federal officer. Later he did not respond positively to
Dearborn's requests in the fall for more troops to evict the British.[26]

Concurrently, the Massachusetts legislature decided that the state should
not officially oppose the embargo without the support of neighboring states.
Napoleon's abdication in March and the subsequent shift of British military
power from Europe to North America, thus enabling British attacks on Maine
and Connecticut in July and on Maryland in August, accelerated plans for a
convention. Despite having argued against efforts that would exacerbate political divisions within the state or between the state and federal government,
Strong called the legislature into session earlier than usual after the British
seized the town of Castine, Maine, in September. He also insisted that the additional militiamen called up to meet federal requisitions should remain under
the command of state officers. Having formally separated the state and federal
defense efforts in Massachusetts, Strong asked newly appointed Secretary of
War Monroe whether Washington would reimburse the state for defending
itself. Monroe replied that compensation would only occur when the state's
militia was placed under federal control.

In response to this exchange, the state legislature issued a report carrying
the name of Representative Harrison Gray Otis, calling for a convention where
states could collectively discuss amending the Constitution and securing their
protection in light of the federal government's inability to do so. The other
New England legislatures supported the measure, as did Maryland's Federalist-
led House of Delegates. Noting that amending the Constitution would take
too long under the circumstances, the measure called for appointing delegates
who would meet with counterparts from other New England states, consult on
their mutual defense, and take steps toward arranging a national convention for

revising the Constitution. The Hartford Convention failed to attract repre-sentatives from all of the New England states, but Monroe took the threat of secession as a serious possibility and ordered several New England regiments that were stationed on the Niagara frontier back to the areas from which they had been drawn. Officially, these units were engaged in winter recruiting, but they also monitored the situation and provided reaction force with orders to secure the Springfield arsenal if necessary. Monroe called again on Strong to pro-vide men and matériel for the federal forces and proposed a campaign to eject the British from Maine and then to capture Halifax.

At the same time, Strong secretly dispatched an emissary to the British governor of Nova Scotia Sir John Coape Sherbrooke. He wanted to explore the terms of a separate peace, given Britain's demonstrated ability to threaten Massachusetts and Maine and Washington's inability to protect them. In par-ticular, Strong wanted to know whether his majesty's government would pro-vide assistance if the New England states arranged an armistice. Upon receipt of Sherbrooke's request for instructions, Lord Bathurst, the British secretary for war and the colonies, authorized him to sign such an agreement and to promise British "arms, accoutrements, ammunition, Clothing and naval Cooperation." London, however, was not willing to engage in direct military assistance by deploying troops as such efforts would have had a counterproductive effect. Bathurst's instructions were dated December 13, and the Treaty of Ghent was signed only eleven days later. For the British, Sherbrooke's arrangement was an insurance policy against the peace negotiations in Belgium collapsing or the Madison administration and/or the Senate's rejecting the peace treaty.[27]

Strong and other Massachusetts Federalists were not overly concerned with the harsh terms that the British initially proposed in their agreement. They did not view London's claim on conquered territory along the border with Canada, including portions of Maine, as unacceptable since Maine was largely Republican and the occupied territory was "a cold barren inhospitable region probably not worth one cent per 100 acres," according to one prominent Federalist. Moreover, Strong was not averse to creating an Indian buffer state in the Ohio region because he believed the American Indian policy had been "extremely unjustified and inhumane."[28]

The Hartford Convention, meanwhile, produced amendments designed to enhance the influence of New England and an implicit threat to conclude a separate peace with Britain if they were rejected. Massachusetts and Connecticut endorsed the convention's proceedings. Delegates carrying these proposals to Washington arrived shortly after news of the Treaty of Ghent and Jackson's victory in New Orleans broke.

Strong continued to serve as governor until May 1816. He died three years later. His sharp and unyielding opposition to the Madison administration's decision to declare war on Britain reflected the intense divisions between Federalists and Republicans that, in the case of Massachusetts, did not abate even in the face of foreign occupation.

North Carolina

In some respects North Carolina, though modest in ambition and backward in thought, was still the healthiest community south of the Potomac. Neither aristocratic like Virginia and South Carolina, nor turbulent like Georgia, nor troubled by a sense of social importance, but above all thoroughly democratic, North Carolina tolerated more freedom of political action and showed less family and social influence, fewer vested rights in political power, and less tyranny of slaveholding interests and terrors than were common elsewhere in the South. Neither cultivated nor brilliant in intellect, nor great in thought, industry, energy, or organization, North Carolina was still interesting and respectable.[29]

William Hawkins (1777–1819), elected governor of North Carolina in December 1811, was a Republican and strong supporter of the Madison administration who backed the decision to declare war in 1812. Following that congressional vote, in which both North Carolina senators and six of its nine representatives voted for war, Hawkins issued a proclamation calling on every citizen "to unite in repelling those aggressions, insults, and injuries with which we have been and are yet assailed." He further noted that war had been "so justly declared against a power who has . . . long since been waging War against the United States by actual and positive aggressions."[30] North Carolina's victims of these "aggressions," though, had been decidedly small. Only twenty-five out of some six thousand American seamen impressed by the British were from the state, and no ship registered in North Carolina had been brought before the British Admiralty Courts as a prize between 1808 and 1812. In fact, the European wars had benefited North Carolina as an exporter of timber and naval stores. For Hawkins and his fellow North Carolinians supporting the war, however, the key issue was honor—that is, a combination of indignation over

British infringements on national sovereignty and a narrative linking 1812 with the conditions that precipitated the Revolutionary War.

Governor Hawkins was appropriately concerned about his state's defenses and the possibility of British raids, but neither Washington nor regional federal military officials considered his fears compelling. Monroe wrote to the chairman of the Senate's Military Committee, "It may be said that it is not probable that the enemy will attempt an invasion of any part of the [Atlantic] coast. . . ."[31] To underscore the remote possibility of such an invasion, he recommended only a hundred men for the defense of North Carolina. Maj. Gen. Thomas Pinckney, commanding the Sixth Military District covering Georgia, North Carolina, and South Carolina, paid scant attention to Hawkins's state. His priority was preparing to secure East Florida, and by the time those plans were abandoned in July 1813, the Creek War had begun to consume his attention and efforts.

When Hawkins asked why more was not done to strengthen coastal defenses, Pinckney explained that his territorial responsibilities far exceeded his resources, and he had decided to protect only the most important and significant ports. Of the seven thousand men that North Carolina raised to fill its share of the national quota, he ordered four companies of militia each to Fort Johnston (south of Wilmington and Cape Fear) and Fort Hampton (Beaufort) to defend against coastal attacks. Pinckney also authorized Hawkins to call out the militia when an attack "obviously threatened" or occurred and pointed out that Wilmington and Edenton (south of Norfolk, Virginia) should have companies ready to be called into action. With minimal assistance from Pinckney, Hawkins relied on voluntary contributions of labor, matériel, and money from city and state funds to improve his state's defenses. Like other governors, Hawkins also sent missives to Washington noting that his state had sent troops to protect other states but that not one soldier had arrived to defend North Carolina. North Carolina, in fact, led the southern states in furnishing recruits.

Hawkins had directed that the state's militia quota be filled "with the utmost alacrity, zeal, and dispatch."[32] Yet, although he and other Democrats preferred a well-regulated militia over a standing army, the North Carolina legislature failed to pass laws in 1811 and 1812 providing funds for the militia's equipment and supplies. Hawkins lobbied for the authority to spend state funds for military purposes without specific legislation, but he did not receive such authority until 1813, when the state treasurer was authorized to borrow funds in 1813 and 1814. This authority provided critical supplies and provisions that were truly the responsibility of the federal government, which later reimbursed the state. In 1814, Secretary of War Armstrong gave Hawkins the authority to call out the militia in federal service without first having a federal officer inspect and muster them.

The only large-scale British attack on North Carolina occurred at Ocracoke and Portsmouth on Beacon Island on July 12, 1813. Adm. John Warren and Admiral Cockburn arrived with five warships and two tenders, hoping to disrupt the shipping that had been using the island as an alternative to blockaded Norfolk. The British, however, found little activity on the island, captured one privateer brig, and departed after requisitioning local livestock. A revenue cutter that had fled when the fleet appeared arrived at New Bern late in the evening, and the local commander sent a dispatch to inform the governor in Raleigh. Hawkins sent a company led by his adjunct general and personally arrived two days later at the head of a troop of cavalry. The governor also sent a special emissary to Norfolk for supplies, but they took eight days to arrive. The citizens of New Bern were particularly appreciative of Hawkins's racing "in such haste to our town, to share in our toil, to mix in our dangers, and to give a more certain combination, force, and effect to our means of resistance. . . ."[33]

The attack caused alarm across the North Carolina coast. Some dismissed the raid and the resulting activity as a tempest in a teapot, but Hawkins used the event to tour the coast, to bolster morale, and to collect information for a report criticizing the federal government for its lack of preparedness. He noted that "every state in the union . . . particularly those most exposed to danger, should place themselves in an attitude to furnish, whenever necessity may require it, prompt and efficient aid."[34] Pinckney used the report to recommend sending twelve infantry companies and two hundred artillerists for North Carolina. The Creek War intervened, however, and little was done until the summer of 1814. Pinckney revisited the coast, concerned that a larger scale attack was possible in the wake of Napoleon's defeat and the redeployment of British troops from the Continent. The government improved defenses and called up additional militiamen. North Carolina troops were also sent to reinforce Norfolk, but following the attacks on Washington and Baltimore, the British bypassed the state on their way to New Orleans.

Shortly before the end of the war, Hawkins completed his third term as governor, a constitutional limit. He subsequently served in the North Carolina House of Commons in 1817 and died two years later.

Pennsylvania

This great State, considering its political importance, was treated with little respect by its neighbors; and yet had New England, New York, and Virginia been swept out of existence in 1800, democracy could have better spared them all than have lost Pennsylvania. The only true democratic community then existing in the eastern States, Pennsylvania was neither picturesque nor troublesome. The State contained no hierarchy like that of New England; no great families like those of New York; no oligarchy like the planters of Virginia and South Carolina.[35]

Simon Snyder (1759–1819) was elected to his second term as governor in 1811 by an overwhelming majority, garnering all but a few thousand of the more than fifty-seven thousand votes cast. The first German American governor of the state and an ardent Democrat, Snyder followed the dictum "Hope for the best, prepare for the worst" when it came to foreign affairs. He forecasted "flattering prospects" in U.S. relations with the warring European powers in 1811, believing that Britain and France would soon end their harassment of American maritime commerce. After seeing efforts fail on that front, Snyder endorsed the Madison administration's war preparations. In doing so, the governor reflected the views of the majority of Pennsylvania Republicans who believed Britain, more so than France, had violated Americans' rights on the high seas. Having supported Madison's economic embargoes and nonimportation efforts to compel the British to end their predatory actions against U.S. ships and sailors, Snyder and his faction in the party saw no alternative to war. In 1809 Snyder remarked that the burdens of war or those of continued embargoes could not compare to "the loss of national independence to be incurred by tame submission to the orders" of a foreign monarch. As the *Pennsylvania Republican* noted as war drew near in April 1812, "The honor of the Nation and that of the party are bound together and both will be sacrificed if war be not declared." So-called old school Democrats (i.e., Republicans) and Federalists in Pennsylvania also supported war at a public meeting that Snyder called at the State House in May, and a month later the declaration of war received solid support from Pennsylvania's senators and representatives in Congress. Without their votes, the western War Hawks would not have had sufficient numbers to pass the measure. As one assessment of the national decision to go to war observed, "However important the role of the frontier west may have been in bringing on the war of 1812, a good share of the credit or blame must be given to the Democrats of Pennsylvania."[36]

Snyder repeatedly exhorted the state legislature to make war preparations, as had his predecessor. He called for the state legislature to undertake a thorough reform of the militia, particularly regarding training and equipment, in December 1810. The legislature, like its counterparts in other states, declined to act on this recommendation. Snyder repeated his request in the fall of 1811 and again in 1812 following that year's military debacles and Madison's reelection, which saw the president receive forty-nine thousand votes compared to twenty-nine thousand for Clinton in Pennsylvania. Snyder also bolstered the state's morale by downplaying these reversals, saying they should be expected from a country that had cultivated the arts of peace and not war, and by noting that Americans would "unshakingly" meet these challenges.[37]

The legislature this time passed resolutions praising Snyder for his ability to encourage volunteers to fill the federal levy, thereby obviating the need for a draft and, as they had in previous sessions, then made minor changes in the militia laws. These efforts, however, fell short of providing the militia with the equipment, training, and leadership necessary to support the regular army. Still, Pennsylvania contributed more militiamen to federal service than any other state and generously subscribed to war loans adopted by the Department of the Treasury to sustain the conflict perhaps, in part, because the war stimulated the agricultural and manufacturing sectors of the state's economy. The governor worked closely with the legislature to allow state-chartered banks to grant loans to the federal treasury, to authorize Snyder to pay any direct tax apportioned to the state while the legislature was not in session, and to give the governor complete discretion in distributing state arms to the militia.[38]

Snyder, unlike Governors Barbour, Hawkins, Tompkins, Strong, and Winder, never faced a British attack on his state's territory, but he did respond to four potential threats. The first came in March 1813 when a British squadron appeared in Delaware Bay. Snyder called for volunteers to defend Philadelphia, and four thousand men rallied to defend the city. A Committee of Defense headed by Charles Biddle was quickly formed and declared operational in mid-April. Concurrently, the War Department authorized the construction of a fort on Pea Patch Island in Delaware Bay. The second threat came later that year when the British squadron on Lake Erie hovered off Presque Isle in July and

August, hoping to launch a preemptive attack on Commodore Perry's base and warships. Although Snyder played no role in this episode, many of the sailors and militiamen in the American forces hailed from the Keystone State, and much of the matériel used to outfit Perry's ships came from Philadelphia and Pittsburgh. The third contingency occurred after the British captured Fort Niagara and burned Buffalo in December 1813. Snyder recommended to Secretary of War Armstrong that Erie should be reinforced, and he was authorized to take command of the regulars at Pittsburgh and to call up a thousand militiamen.[39]

The last and most serious alarm followed the capture of Washington in the summer of 1814, and Snyder called out the militia of thirteen southeastern counties to defend Philadelphia. They gathered on Bush Hill at "Camp Snyder." Snyder asked the federal government to enlarge the fort on Pea Patch and to send regulars and militias into the Delaware Bay area, but Armstrong refused because of the cost. On August 26 a public bipartisan meeting of the reactivated Committee of Defense received $500,000 from local municipalities, and organized a volunteer effort to erect, repair, and man fortifications around the city. The committee ignored the city's government, and Brig. Gen. Joseph Bloomfield, commander of the Fourth Military District and responsible for the defense of Delaware, Pennsylvania, and New Jersey, set up his headquarters in the City of Brotherly Love.[40]

To make matters worse, Snyder also moved his headquarters to the city. He clashed with Bloomfield and his successor in October, Brig. Gen. Edmund Gaines, over the organization of the militia and denounced what he called the "Committee of Offence" for overreaching its authority. The *Democratic Press* also assailed the committee for allegedly drawing up articles of impeachment against Snyder. The governor, meanwhile, used the emergency to recommend the creation of a few regiments, or in effect a state army, to be maintained during times of war. A bill originated in the state Senate along these lines, but the senators discarded it once news of the peace agreement with Britain arrived. It was undoubtedly fortunate that the British had not targeted Philadelphia, where the defenses and coordination (in military parlance, "unity of command") paled in comparison to those of Baltimore.[41]

Snyder's loyalty to the Madison administration led some of his supporters to lobby for his candidacy as vice president on the Republican ticket that James Monroe headed in 1816. Whether Snyder wanted the position is not clear, but as noted earlier, New York governor Tompkins became Monroe's vice president.

Snyder finished his third term as governor in 1817 and was elected to the U.S. Senate in 1818, but he died the following year before taking office.

The importance of these six governors, as well as those of the other states and territories, cannot be underestimated. Their efforts to defend their respective states while contributing soldiers to the U.S. Army and supporting military districts' commanders posed an immense challenge, and the need to coordinate and seek approval from their state legislatures and municipal authorities further complicated their efforts. On occasion, these governors were often the last, and sometimes the only, line of defense for their states and populations. Certainly, Baltimore's defense was more of a local and not a federal success, in which Governor Winder wisely supported and, more important, did not interfere with Senator Smith's plans and actions. Conversely, Governor Tompkins shares the blame for the disaster at Queenston Heights since he selected Van Rensselaer to command the state militia.

Because they focused on state rather than national issues, their actions taken during the conflict do not easily fit into either the Mr. Madison's War or Second War of Independence narratives. This complex set of roles and responsibilities could be viewed as consistent with the emphasis in Mr. Madison's War on the lack of preparation and management of the war effort. Snyder's difficulties with officials in Philadelphia and Winder's deference to Smith in Baltimore fit neatly into this theme. Somewhat differently, Strong's secret negotiations with British officials to take New England out of the war could be viewed as trumping the worst cases of incompetence by either state or federal officials (e.g., Secretary of War Armstrong), even though his motives sprang from his partisanship and his judgment that Washington could not protect Massachusetts and its neighbors. In this sense, these and the other state governors were part and parcel of the political and institutional immaturity of the country as was the lack of a professional staff and capable public servants in the War and Navy Departments.

The history of the governors in the War of 1812, however, also contains threads that are woven into the Second War of Independence interpretation. Barber's, Hawkins's, and Snyder's instincts to "ride to sound of the guns" when the British invaded or threatened their states and their efforts to maintain their militias and raise state armies later in the war demonstrated high levels of patriotism, duty, and courage. On balance, probably neither narrative adequately accounts for the successes and failures of these governors, suggesting a "level of analysis" problem in applying national-level story lines to state-level activities.

Properly evaluating the governors' efforts and the important roles they played in the war probably requires a broader study of American wartime governors in the first half of the history of the United States. Revolutionary War and Civil War governors faced similar challenges as chief executives, and even as de facto "warlords," responsible for the security of their territories and citizens. Confederate governors, like their War of 1812 counterparts, went to war as part of a new country with unproven laws and institutions. Further, civilian and military authorities in Richmond asked the governors to supply recruits but would not commit resources to the defense of their states. These governors also opposed local military officials who forcibly removed military supplies and construction materials needed elsewhere without consulting with them.

As Strong did, the Confederate governors took matters into their own hands and attempted to negotiate a peace with their midwestern Union counterparts and a separate treaty with Britain or France for the defense of the Trans-Mississippi states after Richmond failed to protect them from the Union army's advances. They clearly exceeded their constitutional powers in doing so, but unlike Strong, they kept Richmond informed.[42] However, the Confederate governors faced a different fate than their 1812 counterparts did: they were conquered and subsequently clung to the Lost Cause narrative.

5

DUELING NARRATIVES
Henry Adams's Alternative History of the War of 1812

B y providing a detailed and well-argued critique of the U.S. approach to
and conduct of the war, Henry Adams's *The War of 1812* with its extensive use of what-if commentaries is a major contribution to the Mr. Madison's
War narrative.[1] At the same time, his numerous speculative observations about
alternative decisions and outcomes suggest that the war might have lived up to
its billing as a Second War of Independence. This tension between what was
and what might have been makes Adams's account of the War of 1812 an ideal
subject for exploring the war in which America was neither the victor nor the
vanquished. It also provides a starting point for using this technique more systematically in the following chapters to assess the two narratives and the larger
issue of the war's importance in American history.

Although alternative histories have become fairly popular in recent years,
the War of 1812 has received little attention in this genre. For example, in Robert
Sobel's classic *For Want of a Nail: If Burgoyne Had Won at Saratoga*, the British
victory in the American Revolutionary War precludes a rematch two decades
later. In this tale, James Madison reprises his role as a founding father but of the
breakaway country of "Jefferson," while Andrew Jackson emerges as president of
the United States of Mexico. Robert Crowley's *What If? The World's Foremost
Military Historians Imagine What Might Have Been* does not mention the War of
1812. Its sequel, *What If? 2: Eminent Historians Imagine What Might Have Been*,
offers an echo in "Napoleon's Invasion of North America," where the French
emperor, with Andrew Jackson and Aaron Burr as two of his lieutenants, loses to
the Duke of Wellington in a reimagined Battle of New Orleans. As a result of this
climactic engagement, New England separates from the United States and joins
Canada and British Louisiana in dominating North America.[2]

More directly related to the war, Steve Tally's *Almost America: From the Colonists to Clinton: A "What if" History of the U.S.* features two entries related to the War of 1812—one in which Tecumseh is successful and another where Jackson loses the Battle of New Orleans. Similarly, two historical novels focusing on the War of 1812 feature alternative outcomes to key battles in 1814. David Fitz-Enz's *Redcoats' Revenge: An Alternate History of the War of 1812* depicts the British winning the Battle of Plattsburgh, New York, with Wellington directing operations in North America. Eric Flint's *1812: The Rivers of War* has Maj. Gen. Robert Ross defeated while attempting to dislodge the regrouped American forces fortified on Capitol Hill after the Battle of Bladensburg. Francis Scott Key is on hand to pen slightly different lyrics for the "Star-Spangled Banner."[3]

Henry Adams's *The War of 1812*, however, surpasses these recent alternative histories.[4] This volume, comprising chapters from Adams's nine-volume *History of the United States, 1801–1817*, which was first published from 1888 to 1891, was assembled by the *Infantry Journal* in 1944. It presents a cornucopia of alternative outcomes for many of the war's important battles and military decisions. Historian John Elting writes,

> There is no better general history than Henry Adams's The War of 1812. ... Though a century of continued use has found some errors and omissions in its descriptions of military operations, this book remains an example of honest and careful history. Adams's own unusual career had familiarized him with the inner workings of both the United States and British governments, the hard interrelationships of military power and diplomacy, and the ways in which piddling domestic politics can trip up crucial measures of national policy.[5]

Read from an "alternate history" perspective, Adams more than convinces his readers that individual engagements and the overall conflict could have taken any number of different twists and turns, leading to widely different outcomes. Adams's principal literary device in presenting these what-if scenarios is to describe the historical outcome and then present an "had X done Y" possibility, with X referring to the commanding officer and Y indicating his judgment as to a better course of action. He generally reserved this formulation in analyzing the effectiveness of those American and British senior officers whose performance he found wanting in one or more respects and occasionally noted how their competent opponents could have further exploited the situation. To be sure, not all of his judgments and speculations are shared by the other historians whose works are referenced here to illustrate the range of views on specific historical events and not to suggest a consensus, much less a "correct," view of the events that Adams addressed.

In this sense, Adams's contrarian commentaries run counter to two characteristics of his historical work. First, as part of a wave of nineteenth-century empirical historians, Adams strove to "ascertain what actually happened." Grounded in his understanding of the war's particular events and personalities— and illuminated by his thorough understanding of military tactics, supply efforts, logistics, morale, and discipline, as well as his observations on the conduct of the American Civil War—his speculations go well beyond a basic factual approach to history.

David Hackett Fischer's survey of historians' fallacies suggests boundaries for the proper use of this technique. He begins by categorizing the "fallacy of fictional questions" as one of several errors related to question framing. Fischer writes,

> The *fallacy of fictional questions* is an ancient form of error, which has recently been elevated into an explicit method and proclaimed before the world as a whole new thing in historical inquiry. It consists in an attempt to demonstrate by empirical method what might have happened in history, as if in fact it actually had: . . . if Booths' bullet had missed, . . . or Lee had won at Gettysburg, or Byron had become King of Greece. . . .
>
> . . . But they *prove* nothing and can never be proved by an empirical method.[6]

Fischer, however, notes that such what-ifs can be useful when properly framed. "There is nothing necessarily fallacious in fictional constructs, as long as they are properly recognized for what they are and are clearly distinguished from empirical problems. . . . Fictional questions can also be heuristically useful to historians, somewhat in the manner of metaphors and analogies, for the ideas and inferences which they help to suggest."[7]

Where Adams's speculations fall in these two approaches is a matter of the judgment. His "had X done Y" questions are often posed to critique strategic, operational, and tactical choices; that is, they serve as a heuristic device. At other times, however, they more than imply that the alternative courses of actions that he describes would have changed outcomes; thus, they are framed as empirical judgments. In either case, his repeated use of what-ifs clearly places him beyond the end point of the strict empirical approach and well along the path to alternative history.

Second, some have judged Adams as too protective of military men, but his numerous critiques of American and British generals indicate a discriminating view of senior officers. This quality may reflect his belief that the War of 1812, like the American Civil War, was a necessary conflict for the United States and that mistakes and incompetence on the part of American general officers were serious offenses. However, his less frequent but equally harsh criticism of British generals suggests that as a military historian Adams expected much from practitioners of the art of war and was not shy in calling them to account.[8]

YEAR 1: 1812

Adams wrote extensively on Brig. Gen. William Hull's star-crossed invasion of Canada and his eventual surrender of his entire army to Maj. Gen. Isaac Brock in Detroit. Adams identified a number of alternative outcomes, strongly indicating that Hull's debacle, while tragic, was eminently avoidable. Hull, the governor of the Michigan Territory, led his two-thousand-man army to Detroit believing that its presence there would compel the British to evacuate the region. He arrived in mid-July, crossed into Canada, and turned south. Then he captured the town of Sandwich (Windsor) and prepared to attack Fort Malden, which a British-Indian force half the size of his army occupied. Hull then learned that the U.S. outpost on Mackinac Island at the junction of Lakes Huron and Michigan had fallen and feared a widespread Indian advance from the north. Simultaneously, he found his supply line to Ohio harassed by British and Indian attacks. Hull withdrew to Detroit and pondered a retreat to Ohio. Adams suggested that had Hull opted for either flight or fight, he could have avoided the historical outcome, his surrender of his entire command. "Had he fallen back on the Maumee [River] or even to Urbana or Dayton, he would have done only what Wellington had done more than once in circumstances hardly more serious, and what Napoleon was about to do three months afterward leaving Moscow," Adams observed.[9]

Adams argued that a good general would still have saved Detroit for some weeks. He also noted that during his court-martial, Hull never expressed the opinion that Brock's assault could have succeeded. Adams speculated that the small British force, having failed to take the fort, would have had to retreat a mile and a half under the fire of the fort's heavy guns while the Americans pursued and possibly outflanked them.[10]

Military historian Elting somewhat concurs with Adams, reasoning, "There is little doubt that Hull could have repulsed Brock's assault; there is even less that he would have been eventually starved and bombarded into surrender, with great loss of life among the citizens of Detroit."[11] British historian Jon Latimer points out that Hull had an early opportunity to seize the day when his troops captured the bridge across the Aux Canards stream between Sandwich and Amherstburg: "Thus fell the only defensible position between Fort Malden, which now lay open; the majority of Indians remained neutral, and had Hull reacted quickly he might have taken Amherstburg."[12]

Adams went on to speculate that Brock's speedy arrival in Detroit or Lt. Gen. Henry Prévost's armistice with General Dearborn in the immediate wake of the U.S. declaration of war also might have prevented Hull's surrender of his entire command.[13] He also explored the opposite outcome in which a more aggressive British campaign captured Detroit, advanced into Ohio, and occupied the whole western end of Lake Erie. However, recalled to defend Niagara, Brock left only two or three companies of troops as garrison at Detroit and Malden.[14] If he had followed Adams's course of action, the British general, who favored such an "active defense" strategy, would have disobeyed Prévost's orders to maintain a defensive stance. He also would have risked U.S. forces along the Niagara River cutting his supply line to Lower Canada.

On these two points, Adams illustrated his ability to go beyond the facts. Wesley Turner's study of British generals in the War of 1812 notes that Prévost's armistice with Dearborn did not apply to Hull's command in Detroit. Moreover, Brock, like his predecessor, had planned to seize both Mackinac and Detroit and assessed that doing so would deter American attacks across the Niagara River. Given his limited forces and his two-front war at either end of Lake Erie, Brock's forces would have been stretched in 1812 to take on a more adventuresome foray into Ohio.[15]

Adams was also critical of Prévost's defensive strategy, implicitly arguing that the governor-general could have done more to defend Canada. Although the United States outmatched Canada in population and resources and Canada was fated to be Great Britain's secondary theater of operations given Wellington's operations on the Iberian Peninsula, Adams more than implied that Prévost should have listened to Brock and opted for a more aggressive approach to defending Canada: "Prevost, about the equal of Madison as a military leader, showed no wish to secure the positions necessary for his safety. Had he at once seized Sackett's Harbor, as Brock seized Detroit, he would have been secure for Sackett's Harbor was the only spot from which the Americans could contest control of Lake Ontario."[16] Turner concurs that the armistice prevented Prévost from attacking this key American base on Lake Ontario at the earliest opportunity and that his missives to Brock revealed his caution and pessimism.[17]

Finally, Adams's critique of the naval situation in the war's first year pointed to the possibility that the sole victories that U.S. warships earned at sea might have eluded the republic had circumstances and tactical decisions made by the captains at sea not voided orders from Washington. Later in his historical analysis, Adams showed a distinct preference for single-ship engagements, arguing that the American ships should not have sailed as a squadron. He noted that not long after Capt. John Rodgers and Capt. Stephen Decatur set sail, British Vice Admiral Sawyer sent a squadron from Halifax to prevent the American navy from attacking British convoys. Adams argued that against such a force Rogers and Decatur would have risked defeat by fighting in line of battle.[18]

In his book *Naval War of 1812*, Theodore Roosevelt notes two related what-ifs in his account of the U.S. Navy's first sortie. When Captain Rodgers commanding USS *President* and Captain Decatur commanding USS *United States* left New York, Rodgers shortly encountered HMS *Belvidera*. The *President* damaged the British ship with its first volley and would have been taken the British warship had a cannon not exploded on the *President*'s deck, causing Rodgers to begin yawing to fire his broadsides. The captain of the *Belvidera* used these circumstances to escape. Roosevelt notes that "the distance the chase took the pursuers out of their course probably saved the plate [treasure] fleet . . . had they not chased the *Belvidera* the Americans probably would have run across the plate fleet."[19] Roosevelt does not speculate what effect a successful attack on the fleet might have had on British strategy or morale. Such an encounter probably would have had an equal if not greater impact than did the single-ship victories, which caused the British Admiralty considerable concern and embarrassment and gave the Americans their only substantial success in the first year of the war.

YEAR 2: 1813

Adams's analysis of the western front in 1813 shifted attention from Hull's hesitancy to British Maj. Gen. Henry Procter's plodding behavior. Charged with holding British gains, Procter agreed to support Tecumseh's more aggressive plans to eliminate the U.S. forces under Maj. Gen. William Henry Harrison's command along the Ohio River. Their first effort in January 1813 was a spoiling attack on Brig. Gen. James Winchester's exposed advance force. Winchester, who had moved beyond his assigned position on the rapid of the Maumee River to protect settlers at Frenchtown on the River Raisin, was soundly defeated and saw some of his command massacred. This butchery prompted the Americans' later battle cry, "Remember the Raisin!"

In Adams's telling, Procter's battle tactics were flawed, and he did not capitalize on his victory. He argues that had Procter dashed at once on the defenseless Seventeenth Regiment, he probably would have captured the whole without any losses. Instead, he relied on his three-pound guns, giving the Kentuckians an opportunity to use their rifles with considerable effect.[20] Adams further speculates that had Procter acted quickly, he could have advanced to the rapids and captured Harrison and his force of nine hundred men, his artillery train, and his stores. He judges that in the heavy rain Harrison would not have escaped through the swamp, which had taken him two days to cross.[21]

Sandy Antal presents a more balanced assessment of the effectiveness of Procter's artillery at the Battle of Frenchtown. He quotes one American soldier in the battle who noted that "the British immediately discharged their artillery loaded with balls, bombs, and grapeshot, which did little injury," but also reported that some parts of the pickets defending the town were "completely shattered by the enemy's shot."[22] As for Procter's retreat to Amherstburg after the battle, Antal observes that when he ordered the retreat, Procter was acting on a false report that Harrison was only eight miles away. Hence, Procter did not believe that he had an opportunity to inflict a preemptive attack on Harrison. Harrison was marching toward the action, but he only managed to send an advance force of 170 men to within twelve miles of the town to assist the survivors of Winchester's command. Antal also quotes Procter's explanation: his decision to withdraw "was consistent with prudence and humanity to march off with the prisoners without delay."[23]

While criticizing Procter's judgment, Adams also questioned Harrison's strategy of securing the west, pointing to its political instead of military objectives: "Thus, the Western movement, likened by Henry Clay to a tenth-century crusade, ended in failure. The Government would have been better positioned had it never sent a man to the Maumee, but merely built a few sloops at Cleveland."[24] Here, Adams invoked the "control of the lakes" argument that dominated the campaigns along the Canadian-U.S. border. The side that had a fleet capable of destroying or blockading the enemy fleet and transporting forces for raids or conquest along the lakeshores gained advantages in maneuver and initiative in choosing the time and place of battle.

Disorganization and logistics rather than British military prowess undid Harrison's ambitious, but cautious, winter offensive in early 1813. He blamed his slow advance toward the Detroit frontier on "the imbecility of the public agents and the villainy of the contractors" that left his army poorly provisioned and clothed. He also speculated that if Winchester had waited at the rapids for another week, they could have combined their forces, and their five thousand men would have made an overwhelming advance on Detroit. Harrison planned to follow up his victory in the Northwest by joining the campaign on the Niagara frontier and overrunning that region as well.[25] One Harrison biographer—not referencing Adams—concurred: "Had not Winchester made his unauthorized advance to the Raisin, it is altogether possible that Harrison might have taken Malden and Detroit in 1813."[26]

Adams continued his criticism of Procter in narrating the events that followed Commodore William Perry's victory at the Battle of Lake Erie in September 1813. In commenting on Procter's subsequent decision to abandon Detroit and Amherstburg, Adams quotes Harrison's remark that Procter would have done better to have followed Tecumseh's advice in engaging his forces rather than in retreating up the Thames River: "Nothing but infatuation . . . could have governed General Procter's conduct. The day that I landed below Malden he had at his disposal upward of three thousand Indian warriors; his regular force reinforced by militia of the district would have made his number nearly equal to my aggregate, which on the day of landing did not exceed forty-five hundred. . . ."[27] Adams did not explore what Procter would have done with such a victory if he could not secure his supply route back to Burlington, particularly given the onset of winter and the U.S. campaign across Lake Ontario in early 1813.

Adams's assessment of General Dearborn's and Commodore Isaac Chauncey's campaign against York and Fort George in April–May 1813 also turned on the importance of controlling the lakes. Directed by Secretary of War Armstrong at the main British naval base at Kingston, the American commanders decided the port was too well defended and opted to strike farther west. Their campaign captured York and Fort George but fell short of pursuing the British to Burlington Heights when Brig. Gen. William Winder's and Brig. Gen. John Chandler's brigades were routed at Stoney Creek on June 6, 1813.

Adams correctly noted that this strategy not only sacrificed the direct benefits of seizing Kingston but also put at risk the U.S. base at Sackets Harbor. He
estimated that had the Americans attacked Kingston, as Armstrong initially
intended, they could have continued to protect Sackets Harbor. By sailing 150
miles to the west, they could no longer do so. Had Commodore James E. Yeo
and Prévost attacked, they might have captured the harbor without meeting
serious resistance, asserted Adams, who also attributed the British failure to
take advantage of the situation to Yeo's lack of confidence.[28]

Elting concurs with Adams on Dearborn's campaign. He writes, "The whole
plan was a piece of strategic imbecility—while the Americans were halloing
after minor British posts at the western end of Lake Ontario, the St. Lawrence
would have been clear by mid-May and British reinforcements could move up
from Quebec and Montreal. Moreover, such a move would uncover Sackets
Harbor, the one good American base, to a counterstroke from Kingston."[29]

Adams was equally, if not more, critical of Maj. Gen. James Wilkinson's
ambitious advance on Montreal that fall. He faults Wilkinson for not showing
more personal determination in leading the advance and for failing to mass the
forces under his command to overwhelm Lt. Col. Joseph Morrison's force,
which threatened his rear at the Battle of Crysler's Farm. At that battle, a
smaller British force successfully defeated an American attack and then drove
the antagonists from the field on November 11, 1813. Adams writes that
Wilkinson should have massed his entire force before attacking the British and
judges that even after that battle, Wilkinson should have pressed on to
Montreal and compelled the British to evacuate Upper Canada.[30] He attributes
this failure to Wilkinson's being "a naturally weak man, and during the descent
of the river he was excessively ill, never able to make a great exertion."[31]

Elting's take on the battle is similar. He notes that Morrison fought a careful, methodical battle, using his regulars' disciplined fire power with maximum
effectiveness and counterattacking when the American lines began to fray
away. He agrees that the Battle of Crysler's Farm did not deal a fatal blow to
Wilkinson's force. Elting states that Wilkinson's ongoing rivalry and lack of
communication with Maj. Gen. Wade Hampton, who was leading a supporting advance into Canada, ultimately caused the campaign to collapse.[32]

Donald Graves offered the opposite assessment of Wilkinson's chances of
taking Montreal after the Battle of Crysler's Farm. He notes that Prévost had
assembled a sufficient force to defend the city that "was more than enough to
ward off the less than 6,000 healthy [troops] with Wilkinson when he went

into winter quarters at French Mills."[33] Referring to the shortcomings of both Wilkinson and Hampton, who quit the campaign upon learning of the battle's outcome, Graves places responsibility for the campaign's failure instead on Secretary of War John Armstrong. He asserts that Armstrong should have removed both Wilkinson and Hampton before the 1813 operation started. Hampton had wanted to resign in August, and the more competent Maj. Gen. George Izard probably would have replaced him. Wilkinson's poor health would have provided a useful pretext to replace him with either Maj. Gen. Morgan Lewis or Brig. Gen. John Boyd.[34]

Turning to the war at sea, Adams judged that the key mistake in 1813 was not operational but strategic in that the administration and Congress attempted to defeat the British by building up the American fleet with frigates and ships of the line. In his judgment, the more economical and militarily effective (in today's parlance, "asymmetric") strategy would have been to build smaller sloops to raid British merchantmen. He noted that in 1812 Congress voted to build six frigates and four ships of the line, and in early 1813 it approved building six new sloops of war. Adams agued that had Congress approved the sloops first, the ships might have gone to sea by the end of the year. Even better, had Congress voted for twenty-four or as many as fifty sloops and outlawed privateering, the navy could have kept twenty sloops constantly at sea to destroy British commerce.[35]

Adams did not explain how the Madison administration, criticized for its self-imposed embargo on civilian shipping before the war, would have effectively banned privately owned privateers' pursuing plunder and profit. However, an assessment of the British naval strategy in North America during the War of 1812 suggests that Adams's what-if argument had merit. It considers that from 1812 through early 1815, Britain's attempt to impose a military blockade failed to contain the American public and private navies, resulting in an estimated loss of fifty-two British merchantmen per month. Moreover, in the first two months of 1815 alone, their average losses were more than a hundred vessels per month, and American efforts had not yet peaked.[36]

YEAR 3: 1814

Adams's speculations on events in the last year of the war focused on the rise of Andrew Jackson and his generalship during the defense of Mobile and New Orleans. His first point in suggesting how events might have turned out differently centered on Jackson's elevation to the rank of major general in the

U.S. Army. Adams spent considerable time developing this matter, underscoring his contention that William Henry Harrison would have been given the position had it not been for the maneuverings of Secretary Armstrong. He writes that Armstrong, believing Harrison to be weak and pretentious, left him in nominal command of the Northwest but redeployed his troops elsewhere without consulting him. Harrison responded by simultaneously sending his resignation as major general on May 11, 1814, and writing to Governor Isaac Shelby of Kentucky, who wrote and asked the president to refuse the general's resignation.

At that time, Armstrong and Madison wanted to induct and promote Andrew Jackson into the regular army for his success in the Creek campaigns; however, they had no commission higher than that of brigadier at their disposal. They decided to reward him with a brevet of major general. Armstrong then received Harrison's resignation two days before he was to issue Jackson's brevet and wrote to the president at Montpelier. Madison replied, suggesting that Harrison's resignation opened the way to giving Jackson a commission as major general directly, but he wanted Armstrong to wait a few days until he returned to Washington. Armstrong wrote to Jackson without waiting for the president's return, however, and the president was presented with Governor Shelby's letter supporting Harrison's promotion.

Adams took note of the two men's different perceptions and intentions. Madison believed that Armstrong wanted to appear as army's benefactor by championing Jackson, while Armstrong attributed the president's hesitation to Madison's and Secretary of State Monroe's view that Harrison, rather than Jackson, should take command in Mobile and New Orleans. Adams concluded that this affair deprived the country of Harrison's skill at the moment the British decided to invade the Southeast.[37]

Antal provides more background on Armstrong's animosity toward Harrison. The secretary of war, embarrassed by the reversals in the Old Northwest, was eager for an early victory and wanted an amphibious attack on Amherstburg launched from Cleveland. Harrison, however, planned an impregnable base of operations consisting of fortifications and supply routes through Ohio from which he could overwhelm the British and their Indian allies. Armstrong called his own approach "easy, safe, and economical" and characterized Harrison's as "difficult, dangerous, and enormously expensive."[38]

Jackson biographer Robert Remini paints a more straightforward interpretation of Jackson's elevation. He writes that Jackson's victory over the Red

Sticks at Tohopeka (Horseshoe Bend) "naturally won the notice of the administration, which had resisted granting this supposed backwoodsman a suitable
command." The offer of the rank of brigadier general disappointed Jackson,
though. "Then, suddenly, the problem was satisfactorily resolved. After a long
dispute with the administration, William Henry Harrison resigned his commission in disgust."[39]

Adams did not speculate on what would have happened had Madison
heeded Governor Shelby's letter advocating Harrison's appointment.
Certainly, the feud between the general and the secretary of war would have
intensified. The disdain and neglect Armstrong showed to Brigadier General
Winder after Madison appointed him over the secretary's preferred choice to
defend Washington suggests that Armstrong would have similarly turned his
attention away from the Southeast and would have provided Harrison little
support.

Adams's criticisms of Jackson's performance in his new command, however,
imply that he believed Harrison would have brought better leadership and military acumen to the defense of the Gulf. Adams charged that Jackson did not
properly position his forces and that he failed to understand the British strategy, thereby leaving Mobile and New Orleans exposed to attack.[40] Hence,
Jackson poorly applied the military principles of "mass" and "economy of force"
by having too few troops at New Orleans and too many at Mobile.[41]

Elting's account tracks with Adams's interpretation. He writes that Jackson
"scattered his forces" across the region. Departing Pensacola for New Orleans
in late November, Jackson continued to believe until December 10 that the
British would strike at Mobile before moving on New Orleans. Historian Robin
Reilly also judges that while Jackson remained convinced that Mobile would
be the immediate objective, his larger scheme was to rely on local fortifications
and a mobile defense so that "wherever the British chose to attack, Jackson
intended to be there to command the defenses."[42]

Frank Lawrence Owsley Jr.'s broader study of the war in the Southeast presents a more nuanced assessment of this issue. He notes that the unsuccessful
British attack on Fort Bower had initially convinced Jackson that the British
would first attack Mobile. However, based on documentary evidence from the
period, Owsley concludes, "It was while Jackson was in Pensacola that he
received definite information that the British had a large force of men and
ships at Jamaica and their plan was to make a direct assault on New Orleans,
probably through Lake Pontchartrain. Acting on this information, Jackson

immediately marched most of his army back to Mobile." Owsley also asserts that after the Battle of New Orleans, Jackson initially thought the British would make a second attempt to seize the city but not via Mobile—his hunched proved correct—and he ordered Winchester to send the Third Regiment to New Orleans.[43]

In addition to critiquing Jackson's plans, Adams cited the surprise that the British achieved in landing at Bayou Bienvenue and Jackson's fault in not preventing what could have been a disastrous beginning of the contest for the city. He compared Jackson unfavorably to Hull, Harrison, Smith, and Winder for allowing a large British Army to arrive so close to the city without so much as an earthwork, a man, or a gun between them and their objective. Adams judged that had British Col. William Thornton marched directly on the city after landing at Bayou Bienvenue, he could have achieved complete surprise. However, because Maj. Gen. John Keane, his commanding officer, preferred caution, Jackson had time to respond.[44]

Adams's harsh assessment fails to note that Jackson faced the threat of an amphibious assault from the open ocean, which gave his adversary freedom of action. None of the other American generals cited in his account faced a similar situation. Both Smith and Winder opposed British landings from the Chesapeake Bay, where the terrain forced much longer marches to Baltimore and Washington. Moreover, other historians have emphasized Jackson's task of preparing for an attack from many more avenues of approach than what was achieved on December 23, 1814. Owsley, for example, writes, "The dilemma which no American commander could easily solve was how to cope effectively with the great mobility of an amphibious attack." Further, he points out that "there were seven promising ways to reach New Orleans."[45] Jackson's first concern was the main channel of the Mississippi River, which was guarded by Fort St. Philip. He regarded it as his first line of defense, although he thought the British would probably attack from Lake Pontchartrain and land behind the city. Owsley also describes how militia sentries informed Jackson of the British landing at Bayou Bienvenue within hours. He had fuller information early that afternoon from a reconnaissance patrol and two men who had escaped from the British.

Elting's account, like Adams's, draws a comparison with the attack on Washington: "As aggressive as at Bladensburg, Thornton urged an immediate advance on New Orleans—while Jackson was still unaware of their presence. His troops . . . could reach the city in two hours, catching the American forces in detail."[46] Outside Washington, Thornton had led the initial attack across the bridge at Bladensburg in August; he was expecting to immediately rout the militia to his front, but artillery and musket fire repulsed his initial foray. At New Orleans, Elting echoes Adams's observation that Thornton's commanding officer, Major General Keane, was unwilling to risk an attack based on incomplete information about the forces guarding the city, and he opted to wait until the entire British contingent was in place.

Directly referencing Adams's account, Reilly writes that "Jackson's immediate command of the situation has tended to obscure the extent of the crisis which faced him"; thus, the comparison to other generals is "militarily invalid."[47] Reilly also notes that Jackson had expected that he would have time to oppose a British landing before it came within striking distance of the city. He favorably describes Jackson's decision to preemptively strike the British as "suitably Wellingtonian," or typical of the Duke of Wellington's early defensive campaign on the Iberian Peninsula.

Next, Adams's treatment of the Niagara campaign of 1814 contains a fair number of what-if speculations focusing on two generals he found wanting—British Lt. Gen. Sir Gordon Drummond and General Izard. He introduced the former in the aftermath of Maj. Gen. Jacob Brown's capture of Fort Erie and victory at the Battle of Chippewa, as the American Left Division advanced north toward Fort George. Drummond moved to support Maj. Gen. Phineas Riall, who had retired before Brown's advance. Adams presented a potential turning point that, in his view, Drummond could have taken to end Brown's summer campaign on the western bank of the Niagara River: When Drummond reached Fort George, he sent a detachment of about six hundred men across the Niagara River to Lewiston, threatening an advance on Buffalo. Had Drummond advanced up the American side with fifteen hundred men, Adams argued, Brown would have been forced to recross the river. Failing to provoke Brown, Drummond recalled the detachment and began his march to Lundy's Lane.[48]

Richard Barbuto's analysis of the campaign points out that Brown was indeed more concerned about the British movements on the opposite bank of the river than about those to his north. According to Barbuto, Brown's "intuition told him that since the greatest threat to his plans was the enemy's move on [Fort] Schlosser [opposite Niagara Falls], this must be the British intention. Presumably, the troops at Wilson's Tavern [near Lundy's Lane] were there to distract Brown from the main effort, an attack on Schlosser."[49] Barbuto describes how Brown's remedy for this situation was a mirror image of his opponent's strategy; indeed, he would drive on Queenston to the north and compel Drummond to cease his advance on the eastern side of the gorge.

What the outcome of this pinwheel engagement would have been had Drummond followed Adams's advice is far from clear. The British at this point had control of Lake Ontario and could have supplied Drummond's west bank force via Fort Niagara even if Brown's advance had cut the land route west to Fort George and Burlington. However, at that point Izard was advancing west with the American Right Division, leaving Plattsburgh exposed, and the winter ice on the lake could have made waterborne supply efforts along the Niagara River difficult for the British forces, who were already low on rations. If such a scenario had developed in that theater during the fall of 1814—particularly if Fort George fell to Brown—the British likely would have used their fleet to withdraw their army from the eastern bank of the Niagara, leaving Brown the victor.

Adams made several other isolated speculations about how events might have turned out differently during this campaign. Regarding the climax of the Battle at Lundy's Lane when, late in the evening, the American forces seized control of the hilltop and the British artillery battery positioned there, he wrote, "When the firing ceased, Ripley's brigade held the hill-top with the British guns, and the whole length of Lundy's Lane to the high-road. . . . Had Brown been able to put a reserve of only a few hundred men into the field, his victory was assured; but the battle and exhaustion were rapidly reducing his force. He had at ten o'clock not more than fifteen hundred men in the ranks and most officers wounded."[50]

The decimation of Brig. Gen. Winfield Scott's First Brigade early in the battle deprived Brown of that reserve. Scott's brigade was the first to make contact with the British, and he positioned his troops "too far from the enemy to act with decisive effect" but well within the range of the British artillery, which inflicted heavy casualties. Scott defended his tactical deployment, later writing that "the brigade was, from the first, under a heavy fire, and could not be withdrawn without a hot pursuit." Barbuto, however, judges that "it would have been a simple matter to withdraw the brigade, still in line, to the cover of the woods while awaiting the rest of the division." As Donald Graves points out in his book on the battle, Scott's decision to leave his unit exposed to fire early in the battle and his flawed effort toward the end of the battle to counterattack the British contributed to the high casualty rate and to his troops' considerable degree of bad feeling against him. Some thought he should have been cashiered for being "utterly regardless of human life and willing to make any sacrifice for his own personal renown." Scott began with more than eleven hundred men but had fewer than three hundred after he rested and readied his unit to reengage as a reserve and as Brown intended.[51]

Regarding the subsequent American retreat to Fort Erie, Adams blamed Drummond for the unsuccessful British siege and felt that it could have been avoided entirely had he been more aggressive in his pursuit or had he taken a different strategy. Drummond, he wrote, should have followed General Ripley closely or attacked the retreating army at Fort Erie or crossed the river and moved against Buffalo, obliging Brown to evacuate Fort Erie. But Drummond pursued none of those options. Further, he hesitated to assault the unfinished works at Fort Erie, even though he had half again as many troops as the Americans, who had almost two thousand soldiers.[52]

Turner also criticizes Dummond's failure to follow the American Left Division as it retreated from Lundy's Lane and attributes it to his lack of command experience and the wounds he received in that battle. Barbuto explains that Drummond procrastinated in pursuing the retreating Americans because he needed to replace and resupply his forces: "Preoccupied with those challenges, he gave little thought to finding the Americans and discovering their designs." He also reports that Drummond attempted an indirect strategy to compel his adversaries to surrender or to engage his forces. He planned to attack the American side of the river at Black Rock, to destroy supplies, and to capture guns and boats. However, when the raid was launched on August 3, it encountered a stout defense that the Americans had organized after they had detected suspicious movements on the river's western shores. Only after this unsuccessful attack did Drummond decide to conduct a siege of Fort Erie.[53]

Adams concluded his analysis of the campaign by suggesting that Izard, who became the senior officer in the theater when he arrived with the American Right Division, could have done more to expand the U.S. forces' foothold on the Canadian side of the Niagara. After Armstrong had ordered him to the western front, Izard had missed an opportunity to defend Plattsburgh; instead, Brig. Gen. Alexander Macomb had achieved that honor. Then Izard had a great opportunity to show his abilities in the field. Drummond was at Chippewa, with his army reduced by battle and sickness to about twenty-five hundred men. Izard, who commanded fifty-five hundred regular troops and eight hundred militiamen, had time to capture or destroy Drummond's entire force before the winter. Brown was eager for the attack, and on October 13, Izard moved to Chippewa and stopped. But on October 16, he wrote to the War Department, "I have just learned by express from Sackett's Harbor that Commodore Chauncey with the whole of his fleet has retired to port, and is throwing up batteries for its protection." He went on to say that this development prevented further operations. He planned to engage Drummond if he did not retreat, but if the British fell back to Fort George or Burlington Heights, his pursuit risked being cut off by the large reinforcements the British navy could land to his rear. Izard remained in Canada a few days before retiring to Buffalo.[54]

Barbuto observes that Izard was not a risk taker and was looking ahead to the spring when the American forces would be in a better position to begin a new offensive. Izard knew that neither the recapture of Fort Niagara nor the destruction of Drummond's army would end the war so long as Kingston remained in British hands. He wanted the combined army, with both his and Brown's divisions, to prepare to attack early in the year before more British troops arrived from Europe.[55]

Historian Alan Taylor notes that Izard expected this campaign would be launched far from the Niagara frontier and discounted the value of small conquests of British-held territory: "Izard preferred a campaign in the St. Lawrence Valley, where an invasion could sever the British supply line between Montreal and Upper Canada. In effect, Izard faulted Brown for adopting a strategic folly in pursuit of mere tactical honor."[56]

The British campaign against Washington and Baltimore in the summer of 1814 was another important subject of Adams's conjectures. Not surprising, Adams had much to say about the organization and leadership of the defense of the nation's capital, with his criticism falling largely on Brig. Gen. William Winder. Winder, the nephew of Maryland governor Levin Winder, had recently returned home in a prisoner exchange after having been captured at the Battle of Stoney Creek in 1813. By most accounts he was ill suited to command the newly created Tenth Military District, which encompassed both Washington and Baltimore. Adams penned two what-ifs about Winder, noting that he commanded three hundred infantry regulars of different regiments, with 120 light dragoons; 250 Maryland militiamen; about 1,200 District volunteers or militiamen, with twelve six-pound field pieces. Adams believed "that Brown or Jackson would have gotten good service out of such a force."[57]

He first speculated that Winder would have done better to evacuate Washington and to let the British take the "undefended village." He then suggested that Winder could have proceeded to Bladensburg as soon as he was satisfied—at noon on Monday, August 22—that the British were going there. Yet, Winder ordered his troops to fall back to another location at the Long Old Fields, about seven miles by road from the Washington Navy Yard.[58]

Most historians are critical of Winder's capabilities and performance. Regarding his appointment, Elting writes, "Military competence . . . was a consideration outside the routine deliberations of Madison's cabinet." Walter Lord's classic *The Dawn's Early Light* details Winder's near obsession with personally attending to the most minor issues concerning the defense of Washington: "This passion for trivia and movement left little time for the kind of thinking that went into being a commanding general." Anthony Pitch's more recent account succinctly notes, "His military experience was scant and undistinguished." On the issue of his troop dispositions, British historian Latimer judges, "Winder was indecisive and reluctant to commit his badly trained force." He adds an observation, which others share, that the multiple opinions members of Madison's cabinet offered to Winder made the entire affair a "comic opera."[59]

Adams made one brief comment on British strategy in the Chesapeake campaign that criticized Vice Admiral Cockburn's fixation on Washington as the first objective: "Baltimore should have been first attacked, but Cockburn's influence by diverting Ross to Washington gave the larger city time to prepare its defence."[60] Here, Adams failed to emphasize that Cockburn had impressed the British commander in chief of North America, Vice Adm. Sir Alexander Cochrane—not Major General Ross, the ground force commander—of the feasibility of an attack on the nation's capital. Cockburn provided such a plan to Cochrane on July 17 and followed it with a private letter boasting that within forty-eight hours of landing, Washington would be in British hands. Even so, when the British landed at Benedict, Maryland, Cochrane ordered them to destroy the American gunboat flotilla upriver, leaving the more ambitious march to Washington in question. Cockburn convinced Ross, a cautious commander, to proceed after Cochrane ordered them to return to the fleet.[61]

As for Adams's speculation that bypassing Washington would have improved the British chances at capturing Baltimore, this scenario seems unlikely. British naval movements and raids along the bay in 1813 had triggered substantial efforts to defend the city. As noted previously, after Governor Winder inspected the city's defenses in March 1813, he authorized Maj. Gen.

Samuel Smith of the militia to "take the earliest opportunity of making the necessary arrangement of the militia for the defenses of the Port of Baltimore."[62] Smith improved the troops and fortifications in and around the city.

Perhaps two variables are in question when considering a slightly earlier British attack in the summer of 1814 and before the capture of Washington. The Battle of Bladensburg first had an impact on the Maryland militiamen who were bloodied there; they subsequently fought better at the Battle of North Point, where Ross was killed. Second, after Bladensburg, General Winder was refused command of Baltimore's defenses. He might have had a slightly better chance of asserting his authority and of exposing his lack of battlefield experience absent that battle.

Adams cited the British rationale for withdrawing from the fortifications north of Baltimore after being repulsed. He quoted Col. Arthur Brooke, who assumed command of the ground forces following Ross's death. "'Under these circumstances,' reported Colonel Brooke, 'and keeping in view your Lordship's instructions, it was agreed between the Vice-admiral and myself that the capture of the town would not have been a sufficient equivalent to the loss which might probably be sustained in storming the heights.'" Adams noted that only two days before at Plattsburgh, Prévost had three times the number of troops against a much smaller number of opponents and had come to the same conclusion. Brooke withdrew his army and re-embarked on the fleet.[63]

Adams was more positive in his assessment of Canadian governor-general Prévost's decision to halt the Plattsburgh assault after the British fleet was defeated on Lake Champlain in September 1814. He faced criticism from Royal Navy officers and some of Wellington's subordinates who had participated in the campaign, and a Royal Navy court-martial found him guilty in August 1815. He demanded an army court-martial to clear his name but died days before it was scheduled to begin in January 1816.

Here, Adams is in the company of several other historians. Elting again agreed with Adams and judges that "Prevost's reasoning was sensible: with his fleet destroyed he would not be able to hold Plattsburgh even if he did capture it—and capturing it promised to be a bloody business and a useless waste of good men." Latimer notes, "Certainly it is true that once the lake was lost he had little option but to withdraw, as he could not rely on tenuous road communications, which could easily have been cut now that control of the lake was lost." Fitz-Enz, whose volume echoes Winston Churchill's comment that Plattsburgh was the war's "most decisive battle," argues that Prévost's retreat was consistent with his orders, which read: "It is by no means the intention of His Majesty's Government to encourage such forward movements into the Interior of the American territory as might commit the safety of the force placed under your Command."[64]

Conversely, Canadian historians have been more negative in their assessments of Prévost. J. Mackay Hitsman writes, "The Plattsburgh fiasco was the result of leaving a defensively minded general in charge of operations once the tide had turned and there no longer was any need to hesitate about doing battle merely because several hundred casualties might be suffered in a single action." He then adds an Adamsesque counterfactual: "Had one of Wellington's senior subordinates been sent to command Prevost's reinforced troops in the field, the story of Plattsburgh could have had a different ending." Mark Zuehlke is similarly critical but terse in his assessment: "Seeing the British vessels surrendered or wrecked, Prevost's always tremulous nerve failed completely. He cancelled the attack."[65]

Adams made only one brief point of conjecture concerning naval matters in the last year of the war, and it referred to the nearly two-year-long voyage of the USS *Essex* under the command of Capt. David Porter. His harassment of British shipping ended in a nearly three-hour battle in the Chilean port of Valparaiso on March 28, 1814. Adams presented several what-ifs, arguing that Porter should have sailed for China or the Indian Ocean because he knew that British war-vessels were searching for him. He could have stayed away from Valparaiso, and after being discovered, he might have tried to run out at night or fought even after losing of his main-topmast.[66]

Curiously, the recent monograph *The USS* Essex *and the Birth of the American Navy* echoes this assessment: "Had Porter run west into the Pacific and the Indian Ocean, the element of surprise might have enabled him to capture more British merchant vessels."[67] As for Porter fighting on after the loss of his main-topmast sail, Theodore Roosevelt offered a succinctly contrary opinion in his classic history of the naval war of 1812. He indicated that in his view, Porter's ship was doomed the moment the British attacked: "So the Essex prepared for action, though there could be no chance for success."[68]

Adams's final speculations on the war concern the peace negotiations that took place between the American and British delegations in Ghent, Belgium, in late 1814. He suggested that the Treaty of Ghent, which ended the war on the basis of the status quo antebellum and left several issues to be decided at a later date, resulted from the poor performance of the British delegation. "Had [Lord]

Castlereagh improved the opportunity by sending to Ghent one competent diplomatist, or even a well-informed and intelligent man of business, like Alexander Baring, he might probably have succeeded in isolating [John Quincy] Adams, and in negotiating with the four other commissioners a treaty sacrificing Massachusetts."[69] Although John Quincy Adams insisted that the United States should retain its fishing rights off Canada—rights that were important to his state but his fellow commissioners were willing to sacrifice them—he agreed with a compromise to leave that issue and the British demand for navigation of the Mississippi River for future negotiation. Baring was then a member of Parliament who had opposed the Orders in Council because they were bad for trade. Later as Lord Ashburton, he negotiated the Webster-Ashburton Treaty of 1842, which settled the northeastern boundary of Maine and other bilateral issues.

The British commissioners present at the talks included Vice Adm. James Gambier (Ret.), who was the leader of the delegation, the commander of the British fleet that bombarded Copenhagen into surrender in 1807, and a member of the House of Lords; William Adams, an expert on maritime law; and Henry Goulburn, an undersecretary of the war and the colonies. The American delegation consisted of Minister to Russia John Quincy Adams, Federalist senator from Delaware James Bayard, Speaker of the House of Representatives and Republican representative from Kentucky Henry Clay, former secretary of the treasury Albert Gallatin, and newly appointed Minister to Sweden Jonathan Russell. Canadian historian Zuehlke maintains that Clay, not Adams, was the principal force in the American delegation, successfully playing a game of "brag" with both the British and his fellow Americans. He quotes Clay on the art of diplomacy: "The art of it is to beat your adversary by holding your hand with a solemn and confident phiz, and outbragging him." Zuehlke also credits the Duke of Wellington with a timely intervention and sending Gallatin a "strictly confidential" letter noting that Goulburn had made grave errors in tabling demands the Americans would not accept, actions for which Lord Castlereagh had admonished him. Wellington assured Gallatin that "peace is shortly in view."[70] American diplomatic historian Bradford Perkins credits Lord Bathurst with informing his protégé Goulburn that the cabinet would not press matters and would accept the American proposal to leave the fishing and navigation issues for the future. Perkins judges, "There is every probability that four of the Americans would have surrendered despite Adams' avowal that he would refuse to sign a treaty that did so."[71]

Henry Adams also speculated on what would have happened if Washington had rejected the terms of the treaty: "Had the treaty been less satisfactory than it was, the President would have hesitated long before advising its rejection, and the Senate could hardly have gained courage to reject it. . . . No one had seriously counted on a satisfactory peace, as was proved by the steady depression of government credit and of the prices of American staples."[72] Zeuhlke writes that Madison remained doubtful that peace was possible but thought that continuing the war would accelerate the country's political and economic development. He also notes, however, that predictions in Washington were high that Madison would resign rather than face impeachment if the negotiations failed. Perkins judges that if peace had not come, it seemed certain that New England's sedition as evidenced by the Hartford Convention would deepen and perhaps turn to secessionism.[73]

This review of Adams's speculations about what could have taken place at critical junctures during the War of 1812 when American political and military leaders made poor judgments points to the complementary nature of Mr. Madison's War and the Second War of Independence narratives. Neither shy in his criticisms of what the leaders did nor restrained in his ex post facto recommendations, Adams attempted to strike a balanced tone that would appeal to his readers, many of whom he probably judged would be current and future American military officers. He undoubtedly wanted them to learn from the mistakes of this war by reflecting on his suggestions of what their counterparts in America's second war with Britain could have or should have done.

Adams's criticisms paint a vivid tableau of the bloody ground of Mr. Madison's War. However, his reappraisals of these defeats and disasters also suggest the possibility of a more heroic Second War of Independence. Key defeats—Hull's disaster at Detroit, Winchester's at the River Raisin and his debacle at Crysler's Farm, Winder's rout at Bladensburg, and Jackson's near escape at New Orleans—could all have been avoided. The U.S Navy could also have inflicted higher losses on British maritime commerce if the Congress had built more sloops and fewer frigates.

These "could have been" victories demonstrate the potential that the War of 1812 had for being more than a strange and forgotten conflict. Most important, by Adams's reckoning, the war could have led alternatively to the United States' conquering Upper Canada and the British Empire's capture of New Orleans. Either event would have profoundly shaped the trajectory and dimensions of the young republic.

6

THE BATTLE OF BLADENSBURG
Could Washington Have Been Saved?

The most startling example of Republican military ineptitude in the Mr. Madison's War narrative occurred in August 1814 when four thousand British soldiers routed nearly twice their number of U.S. militia forces and regulars at Bladensburg, Maryland. The subsequent British capture of Washington—and their burning of the Capitol, the president's mansion, and other public buildings—is one of the most iconic events of the War of 1812. It is often viewed as an inevitable result of the early republic's decision to declare war on a global power capable of projecting force on Napoleon's empire on the European continent and on the nascent empire of liberty across the Atlantic Ocean. This single defeat underscored a decade of Jeffersonian military policy and marked the nadir of President James Madison's political fortunes. Yet, as if special providence intervened to attenuate its impact on the national psyche, this sad event was followed within months by the stout defense of Baltimore, celebrated in Francis Scott Key's "Star-Spangled Banner," and Andrew Jackson's spectacular victory at New Orleans—both of which are key episodes in the Second War of Independence narrative.[1]

Immediately afterward and for years to come, blame for the American defeat and retreat was cast on the political and military figures responsible for the defense of Washington. President James Madison, Secretary of War John Armstrong, Secretary of State James Monroe, and Brig. Gen. William Winder, who commanded the newly formed Tenth Military District and was the senior officer present at the battle, received their share of blame and then some. Implicit in these accusations and debates was the assumption that a successful defense of the city was possible.

21

Exploring that assumption requires recounting the historical record of the events that led to this debacle before assessing whether specific changes in command and tactics, as Henry Adams and others suggest, might have altered the outcome. An examination of these factors also provides some perspective on how the defeat at Bladensburg enhanced perceptions of the victory at Baltimore one month later. Finally, it clarifies the role this battle plays in the historical narratives of the War of 1812.

THE HISTORICAL RECORD

The engagement at Bladensburg resulted from the British strategy in 1814 to mount amphibious invasions along the Atlantic and Gulf Coasts of the United States. The British launched attacks in New England to establish a short corridor from Canada to the Atlantic Ocean, in the Chesapeake Bay region to force Washington to pull troops away from Canada, and in the Louisiana–West Florida region—specifically, New Orleans—to gain control of trade exiting the Mississippi River. Concurrently, the British planned a major offensive through the traditional invasion route along Lake Champlain in a replay of Maj. Gen. John Burgoyne's 1777 campaign to separate New England from the rest of the colonies in rebellion.

Forces for this enterprise came from the Duke of Wellington's regiments in France following Napoleon's abdication and the restoration of the Bourbon monarchy. On June 2, 1814, British troops under Maj. Gen. Robert Ross boarded a ship in France's Garonne River for Bermuda. His sealed orders instructed him "to effect a diversion on the coasts of the United States of America in favour of the army employed in the defense of Upper and Lower Canada." He was also proscribed from "any extended operation" that would take him far from the fleet.[2] Aboard were the Fourth, Forty-Fourth, and Eighty-Fifth Infantry Regiments; a brigade of artillery; a detachment of sappers and miners; and other support elements totaling some twenty-five hundred men. They arrived in Bermuda on July 24, and five days later the Twenty-First Royal Scots Fusiliers, numbering eight hundred troops, joined them. Departing on August 3, they entered the Chesapeake Bay on August 15 and launched an operation that Vice Adm. Alexander Cochrane, newly appointed commander in chief of the Halifax Naval Station, and his second in command, Rear Adm. George Cockburn, had spent the preceding six weeks planning.

In early June, Lt. Gen. Sir John Prévost, governor-general of Upper Canada, suggested that Cochrane conduct amphibious raids along the Eastern Seaboard and retaliate for American attacks on Canadian towns, most recently on Dover on May 14. Cochrane endorsed the idea and explained to Secretary of State for War and the Colonies Earl Bathurst in a message dated July 14, "If [British] troops arrive soon and the point of attack is directed toward Baltimore, I have every prospect of success and Washington will be equally accessible. They may be destroyed or laid under contribution as the occasion may require. . . ." Cockburn refined Cochrane's concept of operations and proposed landing on the Patuxent River at Benedict, Maryland, only a fifty-mile march to Washington. He wrote to Cochrane on July 17, "I therefore most firmly believe that within forty-eight hours after arrival in the Patuxent of such a force as you expect, the city of Washington might be possessed without difficulty or opposition of any kind." He also recommended that a small flotilla ascend the Potomac as a diversion and that another force conduct raids farther up the Chesapeake to disguise the invasion's ultimate objective. Cochrane, Cockburn, and Ross conferred on August 12. They agreed to land at Benedict and immediately destroy Commodore Joshua Barney's U.S. gunboat flotilla, which had harassed British naval operations in the bay but was now trapped upriver. The fleet arrived at Benedict on August 18, and Ross's troops disembarked the following day.[3]

The Madison administration was well aware of the transfer of British forces to North America, but it had done little to improve the country's defenses. News of the allied armies' capture of Paris on March 30 arrived in Boston on May 12 and was reported in Washington newspapers on May 18. The cabinet did not meet to discuss the changed strategic situation until July 1, when Madison called for the creation of a separate military district responsible for defending the District of Columbia, Maryland, and part of northern Virginia. This Tenth Military District was to be carved out of the Fifth Military District, which was commanded by Brig. Gen. Moses Porter, a veteran of the Revolutionary War who had done a masterful job of defending Norfolk, Virginia. Secretary of War Armstrong, also a Revolutionary War veteran, supported Moses for command of the new district, but Madison chose Brigadier General Winder.

A lawyer by trade, Winder was initially commissioned in the federal army as a colonel—a purely political appointment. As noted previously, according to one postwar account, Winder's selection was the work of Secretary of State Monroe, who had hoped to become secretary of war and was sometimes addressed as "Colonel," his Revolutionary War rank. Monroe reportedly wanted a weak commanding officer in charge of the capital city so that if and when a British threat emerged, he could personally intervene and take credit for its defense. As for Winder's military experience, while participating in the 1813 invasion of Upper Canada, he was captured in the Battle of Stoney Creek and subsequently imprisoned in Quebec. Winder was clearly unqualified for the job, and his ineffectual efforts over the next two months, including his considerable travel by horseback throughout his new area of responsibility, did not receive Armstrong's support.

At his cabinet meeting, Madison proposed fielding a militia force of two thousand to three thousand men between the Patuxent and the eastern branch of the Potomac River with a larger militia force held in ready reserve. Three days later, Madison called for militias for the new military district with specific quotas from the District of Columbia, Virginia, Pennsylvania, and Maryland totaling fifteen thousand troops. Subsequently, Madison excluded the defense of Washington from cabinet discussions, suggesting he did not believe British military operations would threaten the capital. In mid-August, in a letter to Armstrong regarding potential targets for British attacks on the East Coast, the president noted that "the seat of government cannot fail to be a favorite one." However, his reaction to the British landing in Maryland a week later evidenced his surprise that the British were venturing so close to Washington. Indeed, the shared assumption among high-level military and administration officials that the capital would not be attacked was the root of the problem regarding its defense.[4]

Ross's approach to Washington was cautious and clever, combining a sound tactical formation designed to avoid ambushes and several feints to keep the Americans guessing as to his ultimate objective. After giving his troops one day to recover from their long voyage, he led them on August 20 toward Nottingham, where Barney's flotilla was reportedly anchored. In the lead was an advanced guard of three companies of light infantry, with twenty more troops and two files of scouts moving farther ahead to provide warning. On either side of the advanced guard were parties of forty to fifty men guarding the flanks. Following behind at a distance of 150 to 200 yards was a brigade consisting of the Eighty-Fifth Regiment and the light troops from the other regiments, which also sent out flankers. A second brigade, made up of the remaining troops of the Fourth and Forty-Fourth Regiments, came next; followed by the artillery and a third brigade with the Twenty-First Regiment and a battalion of Royal Marines. A rear guard that was similar to the advanced guard followed at some distance.

Cockburn led the fleet's small craft up the river, protecting Ross's right flank and carrying supplies, and prepared to engage the American gunboats. The British covered about half the distance between Benedict and Nottingham and made camp. The next day was much the same, but as the British halted outside Nottingham, a skirmish erupted. A small band of American riflemen withdrew, and when the British entered the town, they found that Barney's flotilla had retreated farther upstream. Here, Ross considered whether it was prudent to continue and decided to forge ahead to Upper Marlboro, ten miles to the north. Cockburn's river fleet continued up the Patuxent, which angled northeast and away from Ross's line of march. Closing on Pig's Point, Cockburn spied his prey as a series of explosions scuttled the enemy vessels, Barney having removed their armaments and supplies first.

On the morning of August 23, Cockburn caught up with Ross at Marlboro, where, having completed their first objective, they agreed to press on to Washington and leave Cockburn's sailors to hold the town. Shortly, they encountered an American force of infantry and artillery. Ross sent his advanced guard, reinforced with two infantry companies, to dislodge them, but he took his main body to Wood Yard on the road to Alexandria. The Americans fired several cannon rounds at the approaching British before disengaging. That evening, the British saw flames consume Stoddert's bridge, one of two that spanned the river south of Bladensburg, where it was fordable.

At 2 a.m. on August 24, Ross and Cockburn received instructions from Cochrane to proceed not one mile farther and to return to Benedict and re-embark. Having achieved their principal objective—"more than England could have expected given force under his orders"—the vice admiral saw no need to risk engagements that might endanger accomplishing his larger strategic objective, namely, New Orleans. Ross declared they should return to the fleet, but Cockburn convinced him that they had gone too far to retreat and that they would succeed in taking Washington. Ross got his troops moving at 5 a.m. and feinted toward the remaining bridge to Washington. After four miles, they reversed direction and headed north toward Bladensburg.

The Americans' reaction to the British invasion was, in contrast, cautious and chaotic. A little more than two months in command, Winder had fewer than a thousand federal soldiers, sailors, and marines, along with several thousand local militiamen on call. His first move was to order those men coming from the north to assemble at Bladensburg, where Gen. Tobias Stansbury of Baltimore would be in command, and those men from Washington and local towns in Maryland and Virginia to fall in at Wood Yard. Winder also dispatched cavalry detachments from Washington and Maryland to observe and report on the enemy's movements and to harass them if possible. Monroe attached himself to one troop, sending his reconnaissance reports to the president and Winder. The latter took command of the thirty-two hundred men at Wood Yard on August 21 and fell back to the Long Old Fields, eight miles from Washington, the next day. From there he hoped to cover both the river approaches to Washington and Fort Washington should the British turn in that direction. On the following evening, he pulled these forces back into the city, fearing a British night attack.

Ignorance of the size and objectives of the British force, however, further undercut Winder's efforts to mount a defense. Monroe reported that the British numbered some ten thousand in strength while other observers calculated half as many. American military and civilian leaders assumed the larger number was correct, and Winder became even more cautious about engaging the invaders. Beyond Barney's flotilla, Winder believed that Annapolis was the major target. If captured, it would provide an excellent base from which the British could harbor their flotilla, house and supply their army, and strike at either Baltimore or Washington. Secretary Armstrong maintained that Baltimore was the obvious prize, dismissing notions that Washington was threatened. "Why the devil would they come here?" he declared. Madison and Monroe, however, believed the British would march on Washington.

On the morning of August 24, Winder, along with Madison and some cabinet members, were at the Navy Yard in Washington when word arrived that Ross was marching on Bladensburg. Monroe road off to assist Stansbury, followed by Winder, then Armstrong, and finally Madison. Monroe found Stansbury positioning his troops to meet the British. Early that morning, his troops were deployed on Lowndes Hill on the eastern edge of the town. After a conference with his regimental commanders and deciding that the position was not defensible, Stansbury moved his troops across the bridge and began pulling them back toward Washington. But then, he received an order from Winder directing him to prepare to battle the British at Bladensburg. Stansbury deployed six 6-pounders and 150 artillerymen behind a small dirt breastwork three hundred yards west of the bridge and behind the intersection of the Georgetown Pike and the road to Washington. He protected their right flank with 150 riflemen and their left flank with a similar number of Washington militia forces. In the orchard to their rear, Stansbury deployed three infantry regiments, along with three 6-pounders covering the Georgetown Pike. Upon arriving on the scene, Monroe on his own authority and without Stansbury's knowledge ordered two of the regiments to fall back a quarter mile to the rear. This move took them out from under the cover of the orchard and to a point where their fire would no longer support the artillery battery. To the left of these forces stood a thoroughly exhausted cavalry detachment of 350 men who had shadowed the British after their landing at Benedict.

Also unknown to Stansbury, Winder arrived around noon with Brig. Gen. Walter Smith's brigade of the DC militia; elements of the U.S. Twelfth, Thirty-Sixth, and Thirty-Eighth Infantry Regiments; and Commodore Barney's sailors, marines, and artillery—two 18-pounders and three 12-pounders. Winder formed them on the crest of the slope that rose from the river. Their right flank was guarded by Col. William Beall's Maryland Seventeenth Infantry Regiment, which, like Winder's force, had arrived shortly before the British came into view.

Ross's army marched north along the road that paralleled the eastern branch of the Potomac, reaching Bladensburg shortly after noon. A British officer described the scene:

> The American army became visible. The corps which occupied the heights above Bladensburg, was composed chiefly of militia; and as American militia are not dressed in uniform, it exhibited to our eyes a very singular and very awkward appearance . . . seemed country people, who would have been much more appropriately employed in attending to their agricultural occupations, than in standing, with muskets in their hands, on the brow of a bare, green hill. I have seldom been more forcibly struck with anything than the contrast, which at a glance to the rear afforded the moment, with the spectacle which was before me. A column of four thousand British soldiers, moving in sections of six abreast . . . the whole of the light brigade, forming into one extended line, advanced to the attack.[5]

The British swept over Lowndes Hill and then the village, surprised that both were unoccupied by American troops. Artillery and rifle fire repulsed the light brigade's first effort to cross the bridge. Then the British forded the river and gained a foothold on the opposite bank. Soon, the American first line was forced to retreat. Winder moved Stansbury's three regiments forward and drove the British back to the river. For a short while, the second line held until fire from the British infantry and annoying, but inaccurate, Congreve rockets caused them to waver. The British second brigade crossed the river and moved up the Georgetown Pike, threatening Stansbury's left flank, while the first brigade gained ground in the orchard. The Maryland militia broke, although one regiment held, supported by the artillerymen and riflemen from the first line who reformed on a rise behind it. When the British second brigade gained their left and threatened to encircle the Americans, Winder ordered a retreat that turned into a panicked rout. Not knowing that the DC militia and U.S. regulars were to their rear, the American second line fled up the Georgetown Pike toward Montgomery Court House.

The third American line watched Stansbury's regiments collapse and the British column approach up the Washington turnpike. The British attacked around 2 p.m. Barney's heavy cannon and the militia's lighter artillery swept the road and halted their advance while the British light brigade took cover in the ravine approximately halfway between the original positions of the second and third American lines. Twice more the British advanced but were forced back. Ross sent in fresh troops before attempting another assault, this one aimed at the American right flank. It, too, was repulsed with grapeshot, and American sailors and marines charged them, shouting, "Board 'em!"

At this point, Winder assessed that the third line would not hold and ordered Smith's troops to retreat, many of them not even having fired a shot. Seeing the militia take flight, Ross ordered yet another assault that overwhelmed Barney's mixed force, which by now had nearly exhausted its ammunition. Barney ordered his cannon spiked and his men to retire from the field. Wounded, he remained on the battlefield, and the British captured and shortly paroled him. Beall's Annapolis militia also pulled back. By 4 p.m., after more than three hours of combat, the British had won the battle.

Winder and the retreating DC militia under Brigadier General Smith stopped to form a new battle line and encountered Col. George Minor's Virginia Sixtieth Regiment advancing on the Washington Post Road. Minor was late for the battle because the DC Armory had been extremely fastidious in issuing his troops weapons and ammunition. Just as Smith had formed a new battle line to confront the British, Winder ordered the DC and Virginia militias to fall back to Capitol Hill. Once there, Winder conferred with Monroe and Armstrong and decided that the retreat should continue to Tenleytown in the western portion of the district, but at that point most of the DC militiamen had dispersed to look after their homes and families. Ross and the British forces arrived at Capitol Hill around midnight. Over the next two days, they proceeded to burn public buildings, notably the Capitol and the president's mansion, but largely left private property unmolested. The office of the *National Intelligencer* newspaper was an exception in light of its harsh editorial line toward the British, in general, and Cockburn, in particular. An accidental detonation of a munitions dump at Greenleaf's Point, a horrific storm in the evening of August 25, and concerns that American forces were gathering for a counterattack prompted the British to retrace their steps and return to Benedict.

COUNTERFACTUAL POSSIBILITIES

The first step in exploring alternative or counterfactual outcomes that avoid the capture of Washington is to observe that violations of two key principles of war—mass and unity of command—were in large part responsible for the Americans' defeat at Bladensburg.[6] Examining how these errors could have been corrected suggests that the loss of the battle and the city were not inevitable. If events had been different, how might they have influenced Ross's willingness to accompany Cockburn's march on Washington, clearly in violation of Cochrane's directive that they return to the fleet at Benedict? And how would these different events have added to the arduous march that the British column endured through the hot and humid Maryland summer?

The American forces that arrived at Bladensburg on August 24 were sufficient in number to oppose Ross's army but not tactically deployed to do so. Spatially and temporally, the failure to concentrate Stansbury's brigade at the British point of attack was the first lost opportunity to delay the enemy. One account of the battle observes that Stansbury's brigade would have fought longer and better if "Colonel" Monroe had not changed the battle line. He had no authority and little military acumen in ordering two Maryland regiments to pull back to a point where they could no longer support the artillery battery and the riflemen defending Stansbury's flanks and where they would then be exposed to British observers and rocket fire. Certainly, the commanders of these individual units were not under any obligation to obey Monroe's directives, and they should have sought confirmation from Stansbury before undertaking their retrograde movements. And Stansbury, as commanding officer of the Maryland brigade, was irresponsible in not maintaining his chain of command and not noticing Monroe's interference until it was too late. If any of these Maryland militia officers had taken action, they could have prevented the unraveling of the Americans' first line of defense at Bladensburg. In numerous other occasions during the war, American officers questioned or exceeded the orders of their commanding officers. Maj. George Croghan's refusal to quit Fort Stephenson, as Maj. Gen. William Henry Harrison ordered in July 1813, is one example. Another is Brig. Gen. James Winchester's decision in January 1813 to exceed Harrison's orders by marching beyond the rapids of the Maumee River to the River Raisin, where his command was defeated and some of his captured troops massacred.[7]

The Americans' larger failure to mass the DC, Maryland, and Virginia militias, as well as the regular army and naval forces at Bladensburg, belongs to Winder. As noted earlier, following the early July cabinet meeting that created the Tenth Military District and outlined the plan to rely on mobilizing militias to defend the capital city, General Winder sought military commitments from the District of Columbia and nearby state governments; however, he did not challenge Armstrong's view that these forces would only be called out after the British landed. This delay deprived Winder of needed opportunities to develop a working relationship with his subordinate officers who commanded these levies and to devise a set of contingency plans for engaging the British if and when they invaded his district.

Once the British landed at Benedict, Winder ordered his forces to assemble at two separate locations—the Wood Yard and Bladensburg. In doing so, he committed a classic military error and divided his force in the face of an enemy force of unknown size and intentions. He chose an "economy of force" deployment that provided flexibility should the British advance on Washington, by way of either the upper or the lower eastern branch of the Potomac, or on Annapolis, which he initially believed was their immediate objective. Winder did not conclude that the British objective was Washington until the night of August 23, leaving him insufficient time to properly deploy these forces.

Moreover, it is not clear that Winder gave much, if any, thought to choosing a particular location to engage the British where the terrain would be advantageous to his army of militiamen, albeit one salted with a small number of regular forces. Had he done so, Winder would have chosen a place that the Americans not only could defend but also could fall back from and onto a well-defined and defensible rallying point. Bladensburg could have been that point, but Winder's orders to Stansbury on the morning of August 23—advance toward Marlboro and meet the British—indicates that he had not analyzed the terrain or tactics needed to engage a well-trained and organized force. Moreover, when he countermanded those orders and told Stansbury to hold the British at Bladensburg, Winder did not communicate a clear concept of operations that would make the best use of the Maryland and DC militias. Consequently, Stansbury was unaware of the battle line of DC militia and regular units drawn up on the high ground to his rear. Had Stansbury known that a supporting force greater than his own was in place a short distance away, he would have ordered his brigade to meet them on the Washington Post Road rather than retreat down the Georgetown Pike.

Maj. Gen. James Wilkinson's memoirs characterize Winder's efforts as "void of plan or proportion; and the naked truth is the best apology for it, that is, it was formed on the spur of the occasion, by pieces, under the direction of many chiefs, without preconcert, principle or design."[8] That Wilkinson's remarks are self-serving, given that Madison and Armstrong were not willing to put him in command of the situation, does not diminish his accuracy on this point.

The "counter-counterfactual," or historical, rebuttal to this argument is that Winder's decisions during the battle were a critical factor behind the American defeat at Bladensburg. His premature orders to the Maryland and DC militias to retreat—in the case of the latter, even before they had an opportunity to fire on the British—suggest that had Winder properly deployed his force, he would have made the same tactical errors before and during the battle. If so, the Americans' failure to mass at Bladensburg falls to Madison (and probably Monroe), whose political calculations to gain Maryland governor Winder's support by appointing his nephew took precedence over mounting an adequate defense of the nation's capital.

Two what-ifs—one of chance and one of choice—could have removed Winder from the battlefield. The chance event occurred in the early morning of August 24 when Winder's horse threw him while returning to his quarters after conferring with Armstrong. He was alone and injured his right arm and ankle, and he limped into camp several hours later. Winder could have been more severely injured or even killed, preventing him from taking the field later that day. In such a circumstance, whom would Madison have chosen to replace him? Several senior officers were on hand. Madison could have directed Secretary of War John Armstrong, a former Revolutionary War general, to take personal command. Armstrong likely would have declined, however, probably arguing that he was too old for a field command that was well below his level of responsibility. Armstrong had been particularly unhelpful to Winder after the July cabinet meeting and undoubtedly would not have wanted to take responsibility or blame for what he would soon assess as a certain victory of veteran British regulars over inexperienced militiamen.

Armstrong would have deferred to Major General Wilkinson, present in Washington for his pending court-martial to answer charges of neglect of duty and drunkenness while leading the unsuccessful invasion of Canada in late 1813. He was the senior general officer on the scene and an experienced, albeit not entirely trustworthy, field commander. Wilkinson would have jumped at the opportunity to clear his name and reputation. In his testimony to the congressional committee investigating the British capture of Washington, Wilkinson indicated that upon receiving a letter from Monroe on the approaching emergency, he proposed that if his arrest were suspended and his sword restored for a short period, he would take command of the militia. If so, he would have directed the battle at Bladensburg and at that late hour probably would not have adopted either the Fabian harassment strategy or the Capitol-fortress strategies that in his memoirs he claimed to have suggested to Armstrong for defending Washington. Regardless, his unfamiliarity with the situation would have impeded any chances for victory.

Madison, however, might have demurred on appointing the tarnished Wilkinson and turned to Monroe in such an emergency even over Armstrong's certain objections. Madison had given Monroe a commission to lead a campaign to retake Detroit after Hull's surrender in 1812, but the Republican leadership in the Northwest had rallied around Harrison, who also had Henry Clay's support. Both the president and Monroe had declined to challenge Harrison's command. Subsequently, in 1813 Monroe speculated that Maj. Gen. Henry Dearborn should replace William Eustis as secretary of war and that Madison should appoint him, Monroe, as the commanding officer of the U.S. Army; give him the rank of lieutenant general; and allow him to lead the invasion of Canada. This suggestion led some congressmen to wonder whether Monroe had adopted "the baggadocio style of William Hull and Alexander Smyth about the facility of conquering Canada." The secretary of state's role during this national emergency as secretary of scouting and his alleged role in Winder's selection suggest he would have eagerly accepted a commission in 1814; however, his ill-conceived movement of Stansbury's forces indicates that his performance as commanding officer would not have changed the outcome.[9]

One final candidate, a dark horse with probably the best chance of improving the Americans' odds at Bladensburg, was Maj. Gen. John P. Van Ness, the commanding officer of the District of Columbia's militia forces. Unlike the other men, Van Ness was intimately familiar with the forces involved and the tactical situation. When British naval units had investigated the mouth of the Potomac in May, he had taken the initiative to put his cavalry forces on alert. In July, he had insisted that Armstrong keep a small portion of his forces on duty and on the federal payroll given British movements up the Patuxent River. He also had suggested that one of his two brigades be called up on a rotational basis so that a force of some consequence would be on hand in case of a crisis, but Armstrong had refused to do so.

When the British landed and the DC militia was activated, Van Ness did not take the field because he would have outranked Winder. Madison told Armstrong to find him another post, but Armstrong told Van Ness that he was not wanted. Nevertheless, Van Ness led a party of volunteers to Bladensburg to dig trenches where Stansbury's first line made its stand. As an officer in the militia since the Jefferson administration but lacking in combat experience, he showed as much, if not more, initiative in the weeks preceding the British advance and probably would have performed better as a field commander in this situation than Winder did. In many ways, he could have been Washington's counterpart to the Maryland militia's Maj. Gen. Samuel Smith, who beginning in early 1813 prepared Baltimore to resist a British attack by combining regular and militia forces, as well as volunteers, and by building defensive positions around the city. Only a month after the Battle of Bladensburg, Smith successfully defended Baltimore while rebuffing Winder's efforts to take charge.

A number of earlier what-ifs would have prevented Winder's appointment as commander of the Tenth Military District in July. Winder could have been killed, not captured, on June 5, 1813, at the Battle of Stoney Creek. He also might have remained a prisoner in Canada, where he was involved in negotiating a new agreement regarding the treatment and exchange of prisoners. That April 1814 agreement attempted to resolve a dispute arising from British efforts to try twenty-three captured British-born American soldiers who were "naturalized" citizens—a classification that London rejected—on charges of treason. This controversy led to a series of retaliatory measures, with both sides putting officers and soldiers in close confinement and threatening them with execution. Washington had authorized Winder to negotiate the agreement settling this affair, but the Madison administration rejected its terms because the draft agreement excluded the original twenty-three American soldiers and an equal number of British soldiers. Winder was paroled before a final agreement was reached in July, but circumstances surrounding this issue conceivably could have prevented or delayed Winder's exchange and obviated his appointment.

In that case, Madison and Armstrong probably would have given Brigadier General Porter, commanding the Fifth Military District, responsibility for Washington's defense. Porter, like Van Ness, probably would have performed better than Winder did in defending Washington. He had significant experience in organizing defenses of major cities, having commanded in New Orleans in 1805–1806 and then having overseen efforts to improve coastal defenses between New York and Boston when a possible war with Britain loomed in 1807 after the HMS *Leopard* fired on the USS *Chesapeake*. Porter also had substantially more combat experience, having been the regional commander of American forces along the Niagara frontier in the fall of 1812 before participating in Dearborn's 1813 capture of Fort George. Porter commanded the fort until he became Wilkinson's chief of artillery during the invasion of Lower Canada in late 1813. In the spring of 1814, Porter was appointed the commander of the Fifth Military District.

Whether Armstrong would have lent Porter more support than he did Winder is not certain. The secretary of war repeatedly downplayed the British threat to the city because he feared its defense would detract from his operations against Canada—precisely the effect that the British intended. However, Porter was a professional soldier and, like Armstrong, a veteran of the Revolutionary War. His long tenure in the army during both the Federalist and Republican administrations suggests that leaders viewed him as a capable and reliable officer. Had Madison created a separate district and, in Winder's absence, acceded to Armstrong's desire to have Porter in command, the secretary of war conceivably would not have been so resistant to improving the cities' defenses, particularly if Porter followed Smith's example and relied mainly on local levies and matériel.

Porter's artillery and coastal defense background suggests that he would have taken a significantly different approach to defending Washington. Rather than maneuvering his forces to meet the advancing invaders, Porter probably could have built defenses and forced the British to attack them in order to take the city. He would have chosen the ground on which the battle would have occurred and put the militias in fixed emplacements, where they traditionally fared better in combat. The militias that held off advancing British columns at Baltimore, Plattsburgh, and New Orleans were barricaded and entrenched, giving them protection from British musket and artillery fire.

If Porter had chosen a forward defense, the village of Bladensburg and the adjacent Lowndes Hill would have made an excellent position. In fact, the British were surprised that the Americans had not availed themselves of the brick houses and the commanding view that location afforded when they arrived on the battlefield. According to George Robert Gleig's "A Subaltern in America":

> There is a mound on the right of the entrance very well adapted to hold a light field piece or two for the purpose of sweeping the road [approaching Bladensburg along the north bank of the river]. Under these circumstances, we naturally concluded that an American force must be here. Though out of the regular line, it was not so far advanced that it might have been maintained, if not to the last, at all events for many hours, while the means of retreat, so soon as the garrison should be fairly overpowered, were direct and easy. Our surprise, therefore, was not less palpable than our satisfaction, when, on reaching the town, we found that it was empty.[10]

As noted earlier, in preparing emplacements for artillery pieces covering the bridge across the eastern branch of the Potomac, Van Ness had the foresight to recognize that if the British intended on reaching Washington by way of the Patuxent River, they would need to pass through Bladensburg. Stansbury also noted the logic of garrisoning the hill to defend the village but decided on the morning of August 24 that he did not have sufficient troops to do so. However, Porter had nearly two months to make advance preparations and would have recognized the strategic importance of the village with its natural defensive advantages. Like Van Ness, he would have used civilians and military volunteers to improve on those advantages with trenches and breastworks for a force that would have included at least one Maryland and one DC brigade, as well as the soldiers, sailors, and marines who fought in the battle. If well led, they might have proved too tough to crack, forcing the British to reconsider moving on Washington. Alternatively, if dislodged after hours of combat, they could have retreated either to the north and posed a threat to Ross's rearguard or to a rallying point on the heights across the eastern branch, where Winder's final line stood. In the latter case, another engagement might have been fought on the following day, and if pushed back again, Porter could have made a final stand closer to the city.

As an alternative or as a fallback position, Porter would have constructed defenses in Washington. The Naval Yard along the river would have been one logical site, along with Greenleaf's (now Haines) Point and Capitol Hill. Both Armstrong and Wilkinson cited the Capitol in their memoirs and observed that the legislative building could have been successfully defended with naval and militia artillery concentrated on the first floor and several thousand infantry filling the upper floor and adjacent buildings, and with the cavalry held in reserve for a charge when the British attack showed signs of breaking.[11]

Armstrong and Wilkinson also argued that a strategy of harassment—hit-and-run attacks on the flanks and rear of the British column—rather than a meeting engagement or a purely defensive strategy would have been more appropriate under the circumstances. Winder hinted that he would follow this course of action shortly after he was appointed, but he made no concerted plans or efforts to do so after learning that the axes he needed to fell trees and destroy bridges were not available. In his testimony to Congress after the battle, Armstrong claimed that he had instructed Winder to place a strong force at Nottingham or another point on the Patuxent, to obstruct the road by tearing down the bridges and throwing up abbatis, and to make small attacks on the enemy's front, flanks, and rear. Armstrong cited the defeat of the British column that marched to Lexington at the outset of the Revolutionary War as proof that such a strategy was appropriate for the largely militia forces at hand.

Wilkinson also testified, and later wrote in his memoirs, that he had offered to pursue such a strategy if given command of the situation. In particular, he noted that Winder should have deployed Smith's DC brigade on the heights to the north of Marlboro and should have attacked the rear of the British Army as it turned west toward Wood Yard. Both Armstrong and Wilkinson also observed that the route that the British took through Maryland was heavily wooded and cut by ravines and ridges that would have been ideal locations for ambushes. The terrain provided natural defensive positions that could have been exploited during the days it took the British to move from Benedict to Bladensburg. Wilkinson added that the principal reason this strategy was not adopted was that Monroe and Madison wanted to distinguish themselves in a major battle, the former with an eye toward the 1816 presidential election and the latter with an eye toward posterity.

Earlier accounts of the battle presented mixed views on the effectiveness of an American harassment strategy against Ross's force. William M. Marine's 1913 volume on the British invasion of Maryland cites a British officer's observation that "instead of concentrating their forces in one place, they ought to have harassed us with continuous skirmishing; felled trees of each side, and thrown them across the road; dug deep ditches at certain intervals; in a word, it was their wisdom to adopt the mode of warfare to which their own habits, as well as the nature of the country invited them." Similarly, John M. Stahl's 1918 account makes the case that Winder should have taken exactly this approach: "It was this strategy—avoidance of a pitched battle and the constant harassment of mobile parties taking all advantage of every natural feature of the theatre of operations—that should have opposed the British that landed at Benedict and which doubtless would have been successful."[12] In fact, the DC and Maryland militias made several tactical movements that could have resulted in such engagements in the handful of days between the British landing and the battle at Bladensburg. On two occasions, at Marlboro and the Wood Yard, they deployed for combat only to be withdrawn.

However, John S. Williams, who commanded a brigade of the DC militia during the War of 1812, speculated years later that had Winder been inclined to engage the British in this fashion and avoided a pitched battle, Armstrong would have forced his resignation because such a course of action would have been regarded as dishonorable. Williams wrote,

> The mass of mankind are not disposed to tolerate a Fabian policy or "masterly inactivity," and very naturally, because it is much more likely to be the result of sluggishness or timidity than of sagacious foresight and calculation. They love and admire promptness, energy, and determination. The vicinity of danger, too, occasions a kind of excitement which almost irresistibly impels men to run into it if they can not run away from it, and to do anything but calmly await its approach.[13]

Moreover, unlike New England's Minutemen in the Revolutionary War, the Maryland and DC militias were not trained or proficient in these tactics and could not have been counted on to competently execute them in combat. The units under Winder's command had never trained or fought together, and breaking them down into smaller detachments probably would have further complicated communications, command, and control.

However, a combined harassment and fortification strategy was used in the Battle of North Point outside Baltimore on September 12 to good effect. There, weeks later, Ross's force of four thousand engaged three thousand Maryland militiamen, including some who had fought at Bladensburg.[14] Unlike Winder, Maj. Gen. Samuel Smith, whom Baltimore's Committee of Vigilance and Safety looked to and Governor Winder appointed to lead the city's defense, adopted a forward defense. At the mouth of the Back River and Bear Creek, he positioned Brig. Gen. John Stricker's Third Brigade of the Maryland militia. As the British advanced guard made contact with the riflemen who made up the American skirmish line, Ross rode ahead to assess the situation. A sniper shot him from his horse, and he died shortly thereafter. His second in command, Col. Arthur Brooke, moved the British infantry forward and with artillery and rocket fire attacked the American line. He successfully maneuvered the Fourth Regiment to collapse the Americans' right flank, before ordering a general advance that culminated with a volley round and a bayonet charge. Although some of the Maryland units routed, most withdrew in good order and rallied at a reserve line three hundred yards to the rear. Uncertain of the size of the American force before him, Brooke reassembled his forces while probing the second American line. The British had suffered three hundred casualties compared to two hundred for the Americans in the battle, which lasted less than an hour.

Stricker used the approaching nightfall to retreat to higher ground six miles to the rear and a half mile forward of the left flank of Baltimore's main fortifications on Hampstead Hill. Brooke followed at 4:30 a.m. on September 13, but numerous felled trees delayed his march as the British took time to reconnoiter and secure their route, fearing they marked potential ambush sites. At 10 a.m. Brooke first saw the Hampstead Hill defenses holding eleven thousand troops and realized that his force could not take them in a daylight attack. For the rest of the day, the British marched and countermarched, looking either for a way to outflank the Baltimore defenses or for its weak points. Brooke ultimately decided against launching an attack to coincide with an amphibious assault on the harbor, and the latter proved disastrous for the British. Early on the morning of September 14, Brooke's force withdrew toward North Point and re-embarked their ships.

The Battle of North Point suggests that Winder or another commanding officer could have successfully engaged the same British force that had made a much longer march from Benedict to Washington. As Wilkinson indicated, numerous sites for such engagements could have been found along the British line of march. Combined with the high temperatures that punished the invading British forces in August, such firefights might have strengthened Ross's reluctance to march beyond Marlboro once Barney's flotilla had been destroyed. They would also have made him more responsive to Cochrane's directive to return to the fleet once that primary objective had been completed. The British certainly regarded Baltimore and New Orleans as more strategically important and more lucrative targets than Washington was. Risking mounting casualties in such engagements to reach Washington would not have been lightly tolerated. For the Americans, a series of clashes might have also masked their overall weaknesses, and avoided risking defeat in a single major engagement.

CONSEQUENCES

If the American forces had successfully deterred or defended against a British attack on Washington, what strategic effect would such outcomes have had on British plans to conduct other amphibious offensives along the Atlantic and Gulf Coasts? In all likelihood, the British would have pursued their campaign. Capt. James Gordon's Royal Navy flotilla ascending the Potomac would have still reached Alexandria on August 27 and probably would have been unaware of Ross's defeat. Whether the Virginia militiamen and citizens, possibly with reinforcements, would have surrendered as quickly as they did is uncertain. More important, Cochrane, Cockburn, and Ross would probably have attacked Baltimore except in the unlikely event that their defeat at Bladensburg had resulted in extraordinarily high casualties, including some senior officers. If so, Cockburn's advice to advance on Washington would have probably been discounted, and the move on Baltimore might have been limited to a reconnaissance in force. Landing as they did at North Point and engaging the Maryland militiamen, whose morale would have been lifted by a victory so close to Washington, the British would have proceeded to within sight of the Hampstead Hill fortifications and returned to the fleet. With fewer troops, neither Ross nor Brooke would have risked a frontal attack by day or by night. At best, they might have made a display of force in front of Fort McHenry to assess the harbor defenses or possibly might have conducted a punitive bombardment, but they would not have launched anything as dramatic as the attack that inspired the "Star-Spangled Banner."

Alternatively, if Ross had not been killed at North Point, he would have waited for reinforcements. London had sent Maj. Gen. Sir John Lambert and twenty-two thousand troops to Bermuda to provide additional support for Chesapeake Bay operations. In history, Ross's death and Cochrane's decision to sail for the Gulf prompted the British to send these troops to Jamaica, where they were met by Wellington's brother-in-law and Ross's replacement, Maj. Gen. Sir Edward Pakenham. The contingent arrived shortly after the main body of British forces landed outside New Orleans. If Ross had remained in command, however, he might have waited for Lambert to arrive in the Chesapeake Bay. According to one of his staff officers, Ross was "very cautious in responsibility—awfully so, and lacked that dashing enterprise so essential to carry a place by coup de main."[15] With these additional forces, Ross could have done what Brooke could not do—that is, launch a frontal attack on Hampstead Hill while simultaneously launching an amphibious attack on the harbor. But even with five thousand men, Ross would have attacked uphill against an entrenched opponent at a numerical disadvantage. Given the Maryland militiamen's plucky performance at North Point as compared to Bladensburg, Ross might have suffered a defeat comparable to Pakenham's at New Orleans. In that case, the place of the "Star-Spangled Banner" in history would have remained unchanged, and the British might have abandoned its plan for a subsequent attack on New Orleans.

A successful defense of Washington would also have had a political impact. On the one hand, those responsible—Winder (or Winchester or Porter), Armstrong, Monroe, and Madison—would have shared in the glory and political benefits. Winder could have made a stronger argument for taking command at Baltimore, but he almost certainly would have lost that argument given the local popularity of Major General Smith. Armstrong would not have resigned, depriving Monroe of the opportunity to serve as secretary of war. Madison's political fortunes and historical reputation as commander in chief would not have been tarnished by the British torching of Washington's public buildings. On the other hand, without his stunning success at New Orleans, Andrew Jackson's star would not have shone so brightly, and his political fortunes might have fallen well short of a White House that had not been burned by the British.

A British defeat at Washington would also have weighed heavily on the British calculations regarding a peace agreement. Whereas their summer offensives were designed to support the imposition of harsh terms, including territorial gains, their lack of success at Baltimore and Plattsburgh undercut these demands. It also weakened their position on the European continent, where strains were emerging among their allies. Unlike the Battle of New Orleans, American victories on the Patuxent, Potomac, and Patapsco Rivers in the summer of 1814 would have mattered. They could have given additional impetus to London's decision to take a more conciliatory approach to the peace talks, perhaps yielding the Treaty of Ghent weeks earlier. If so, the Second War of Independence narrative might have emerged as the clearly dominant interpretation of the War of 1812.

— 7 —

VICTORY OR DEFEAT,
AND FOR WHOM?

Alternative Outcomes for the War of 1812

W hen the United States declared war in 1812, American leaders were exceedingly optimistic that conquering Canada would coerce Britain into lifting its Orders in Council and ending impressment. Thomas Jefferson wrote that seizing most of Canada would be a "mere matter of marching." New York governor Daniel Tompkins predicted that "one-half of the Militia of [Canada] would join our standard." Henry Clay had previously boasted that "the militia of Kentucky are alone competent to place Montreal and Upper Canada at our feet." So deeply did Republicans hold these expectations of conquest that Virginia's John Randolph mocked their claims: "[N]o expense of blood, or treasure, on our part—Canada is to conquer herself—she is to be subdued by the principles of fraternity."[1]

When American and British negotiators first met in the Belgian city of Ghent in August 1814, the United States had utterly failed to make good on these boasts, and the belligerents' fortunes and expectations had been reversed. Britain had entered France, sent Napoleon into exile, and initiated military operations against New England and the Chesapeake Bay with further invasions planned along the Gulf Coast. British negotiators believed their military supremacy and prospects were so bright that they could dictate the terms of a peace treaty. They included a buffer state for the Indian nations, an adjustment of the U.S.-Canadian border to permit a direct land link between Quebec and the Atlantic, and the cessation of American rights to land and to dry fish off the Northern Banks. Further, the treaty would not address the issue of impressment. British negotiators clearly stated that London "did not think that it was a point necessary to be discussed."[2]

Yet, the pendulum swung decidedly to center over the next four months, yielding a treaty based on the principle of status quo antebellum. Negotiators set aside core issues, such as impressment, while leaving others—fishing rights and navigation of the Mississippi River— for bilateral commissions to solve. The Americans' successful defense of Baltimore and Plattsburgh were key events in this brief period, along with the deterioration of the British negotiating position in Paris and the prospect of a new continental war. Equally important were the persistence of the American negotiators—John Quincy Adams, James Bayard, Henry Clay, Albert Gallatin, and Jonathan Russell— who arrived with little prospect of success, and the wisdom of Lord Castlereagh, who reined in his overzealous delegation and accepted the terms of an honorable peace.

These dramatic shifts in expectations suggest how differently the war could have ended. Both sides had hoped to gain far more alternatively at the beginning and at the end of the conflict when they, respectively, sustained surprising defeats. To explore these possibilities requires a more ambitious and holistic approach that examines not only the potential outcomes of battles but also the entire war itself. *Alternative futures analysis*, which identifies two key factors that when juxtaposed create four equally plausible scenarios, as well as the basis for story lines leading to those outcomes, is a useful tool for this purpose.[3]

In the case of the War of 1812, those two main factors are the war in Europe and the quality of generalship. For such a strategic inquiry, it is necessary to recall that the War of 1812 was a function of Britain's struggle with Napoleon. London's willingness to curb American rights on the high seas was the issue on which the Jefferson and Madison administrations refused to yield. Once the war began, the availability of British forces for duty in North America became a central component of both American and British strategic planning. As noted in chapter 2, Sun Tzu cites generalship as one of the major, and possibly the most important, gauges of military strength in that it determines how the others—geography; weather; rules, or military doctrine; and national leadership— are addressed in planning and executing military campaigns.

THE WAR IN EUROPE

The War of 1812 was an offshoot of the Napoleonic war in Europe. The dueling blockades of Britain and France precipitated the harassment of American oceanic commerce that triggered President James Madison's efforts to deny London and Paris the benefits of trade with the United States. In particular, British domination of the high seas after the Battle of Trafalgar in 1805 narrowed the maneuvering room of such neutral powers as the United States to pursue their interests without antagonizing France or Britain. America also bore the burden of practice of "impressment," or "man stealing" as it was more pointedly described in U.S. domestic politics, as the price of doing business on the high seas. Even after war was declared in 1812, events in Europe shaped the character of the war in North America. Britain was unable to shift naval and land forces to the North American theater to defend Canada or attack America until it checked Napoleon's military power and continental ambitions.

The year 1813 was a critical turning point in this regard and one that could have gone against Britain rather than in its favor. France's retreat from Russia was a massive setback but not a knockout blow for Napoleon as the size of his empire and his talents left France with the means to raise new forces and successfully defend, or even expand, its realm. Austria, which refused to take sides at this time, as early as March 1813 proposed an agreement creating an independent central Europe with France in control of its "natural boundary" on the left bank of the Rhine.

Napoleon was noncommittal on this proposal until his army had endured months of inconclusive fighting in Germany. Following his victory at Bautzen in late May, he agreed to the Armistice of Pleischwitz, which began on June 2 and was extended until August 16. The emperor was worried about his shortage of cavalry and, more important, the possibility that Austria would join the allies. Britain signed treaties with Russia and Prussia on June 14 and 15; the Duke of Wellington won a strategic victory at Vitoria, Spain, on June 21; and on June 27, Austria joined the allies. The latter development prompted some of Napoleon's key aides to press for a peace treaty.

However, Napoleon saw the agreement as a trap and refused to yield territory when he had not been defeated on the battlefield. In particular, he refused London's demand that he restore the dynasty in Spain. This error proved to be graver than was his invasion of Russia a year earlier. Austrian foreign minister Klemens von Metternich reportedly told Napoleon at their last meeting, "Sire, you are a lost man." The combined forces of the Sixth Coalition deployed in Germany totaled 600,000 men against 370,000 for France and its allies. Following a series of French defeats, Bavaria allied itself with Austria, and on October 19, Napoleon lost the Battle of the Nations at Leipzig. Only the weakness of the allied pursuit allowed the war to continue, albeit briefly, into 1814.[4]

The defeat of France and Napoleon's abdication released British forces for operations in North America, but French decisions in 1813 might have alternatively shortened or prolonged the War of 1812. Clearly, Napoleon could have accepted a peace agreement in the summer of 1813 without abandoning his grander plans for a continental empire. He had signed peace agreements in the past, only to break them when he thought doing so was to France's advantage. The Treaties of Tilsit in 1807 with Prussia and Russia were voided five years later, but for a time they permitted Napoleon to pursue his ambitions against Austria and Britain. A peace agreement in 1813 would have given France a respite, albeit with a smaller but still significant continental empire, as well as time to rebuild its forces. Napoleon might have judged that his enemies' alliance would almost certainly dissolve once the war ended and France ceased to be the focus of their attention. Indeed, the diplomatic problems Britain experienced with its allies after Napoleon's abdication in 1814 suggest that such a calculation would have been correct.

For Britain, a peace in 1813 would have permitted the British Army to undertake offensive operations in North America six to twelve months earlier. Indeed, while American Republicans thought that an armistice would prompt France and Russia to support American maritime rights, they also believed it would lengthen the war with Britain by lessening London's commitments in Europe.[5] The time that the British needed to extract forces from Spain and sail across the Atlantic would have prevented any reinforcement of Upper Canada, where American forces defeated Gen. Henry Procter and Tecumseh at the Battle of the Thames in October 1813. However, the British could have launched amphibious operations against the Atlantic seaboard, in the Chesapeake Bay, and in the Gulf of Mexico earlier than they actually began.

Conversely, Napoleon's decision could have significantly delayed such a strategic military pivot from Europe to North America. Gen. Baron Antoine-Henri Jomini of France, whose writings became coda for military strategists in the nineteenth century, judged Napoleon's decision to agree to the armistice in June 1813 as the greatest mistake of his career. He argued that Napoleon could have achieved a decisive military victory and brought the war to an end by continuing his offensive after the Battle of Bautzen. Allied morale was low, and the Prussian and Russian military staffs disagreed on the future conduct of the war.[6] Initially, Napoleon had ordered a pursuit of his adversaries and came close to cutting off their withdrawal but reversed himself when his newly formed conscript army began to show signs of exhaustion after months of campaigning. In addition, Napoleon's confidence may have been shaken after a cannon shot passed close to him and killed Grand Marshal Géraud Duroc, for whom he had great affection. If, however, Jomini was correct, one more French victory could have forced Berlin and Moscow to come to peace on French terms. With his eastern front stable, Napoleon could have turned his attention not only to refitting and resting his forces but also to planning a forceful return to Spain.[7]

Had London faced a longer, and possibly unsuccessful, war in Spain, the British might not have succeeded in fending off repeated American invasions of Canada, much less launching counteroffensives of its own. Governor-General George Prévost's defense of Upper and Lower Canada could have become untenable over time absent British reinforcements. London might have faced difficult decisions on military and diplomatic issues with the United States in 1814, a situation that would have been quite the opposite of their bullish prospects after Napoleon's abdication.

GENERALSHIP

The second key factor to consider is the talent pool of generals that was available to America and Britain. Napoleon remarked that in war, men are nothing; one man is everything. Commodore James Yeo, who commanded British naval forces on the Great Lakes during the war, also commented on this issue: "The experience of two years active service has served to convince me that tho' much has been made by the mutual exertions of both Services, we also owe as much if not more to the perverse stupidity of the Enemy; the Impolicy of their plans; the disunion of their Commanders, and lastly, between them and their Minister of War." Donald R. Hickey's assessment of the American campaign to invade Canada in 1812 elaborates on this point: "The principal reason for America's failure was poor leadership. The administration's strategy was ill-advised, the War Department failed to give proper direction to commanders in the field, and most of the army's senior officers were incompetent." Finally, J. P. Riley's study of the Napoleonic war on both sides of the Atlantic in 1813 similarly observes, "At the end of the day, the personal qualities of the allied field commander may well be the major factor in determining the success or failure of a coalition force at an operational level."[8]

In a broad sense, the War of 1812 witnessed a race between the greening of a new postrevolutionary generation of capable American field commanders and the availability of seasoned British commanders freed from the conflict in Europe. Madison and his first two secretaries of war, William Eustis and John Armstrong, relied heavily on elderly Revolutionary War veterans in 1812 and 1813 who proved inept in executing their duties: Brig. Gen. William Hull, Maj. Gen. Henry Dearborn, Maj. Gen. Wade Hampton, and Maj. Gen. James

Wilkinson. Ironically, America's subsequent and more successful major generals—Jacob Brown, William Henry Harrison, and Andrew Jackson—began the war as officers in their respective state militias.

The British began the war with Prévost and Maj. Gen. Isaac Brock, respectively, commanding Lower and Upper Canada. Prévost remained at his post until the end of the war and returned to Britain to answer charges concerning his retreat from Plattsburgh. After Brock died at the Battle of Queenston Heights in October 1812, Maj. Gen. Roger Hale Sheaffe replaced him on the Niagara until June 1813, when Maj. Gen. Francis de Rottenburg succeeded him after the Americans captured Fort George. In December 1813 de Rottenburg was transferred to Lower Canada in anticipation of Prévost's invasion of New York. Lt. Gen. Gordon Drummond, who succeeded him, proved to be more aggressive and competent than either Sheaffe or de Rottenburg was. Finally, Procter, who commanded the British forces at Detroit, failed to expand British gains into the Ohio River Valley in 1813 before his defeat on the Thames later that year.

Napoleon's abdication in the spring of 1814 released British forces under the command of Wellington's two lieutenants—Maj. Gen. Robert Ross at Washington and Baltimore and Maj. Gen. Edward Pakenham at New Orleans. After Prévost's defeat at Plattsburgh, the British government considered sending Wellington to Canada in late 1814, but his arguments about the difficulties of defeating the United States and growing concerns about the situation in Europe convinced them otherwise. Nevertheless, speculation about what Wellington could have accomplished in North America is one of the great what-ifs of the War of 1812.

In a more narrow sense, the War of 1812 consisted of a series of duels between individual American and British commanders. Both sides had good and bad field commanders, and mismatches occurred. Brock led smaller numbers of British regulars and Native American warriors to victory over Hull's larger force of regulars and militiamen at Detroit in 1812. A year later, Harrison bested Proctor at the Battle of the Thames. On other occasions, comparable commanders parried each other, resulting in a stalemate. Drummond and Brown fought to a draw at Lundy's Lane. Ross, who combined prudence and persistence in his long march from Benedict to Washington, planned an attack on Baltimore that Smith's well-prepared defenses repelled. Similarly, Jackson at New Orleans combined a spoiling attack on the newly arrived British forces with a well-constructed defensive line that militiamen and regulars manned to defeat "Wellington's finest." But Jackson was not in a position to follow up and drive the British from the vicinity and simply waited for the enemy to retreat to their fleet.

The availability of specific commanding officers, good and bad, was as much a matter of chance as of choice. When war was declared in 1812, the British were fortunate to have the more operationally competent and aggressive Brock and the more cautious Prévost in Upper Canada, where the Americans chose not to advance. Mortality was also a critical factor throughout the war. Brock's death at Queenston Heights quickly deprived Upper Canada of its most capable commander, one who defended a vast unsettled region with extremely limited forces. Ross's death at North Point, followed by Pakenham's death at New Orleans, took two of Wellington's lieutenants from the ranks of experienced British combat commanders. These losses would have been more important had the war dragged on beyond the first months of 1815. Similarly, the death of Brig. Gen. Zebulon Pike, who was crushed by a stone flung from an exploding armory at York, cost America one of its most promising brigadiers. Brown and Brig. Gen. Winfield Scott were both casualties at Lundy's Lane; their absence undoubtedly had an impact on the subsequent American retreat to Fort Erie and the failure of the 1814 offensive along the Niagara frontier. In 1813, two associates who had been humiliated in a duel where Jackson had served as their opponent's second severely wounded the future major general. Jackson's wounds resulted in a massive loss of blood and kept him in bed longer than a month. Shortly thereafter, Jackson left to campaign in the Creek War, still suffering ill effects from his wounds. That he might have died in the duel or at some point shortly thereafter, depriving the nation of its most aggressive general and the hero of New Orleans, is not hard to imagine.

A far more significant what-if than Jackson's untimely demise concerns Alexander Hamilton, whom Aaron Burr killed in a duel in 1804. A former chief of staff for George Washington and briefly a combat commander at Yorktown, Hamilton was a contemporary of the Revolutionary War veterans who served in high positions in both the Madison administration and the army in the War of 1812. In 1798 he authored a series of newspaper essays advocating the creation of a large army capable of resisting French imperial designs in North America. Hamilton declined to join the Senate or to become secretary of war, hoping to become commander in chief of a revitalized army. When the John Adams administration gave that position to Washington, Hamilton became inspector general with the rank of major general. After Washington's death in late 1799, Hamilton served as "Senior Officer of the United States

Army" until June 1800. A contemporary observed at the time, "He was quali-
fied, beyond any man of the age to display the talents of a great general."
Jefferson, however, feared that "our Buonaparte" might use the army to invade
Virginia and suppress dissent against the Alien and Sedition Acts and other
Federalist efforts to curb radical Jacobin tendencies.[9]

During his brief tenure, Hamilton organized the army in elaborate detail,
planned defenses against a French invasion, and considered an operation for
conquering Spanish colonies in Louisiana and Mexico.[10] If he had avoided his
duel with Burr or survived it, Hamilton would have been a logical and eager
candidate for either secretary of war—following the bumbling campaign in
1812—or, more likely, as commander in chief of the army given his previous
position and long interest in martial affairs and glory. Indeed, Hamilton's
detailed understanding of military organization and operations would have been
a powerful tonic for the army after its early defeats. Madison might also have
viewed his participation in the war as a force for unifying Republicans and
Federalists, particularly those in Hamilton's adopted home state of New York,
given the American strategy of conquering Canada as a means of compelling
Britain to cease its predatory maritime policies. Although he was a long-
standing opponent of Jefferson and Madison's party, they might have chosen
to follow the old adage "Keep your friends close and your enemies closer" by
offering him a prominent role in the war.

Scenarios

The juxtaposition of these two key factors—the war in Europe and the quality
of generalship—creates four what-if scenarios with which to explore alternative outcomes for the War of 1812. In figure 2, the vertical axis displays the
duration of the Napoleonic wars in Europe (long to short), and the horizontal
axis shows the advantage in British and American generals.

The basis of each scenario is first discussed in terms of generalship and the
duration of the war. This discussion also identifies and analyzes other events
that would have shaped the outcome. A what-if narrative for the scenario sets
the stage, identifies the main actors, and describes how key decisions and events
took a different turn than they did in history. Such narratives are a necessary
part of alternative futures analysis, which while ground in knowledge also
requires imagination based on historical trends and precedents. For purposes of
readability and realism, the scenarios are written from the perspective of the
victorious commanding general whose efforts were critical in deciding the con-

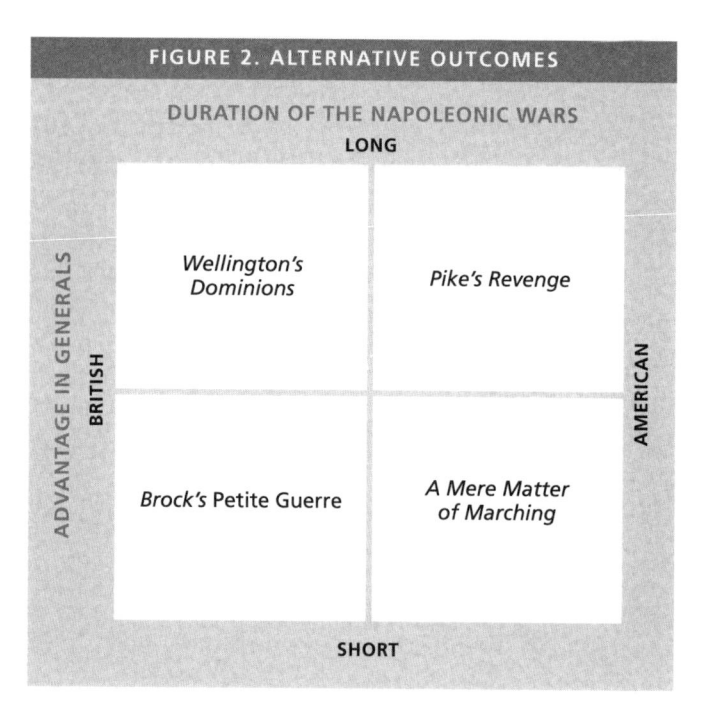

FIGURE 2. ALTERNATIVE OUTCOMES

DURATION OF THE NAPOLEONIC WARS

LONG

Wellington's Dominions

Pike's Revenge

Brock's Petite Guerre

A Mere Matter of Marching

SHORT

ADVANTAGE IN GENERALS

BRITISH

AMERICAN

flict. The scenarios predicated on an early end to the war in Europe precede those depicting a prolonged continental conflict; the British accounts are presented before those of the Americans.

Brock's Petite Guerre

Maj. Gen. Isaac Brock's capacity for leadership and his firm belief that Upper Canada could be defended are significant factors in this scenario, which requires postulating that he escaped death at the Battle of Queenston Heights on October 13, 1812. Brock defeated Hull at Detroit, a feat that improved morale among his troops and proved to Prévost that the portion of Canada north of the Great Lakes and west of Montreal was defensible. If he had not been killed at Queenston Heights, Brock could have led a campaign that not only kept the region free from American control but also defeated American forces in the West and secured an early victory for Britain in the War of 1812. His continued success could have turned Prévost's initial inclination to abandon the region and mass his forces for the defense of Lower Canada into a bolder offensive strategy that supported Native American claims in the Old Northwest, which became a key British demand at Ghent. Relying on light infantry and his Native American allies, this scenario argues Brock could have waged a successful *petite guerre* (small or guerrilla war) in the West.

Brock would have been a more aggressive commander than was his replacement, Major General de Rottenburg, or his subordinate, Colonel Procter, who commanded British forces west of Burlington after Detroit fell. With his ally Shawnee chief Tecumseh, Brock could have thwarted Harrison's counteroffensive before it gained traction and precluded the naval race on Lake Erie that the Americans won in 1813. Like Procter, he probably would have defeated Maj. Gen. James Winchester but then sought out Harrison's larger force rather than retreating to Detroit.

This success, in turn, could have convinced the British to mass those troops freed from the Napoleonic wars for an invasion of New Orleans and to widen their offensive against the heartland of the American War Hawks, whose support was central to Madison's decision to declare war shortly before his reelection in 1812. With Canada secure, the British would have had less reason to harass the Chesapeake Bay in hopes of pulling American forces away and could have immediately applied their efforts to attain the larger strategic objective of gaining access, if not control of, the Mississippi River. Maneuvering their force by sea for an amphibious offensive at New Orleans earlier in the war would also have taken advantage of James Wilkinson's presence as commander of U.S. forces in that region. Wilkinson, in history an agent of Britain's ally Spain, might have found a pretext to surrender the city to a far superior force at that point in the war.

An early termination of the war in Europe would have been a precondition of this offensive. Had Napoleon and the allies turned the Armistice of Pleischwitz into a permanent peace agreement that included an arrangement regarding Spain, British troops could have been released for duty in North America and could have arrived early in 1813. Sending the bulk of those forces deployed in Spain to the Gulf of Mexico, perhaps via Jamaica (as they did in 1814), would have made more strategic sense than sending them to Canada, where they would have had to wait until the spring to begin military operations. An attack on New Orleans would have been a masterful strategic move, possibly forcing the Madison administration to capitulate early in the war. No doubt to placate Prévost, London also would have sent a smaller number of troops to Lower Canada to seize enough territory to create an overland supply route from the coast of Maine to Quebec, as they did in 1814.

20 February 1814
Letter to Lord Bathurst, Minister of War
From Maj. Gen. Isaac Brock

Your Lordship,

As directed by Governor-General Prévost, I have the honour of providing you with a first-hand account of His Majesty's successful campaign to defend Canada and end the war with the United States on favourable terms. You will forgive me if I begin by mentioning our initial victories at Mackinac, Detroit, and Queenston Heights in 1812, of which you are fully aware. It is important to note that these crucial battles allowed His Majesty's forces to take limited offensive actions to disrupt the enemy's continuing plans to conquer Canada. As our adversaries planned additional attacks across the Niagara in the fall of that year, Commodore Yeo, with my encouragement and support, successfully attacked Sackets Harbour. We caught the enemy by surprise, destroying his base, supplies, and vessels and most importantly preventing any offensive actions from that quarter for the remainder of the conflict. This victory almost certainly also prevented the Americans from enjoying freedom of manoeuvre on Lake Ontario and from diverting men and matériel to build a naval base and warships on Lake Erie.

By taking this initiative, we enjoyed freedom of action in initiating and sustaining le petite guerre in the Ohio River Valley through the rest of the war. American general Winchester's imprudent advance to the Raisin River provided us with an opportunity to defeat his force in a surprise attack by a mixed force of British, Canadian, and Indian forces, the latter led by our ally, Chief Tecumseh. In addition to its immediate benefits, this battle provided us with a model with which to prosecute the war in the West. As our enemy built stockades and husbanded men and supplies for an offensive to retake Detroit, His Majesty's forces and their native allies besieged these forts but resisted the temptation to capture them, instead ambushing relief forces and attacking more vulnerable locations. The complete destruction of General Clay's column, which was attempting to relieve Fort Meigs in the spring of 1813, was followed several months later by the Second Battle of the Raisin. There, our forces repeatedly ambushed General Harrison's army of five thousand over a period of several days, defeating it in detail. Some in the American government and press have, perhaps unfairly, characterized this engagement as a repeat of our own Gen. Edward Braddock's defeat outside Fort Duquesne in 1755 and of American Gen. Arthur St. Clair's disastrous performance on the Maumee in 1791. I had the honour of accepting General Harrison's surrender but returned his sword. As reported in the American and British press, I joined Harrison and his officers at a military funeral for his subordinate, Kentucky Congressman and Col. Richard Johnson, whose cavalry charge at a crucial moment nearly turned the tide of the battle.

Needless to say, our efforts in Ohio would not have won the war absent the termination of hostilities in Europe that released additional British forces for operations in North America. The Treaty of Pleischwitz in June 1813 effectively ended, for now, the war in Europe, giving Napoleon his "natural borders" for France; established a neutral Prussia and Spain; and settled a peace with Austria, Russia, and His Majesty. Even if it should prove to be only a brief respite from warfare on the Continent, the agreement released sufficient British forces to reinforce Canada and strike New Orleans.

Governor Prévost has already expressed his thanks for your confidence in the strategy proposed for winning the war in North America. Allow me to emphasize that Lt. Gen. John Sherbrooke's movement of His Majesty's recently arrived forces from Nova Scotia to Maine in September of last year—completely surprising the Americans—not only seized sufficient territory in northern Maine to provide a direct land route to Quebec but also forced the Madison government to direct its attention to defending the northern border of the United States, leaving us considerable liberty in expanding our gains in the West.

To that end, Chief Tecumseh's warriors accompanied my forces to reclaim the site of Prophetstown at the juncture of the Tippecanoe and Wabash Rivers. We pushed down the Wabash to invest Fort Harrison, where a demonstration of our numbers and the knowledge that no help would be coming so late in the season convinced the commander to surrender the installation without needless loss of blood. From this position, Tecumseh and I were able to effectively supply and advise the Creek Indians who were struggling to preserve their lands and way of life in the Mississippi Territory of the United States. Our presence on the Wabash, in particular, kept the Kentucky and Tennessee militias focused to the north. Indeed, our victory over a hastily assembled force of Tennessee militiamen led by General Jackson, who was all too eager to engage British troops and left his flanks poorly guarded, eliminated the last significant American force west of the Ohio.

However, the coup de main of His Majesty's strategy was the arrival of Vice Admiral Cochrane's fleet with Major General Ross's forces at New Orleans in December. As their dispatches have undoubtedly informed you, the suddenness with which they moved from Lake Borgne and through the bayous to the outskirts of the city took the city and its defenders completely by surprise. American Secretary of War Armstrong's decision to leave his Revolutionary War comrade, General Wilkinson, in command of New Orleans rather than transferring him to New York, where General Dearborn remained in command, appears to have saved numerous lives and the needless destruction of property. Recent reports suggest that General Wilkinson's selfless decision to remain as a private citizen and to serve as liaison with the civil authorities has had a most beneficial impact on security and safety in the city.

By severing the larger Louisiana Territory west of the Mississippi from the rest of the United States, His Majesty's military forces were able to dictate the terms of the recent peace agreement signed in Boston last month. Pending ratification, it will leave us in control of our reestablished colony of New Ireland in northern Maine, strengthening the defence of Canada. It will give our Indian allies legal and military protections of their territories through the work of joint commissions to be established this year. Finally, it will give the American government the generous suspension of the Orders in Council first offered by His Majesty's government in June 1812. With the cessation of hostilities in Europe and the lifting of Napoleon's paper blockade on the Continent, the Americans will be fortunate to return to the peaceful and profitable commerce they enjoyed prior to these unpleasant and unfortunate hostilities. I am confident that they will take this agreement given the untenable position they now find themselves. Indeed, whereas the Madison government and its so-called "War Hawk" faction in Congress sought to use an attack on Canada to defeat Britain, His Majesty's government used a successful campaign across a comparable span of territory west of the Appalachian Mountains to defeat the United States. As they say, turnabout is fair play.

I Remain Your Humble Servant,
Maj. Gen. Sir Isaac Brock

A Mere Matter of Marching

This scenario takes its name from Thomas Jefferson's optimistic assessment that capturing Canada would have been "a mere matter of marching" for the American militia, which would bring the War of 1812 to a speedy conclusion in less than two years. It postulates that Hull's subordinates could have taken charge of the defense of Fort Detroit in light of the imbecility and cowardice of their commanding officer and held out until Harrison arrived and broke the British-Indian siege. Both Brock and Tecumseh fall at Detroit, rather than at Queenston Heights and the Thames River, respectively, leaving the Americans with a decisive edge in generalship.

Harrison probably would have followed up by massing Hull's army with his own and launching an offensive against Burlington, thus cutting off the British Fort Erie and Fort George from their supply route around the western side of Lake Ontario. The American forces invading across the Niagara River could have then captured both forts. Prévost almost certainly would have responded by planning to withdraw the majority of his forces from Upper Canada in the spring and concentrating on the defense of Lower Canada.

However, had Harrison literally stolen the march on the British by launching an early spring offensive and coordinating a two-pronged surprise attack with Commodore Isaac Chauncey and General Brown (who as in history did so against York) in the spring of 1813, the Americans could have taken Kingston. The loss of this city, home of the major British naval base on Lake Ontario, would have given the United States the "control of the lakes" that Wellington noted was critical to controlling North America. Moreover, such a campaign might have eliminated any British opportunity to transfer forces from Europe following a peace agreement in 1813.

Sweeping aside the residual garrisons and militia in Upper Canada would have left Harrison poised to strike at Montreal and following the same route that Wilkinson had taken in 1813. Knowing that capturing this well-defended city would require a prolonged siege and possibly a direct attack, Harrison could have maneuvered a portion of his forces to conduct a feint from northern New York, hoping to draw out the defenders. He could also have baited Prévost to attack the American militia at Crysler's Farm as the force prepared to bypass the eight-mile Long Sault Rapids before following the St. Lawrence River down to Montreal. Capturing the city would have given the Madison administration significant leverage in bringing the war to an end on its terms.

National Intelligencer
September 9, 1813
"General Harrison's Address to a Joint Session of Congress"

The road to Montreal began in Frankfort. It was there in August 1812 that I met with Governor Scott, Governor-elect Shelby, Speaker of the House Clay, and other dignitaries to accept, reluctantly I might add, a commission as major general and a charge of leading three thousand Kentucky militiamen to relieve our besieged forces at Fort Detroit. Four weeks later, we broke through the British and Indian forces surrounding the fort and were warmly welcomed by Lewis Cass of Michigan and his fellow officers. I congratulated them for their courage in defeating several attacks, including one where British general Brock was killed storming the barricades. Shortly thereafter, we crossed into Canada, captured Fort Malden, killed the Shawnee chief Tecumseh in the process, and accepted the surrender of General Procter. We made prisoners of his regulars, released the Canadian militia, and made peace with the Indian chiefs who had not fled to the north and east.

With several months remaining before winter, I put General Winchester in charge of the Detroit area and struck out for Burlington Heights on Lake Ontario. Our advance and capture of that strategic point was facilitated by several factors, including the decision of the resident Indian tribes to abide by the peace, the withdrawal of British forces from the Ontario Peninsula as ordered by British governor-general Prévost, and General Van Rensselaer's capture of Fort George. Winter arrived with our forces safely billeted and well provisioned at the western end of Lake Ontario, where I augmented my forces with those of Brigadier General Smyth. General Van Rensselaer was given local command of the Niagara frontier.

When spring freed the lakes and rivers of ice, we continued our advance on York, the capital of Upper Canada, expecting considerable resistance from the British. Under the direction of Secretary of War Eustis, Major General Dearborn took advantage of the British effort to blunt our efforts by launching an amphibious invasion of Kingston in April 1813. The enemy was caught completely off guard. Brigadier General Pike, who commanded the army units seizing Kingston, its harbor, and much of the British fleet on the lake, so completely achieved his objectives that the enemy before us—led by British lieutenant general Sherbrooke—found itself effectively surrounded and surrendered to avoid unnecessary loss of life.

From Kingston, we proceeded down the St. Lawrence toward Montreal. Major General Dearborn seconded Brigadier General Pike and his forces to my command and traveled to Albany to organize a feint toward the Canadian border north of Plattsburgh. My western forces, augmented by Brigadier General Smyth's command, moved by land up the northern bank of the river with Pike's division proceeding by bateaux and by land along the southern bank. Our forces totaled six thousand regulars and militiamen, including many from Kentucky who chose to "march on Montreal" rather than return home when their enlistment tours ended. We were evenly matched with Prévost's forces guarding Montreal. Hence, I needed to tempt him to engage us in the field as his defenses in that city and supply line by river to Quebec gave him the advantage if I attempted to storm the city or take it by siege. I spread rumors through the towns that we passed that our militia was eager to return home and that disease and supply shortages were rampant among our forces.

Prévost took the bait, sending half of his forces—including many Voltigeurs, or French Canadian militia—under Major General de Rottenburg to make a stand at Crysler's Farm, where our river-borne forces needed to disembark to circumvent the nearby eight-mile Long Sault Rapids. Our numbers and strategy prevailed as they attacked Pike's division, which was entrenched on the northern bank of the river, and I hit them on their right flank and rear with my Western Division and Smyth's forces. Our victory compelled Prévost to pull back to Quebec, and we entered Montreal on June 24. Our occupation of the city was facilitated by an agreement with the gallant and honorable Lt. Col. Charles-Michel de Salaberry, who was captured at Crysler's Farm and persuaded to act as a liaison with the city's officials and populace with my firm word that all persons and property would be respected. Sadly, I had to make good on that promise by executing several American regulars and militiamen who chose to prey upon the populace.

To my surprise and delight, that was the end of our military operations in Canada. Across the ocean, the peace signed by France and the Russian-Austrian-British alliance freed the British forces that had arrived in the city of Quebec as we took Montreal. Unsure that he could retake the latter city, General Prévost arranged an immediate cease-fire and entered peace negotiations with the United States. As you know, those negotiations produced the Treaty of Montreal, which restored that city to the British but left Upper Canada, newly renamed the Ontario Territory, in our hands. Just as important was the British agreement to permanently repeal their Orders in Council and to cease their impressment practices against American merchant vessels. No doubt their need for our grain and beef to feed their remaining troops in Portugal— there as a hedge against a renewal of war in Europe—as well as for our markets for their manufactures also weighed heavily in their decision to end this war. Finally, having secured the Michigan and other territories, we can continue to build and expand this empire of liberty. We, thus, ended this war with security, peace, and honor.

[Editor's Note: General Harrison is to be forgiven for not mentioning the significant contribution to the war effort played by the officers and sailors of our navy on the high seas. Their victories over British warships helped raise morale at home and demonstrated our capacity to defend our interests abroad. General Harrison's failure to mention the shortcomings of General Hull during the early phases of the Detroit campaign are also understandable given the pending outcome of the latter's court-martial.]

Wellington's Dominions

One of the great what-ifs of the War of 1812 involves Wellington's refusal to take command in North America following the British offensive failures at Plattsburgh, Baltimore, and New Orleans. He refused the opportunity, believing that Britain would find it difficult to gain control of the Great Lakes and should instead come to terms with the United States.

In this scenario of a longer war in Europe, Napoleon refuses a temporary truce after the Battle of Bautzen, instead pursuing and defeating Austrian and Russian forces. He compels them to sign a separate peace treaty, allowing him not only to focus on Wellington in Spain but also to rebuild the French Army and prepare it to resume operations in the East. The Iberian War, however, proves costly and indecisive, and Napoleon finally agrees to a separate truce with London in the spring of 1815 that releases more British reinforcements for duty in North America under Wellington's command. Before the truce, London sent some forces to North America as it did in 1814, but not the reinforcements that joined Pakenham in Jamaica after Ross's death at Baltimore. In this telling, Pakenham retreats to Halifax after Baltimore to bolster Canada's defenses; and it is only in June 1815 that he sails to attack New Orleans in conjunction with Wellington's offensive in Canada.

In this longer war scenario, history remains unchanged through the end of 1814, except that the negotiations at Ghent collapse. Madison's determined opposition to acceding to British demands is bolstered by American victories at Baltimore and Plattsburgh, compelling Wellington to agree to take command in North America. Given the importance that he placed on control of the Great Lakes, Wellington's strategy would have been to capture the U.S. naval base at Sackets Harbor, putting an end to the naval arms race on Lake Ontario. An offensive that combined a ground assault supported by Yeo's fleet could have accomplished this objective. With Izard and Brown preparing for an invasion up the St. Lawrence River (see chapter 3), Wellington's operation probably would have succeeded. He would have also exercised the opportunity presented by Massachusetts governor Strong to establish a de facto cease-fire in New England (see chapter 4).

The impact of these two developments would have prolonged the war well into the spring of 1815. By bringing additional manpower to bear in Canada, the British could have compelled the Madison administration to reopen negotiations, probably demanding boundary adjustments along the southern border to Quebec and possibly in the West to reward their Indian allies. The British, in particular, probably would not have returned the territory they had seized in Maine to create an overland route to Quebec.

However, a longer war against the United States would have created a larger strategic problem for London arising from Napoleon's resumption of hostilities in 1815, echoing his escape from Elba in history. Needing to return Wellington's divisions to Europe, the British government would have decided that the game was not worth the candle and agreed to some American conditions.

24 December 1815
Letter to Lord Bathurst, Minister of War
From the Duke of Wellington, Governor of the British Dominions of North America

Your Lordship,

I write to inform you that the American delegation in the City of Quebec delivered to me this morning written confirmation that President Madison has agreed to terms for the peace treaty and to continuing the current armistice until Congress ratifies the agreement post haste. Those terms include:

- *British possession of Forts Niagara and Mackinac, as well as New Ireland in eastern Maine; American possession of Amherstburg.*

- *The neutrality of the Confederation of New Columbia consisting of the independent states of Massachusetts, Connecticut, Rhode Island, New Hampshire, and Vermont for a period of ten years, after which time they may individually or collectively apply for readmission to the United States of America.*

- *A prohibition of American armed vessels on the Great Lakes for the same period.*

- *And, finally, the establishment of bilateral commissions to settle issues regarding American access to fishing grounds off Halifax, the future status of Louisiana, British access to the Mississippi River, and the protection of Indian tribal lands west of the Greenville Line.*

On these points, I had instructed our negotiators not to press the Americans, given the complicated history of these issues and my pressing need to return to the Continent with substantial forces.

Certainly, this agreement is less than what His Majesty's Government hoped for when more of our troops were released from combat in Europe following Napoleon's armistice. By the time negotiations began in earnest in Ghent, we had been rebuffed at Baltimore and Plattsburgh. To make matters worse, Lord Castlereagh's prolonged illness last winter contributed to the collapse of the negotiations and by extension to my appointment to this post.

That His Majesty's Government achieved these tangible gains is the direct result of our winter and spring campaigns and the political effect they had on the United States. We were fortunate that General Pakenham captured New Orleans in June, assisted in no small part by General Jackson's inability to cover all of the avenues of advance open to us in taking the city by surprise.

Based on my judgment that control of the lakes was key to victory in North America, I directed that our next step should be to advance on Sackets Harbour, the enemy's main naval base on Lake Ontario, before the onset of winter. The advance had three prongs. First, fifteen thousand men headed directly south from the confluence of the lake and the St. Lawrence River. Second, another ten thousand moved in parallel to the main advance several tens of miles to the east, blocking any American reinforcements from Plattsburgh. Third, five thousand troops boarded Commodore Yeo's fleet and landed just north of Sackets Harbour and, under the protective guns of the fleet, quickly built a strong defensive position that I judged would command the enemy's attention while our main forces advanced.

I must admit that our intelligence sources failed to warn us that the Americans were advancing north from the harbour with the objective of establishing a strong position on the St. Lawrence in order to cut the logistics line to our forces in the West. Under the capable Major General Brown, the American troops suddenly found themselves surrounded on three sides. In a series of clashes that ran for the better part of a week, British forces succeeded in pinning them against the eastern shore of Lake Ontario, while Yeo's fleet kept American commodore Chauncey's vessels bottled up. Here, I must call to your attention the contribution made by Lt. Gen. Sir George Murray, whose presence in Canada before my arrival was instrumental and critical in the development and execution of our strategy. Commanding the forces guarding our left flank, he attacked at a critical point in the engagement, causing great confusion amongst the enemy. Realizing the hopelessness of his position, General Brown surrendered his forces. We advanced on and captured Sackets Harbour. The American fleet bravely engaged Commodore Yeo's ships, which suffered substantial damage but ultimately prevailed.

Our success in the field and on the lake reactivated the political efforts of those in New England to achieve the objectives laid out at the so-called Hartford Convention. They amounted to compelling the Madison government to contribute more significantly to the defence of the participating states that I mentioned above and to seek an accommodation with Great Britain. As you know, Governor Strong of Massachusetts had already opened communications with His Majesty's Government. With Madison unable and unwilling to provide more protection to New England, Strong engaged in direct talks with my staff to arrange a truce and a resumption of commerce between New England and the British Isles and Canada. Our victory substantially aided his efforts to bring along his neighbouring governors and assemblies into this agreement and a separate pact to suspend for an indefinite period of time their participation in the federal government of the United States.

Following our victory, I invited Governor Tompkins of New York to enter into negotiations for a local cease-fire. The strategic imperative of returning the bulk of our forces in the Canadas after Napoleon once again declared war on the Great Powers of Europe compelled me to be somewhat lenient in dictating the terms of a peace treaty. I made clear to the representatives from Albany that it was my intention to withdraw from New York State, with the exception of Fort Niagara, as soon as possible. When they were subsequently joined by a delegation from Washington, I offered the generous terms indicated above, and they were quickly accepted. Implicit in this agreement is the understanding that His Majesty's 1812 offer to rescind the Orders in Council would be honoured. On the issue of impressment, I have indicated that sailors will not be removed from U.S.-flagged ships on the high seas, but crews in British ports and British-controlled ports are subject to such levies.

I pray these arrangements meet with the approval of His Majesty and His Government. It would be prudent to confirm the terms of this settlement so that upon my arrival in London we can discuss how to restore peace in Europe by defeating Bonaparte in as expeditious a manner as possible. In conclusion, whatever gains my presence in North America, they must be viewed as secondary, if not trivial, in comparison to our current perilous position on the Continent.

I am, &c,
Wellesley

Pike's Revenge

This scenario also posits a longer war in Europe but one where the British Army is pushed from Spain after Napoleon signs a separate peace with Austria and Russia. Without reinforcements from Europe, Prévost is left to fend for himself. An American victory results from better generalship from General Pike, who is not killed at York in the spring of 1813 and replaces an ailing Dearborn as de facto commander of U.S. forces in the Northeast. Pike would probably have fared better than his elderly and sickly superior officer did in exploiting the capture of Fort George to march on Burlington.

Capturing that strategic position at the western end of Lake Ontario would have permitted him to focus his resources on Kingston, Armstrong's preferred objective in 1813. Following Perry's victory on Lake Erie and Harrison's success at the Battle of the Thames, a combined American Army would have advanced on Montreal. Hence, Armstrong has no reason to call upon his Revolutionary War comrade General Wilkinson to lead the advance into Canada (that failed in 1813).

On the British side, Prévost is denied Wellington's Invincibles and has no opportunity to threaten Plattsburgh. Consequently, the Madison administration is not faced with multiple contingencies in the Chesapeake Bay and the Gulf of Mexico, where British amphibious forces in 1814 attempted to divert U.S. forces from Canada and to threaten vital U.S. interests.

Overall, this strategic situation allows Washington to mass its forces against Canada as was originally proposed in the summer of 1812, but Generals Hull, Smyth, and Dearborn horribly executed the plan. And rather than being dispersed from New York to Michigan, the U.S. Army could have massed for a strike at Lower Canada. As with the historic War of 1812, events in Europe would have dictated the conditions of peace in this scenario but not to the benefit of Great Britain.

Excerpts from A Soldier's Reflections on Our Recent Conflict
By Maj. Gen. Zebulon Pike, U.S. Army (Ret.)
New York City, 1837

As fate would have it, our capture of York in April 1813 was the first victory in a long and difficult struggle to extinguish the threat Britain posed to our country. We seized the capital of Upper Canada by combining surprise with audacity, catching the British unprepared, quickly subduing resistance, but exercising restraint in our occupation of the city and in our treatment of its citizens. To be sure, the enemy's perfidy in blowing up the power magazine in their principal fortification, killing and hideously wounding many of our soldiers as we seized it, was sufficient cause and justification for treating them more harshly. I, too, felt the desire for retribution after watching my young adjutant, the son of a close friend, crushed to death by a massive block that missed me by only a few yards. Nevertheless, I ordered our troops to be firm, but civil, with our prisoners and toward the population. They complied with this order even after discovering two scalps, possibly from American settlers, hanging in the provincial assembly hall. . . .

Our capture of Fort George one month later was followed by the successful pursuit of the retreating British, Canadian, and Indian forces. At Beaver Falls, we foiled a night raid on our camp with diligence and alacrity. The next morning, we overtook the British before they reached Burlington. With General Dearborn ill and hospitalized in Fort Niagara, I convinced Commodore Chauncey to double back across the lake and strike at Kingston. Our sudden appearance caught the enemy by surprise, and we succeeded in capturing the city and the naval base. This signal victory gave us supremacy over the lake for the remainder of the war, allowing Chauncey to use his fleet exclusively in support of the army's operations and giving us a permanent presence astride the British supply line to its scattered forces to the West. . . .

Events on Lake Ontario enabled General Harrison and Commodore Perry to quickly seize control of the Detroit area. General Procter fled Detroit but was successfully pursued and defeated at Monrovia on the Thames River. Most of his Indian allies returned to their settlements along the Grand River, though Tecumseh and his closest warriors fled south to join in the Creek War.

We more than sustained ourselves that winter in Kingston, living off the provisions and supplies that had been intended for the British and Canadian garrisons across all of Upper Canada. Two convoys of bateaux arriving in the city, unaware that it had been captured, also fell into our hands. My promotion in January 1814 to the rank of major general with orders from Secretary of War Armstrong to continue the northern campaign sent us down the St. Lawrence to Montreal. I ordered flanking columns of infantry and cavalry to screen the banks of the river while a flotilla of galleys and bateaux carried the bulk of the infantry and our artillery, as well as supplies. Governor-General Prévost had opted for a tight defense of Montreal that permitted me the time to carefully construct siege works around the city. Only when every battery was finished and every route into the city was blockaded did I order the systematic destruction and capture of the British fortifications.

After two and a half months, the city had consumed its remaining grain and other provisions. With no relief in sight, the British commanding officer, General Sheaffe, surrendered. As he had commanded the defenses in York the previous year, I felt no shame or regret in denying him a customary parole or transfer to more comfortable quarters in some town in New England. I sent him under guard up the St. Lawrence and across the lake to confinement at Sackets Harbor for the duration of the war. . . .

The fall of Montreal coincided with the retreat of the Duke of Wellington from Spain to Portugal. The separate peace that the Emperor Napoleon had signed with Austria and Prussia the previous summer had permitted him to reinforce his army on the Iberian Peninsula. With sufficient numbers, his commanders crushed the irregular forces supporting Wellington and engaged the Duke in a successful war of attrition. No doubt, these developments aided our cause by depriving Prévost of any hope of receiving reinforcements.

The British government suddenly expressed heightened interest in bringing the war to an end. A British emissary was sent from Halifax to Montreal with extraordinary authority to end the war on terms generally unfavorable, but not embarrassing, to London. The British agreed to cede Upper Canada to the United States, to significantly increase licensed trade by American merchantmen throughout the British Empire, to rescind the Orders in Council (as London offered in 1812), to quietly cease impressment of sailors aboard American merchantmen, and to restore American fishing rights on the outer banks of Canada. Thus was the honor of the United States of America upheld by President Madison's courageous decision to declare war on Great Britain in 1812.

The implications of these alternative histories, had they come to pass, are largely territorial and political. In the two American victories, the United States conquers and retains Upper, but not Lower, Canada. Upper Canada could have been easily assimilated given the substantial numbers of "Late Loyalists," or Americans who immigrated to Canada well after the Revolution, mostly for the promise of cheap land. It is safe to assume that several states could have been fashioned out of such a large territory and that a significant victory would have bolstered the political fortunes of Madison and his generals. How this twist in history would have shaped the 1821 Missouri Compromise—triggered by the modalities surrounding the admission of Alabama, Maine, and Missouri to the Union—is also worth considering. Meanwhile, not having occupied Lower Canada would have avoided the significant political challenge of assimilating a Catholic and French-speaking ethnic minority into the largely Protestant and English-speaking Union.

The British victory scenarios could have had equally important ramifications. In the case of Brock's Petite Guerre, the resulting British hold on North America could have given London, rather than Washington, the best opportunity to capitalize on the Spanish Empire's collapse and the subsequent turmoil in Mexico. These vast acquisitions are less certain in Wellington's Dominions given the British desire to rapidly withdraw their forces from North America and send them to Europe after Napoleon resumes war on the Continent. However, the temporary, and possibly permanent, separation of New Columbia from the rest of the United States could have had an equally significant impact on the political development of the United States. London might have enticed the former New England states to remain outside the Union by creating a federal structure similar to that set laid down in the British North America Act of 1867, albeit several decades earlier. This development, in turn, could have preserved the aristocratic elements of Federalism and deprived the United States of a powerful center of abolition sentiment. It is worth speculating as to whether such a redivision of North America after the relatively short War of 1812 would have spared what remained of the United States a longer and bloodier Civil War half a century later, albeit at the cost of preserving the institution of slavery well past 1865.

Narratives integrating these wars into the national experience would in most cases run along the lines of the Second War of Independence for the American victories and Mr. Madison's War for the British victories, underscoring their complementary nature. The significant defeat of Wellington's Dominions, with its separation of New England from the Union, could have also produced a more negative tale. Had Strong's gambit with the British turned into a permanent relationship, the departure of these original states, combined with the permanent loss of Louisiana, probably would have engendered a defeatist narrative. Such a story line would have identified scapegoats for this national disaster and would have included Madison and his cabinet along with his incompetent and unsuccessful generals. Strong and Wilkinson would be vilified in terms worse than has the unsuccessful Benedict Arnold, whose treason did not permanently change the course of the Revolutionary War or the shape of the early republic.

A WORST-CASE SCENARIO
FOR THE WAR OF 1812

O! say does that star-spangled banner yet wave,
O'er the land of the free and the home of the brave?

Francis Scott Key's rhetorical question in the first stanza of the national anthem unintentionally echoed a deep concern of the American political class in the early years of the republic. Federalists and Republicans believed that war itself was a threat to liberty, albeit from different ideological perspectives.

For the Federalists, the threat came from democracy in the classic meaning of the term. Rule by the people—the ordinary, uneducated, unrefined people who lacked the upbringing and perspective of the gentry—threatened the republic from below. Revolutionary France was their proof. President John Adams remarked, "The French are no more capable of a republican government than a snowball can exist a whole week in the streets of Philadelphia under a burning sun."[1] Fisher Ames, a Federalist representative from Massachusetts to the U.S. House of Representatives from 1789 to 1797, expressed this concern more pointedly in an 1805 essay titled "The Dangers of American Liberty" in which he analyzed "the tyranny of what is called the people."

A democracy cannot last. Its nature ordains, that its next change shall be into a military despotism, of all known governments, perhaps, the most prone to shift its head, and the slowest to mend its vices. The reason is, that the tyranny of what is called the people, and that by the sword, both operate alike to debase and corrupt, till there are neither men left with the spirit to desire liberty, nor morals with the power to sustain justice. . . . A military government may make a nation great, but it cannot make them free. There will be frequent and bloody struggles to decide who shall hold the sword; but the conqueror will destroy his competitors and prevent any permanent division of the empire. Experience proves that in all such governments there is a continual tendency toward unity.[2]

Ames penned this warning after Bonaparte's coronation as Napoleon, emperor of the French, in December 1804. Then, in August 1805, the Grand Army marched into Bavaria and in October captured Ulm. This maneuver was not so much a battle as a strategic victory so complete and overwhelming that its outcome was never seriously contested. The nearly bloodless conquest underscored the threat that tyranny posed to all of Europe.[3]

As for the Republicans, they feared that the Federalists' plans to raise a standing army and a capable navy mimicked how monarchs used such oppressive instruments to subdue popular legislatures. The Founding Fathers, including Samuel Adams, voiced this well-established classical liberal tenant:

A standing Army, however necessary it may be at some times, is always dangerous to the Liberties of the People. Soldiers are apt to consider themselves as a Body distinct from the rest of the Citizens. They have their Arms always in their hands. Their Rules and their Discipline is severe. They soon become attached to their officers and disposed to yield implicit Obedience to their Commands. Such a Power should be watched with a jealous Eye.[4]

Embodied in President Thomas Jefferson's defense establishment, this liberal orthodoxy called for militiamen or citizen-soldiers and small gunboats, as opposed to a professional army and a navy equipped with oceangoing warships, to guard the young American republic. Jefferson feared that war would empower the central government and threaten the individual republican states. Hence, his faction opposed strengthening the defense establishment as the Adams administration proposed and partially enacted during the Quasi War with France. Jefferson also feared that this new military force under the command of Inspector General Hamilton would be used to suppress internal dissent, remarking that "our Bonaparte" might "step in to give us political salvation in his own way."[5]

Jefferson's successor, James Madison, shared these concerns, and from the outset he engaged Britain with diplomacy and coercive economic measures.

When this approach failed, Madison fought the War of 1812 in a manner so as to preserve these Republican principles. Gordon Wood notes that Madison knew that a Republican leader should not become a Napoleon or even a Hamilton. The first president to fight a declared war looked past the lost battles and the political and bureaucratic obstacles that he faced.[6] Wood sums up Madison's success in the War of 1812 by stating, "The grand republican experiment had survived."[7]

But what if a defeat had caused this experiment to fail? Henry Adams assessed that the twin disasters of a defeat at New Orleans and a breakdown of the peace negotiations would have led to the federal government's collapse, leaving Jackson as a dictator over the Southeast and New England estranged from Washington.[8]

These musings suggest the outlines of an even darker scenario for the United States in the War of 1812. This worst-case scenario does not entail losing the war to Great Britain, but it does imagine the creation of a less liberal form of government with some of the characteristics of the democratic despotism that Adams and Ames feared. Such a low probability outcome would have required simultaneous military and political crises that would have been well beyond the capabilities of the political elite and institutions to resolve in their existing conditions. These crises would have altered the political DNA of the republic so that it would not only survive the war but also emerge victorious and prepared to pursue Jefferson's "empire of liberty," albeit with more empire and less liberty. Such a turn in the war would certainly have struck its proponents as improbable. But so too would have been the idea that after three years of war, the United States would have failed to conquer Canada while the British Empire was preoccupied in a life-and-death struggle with Napoleon.

As was true with the scenarios presented in chapter 7, the worst-case scenario rendered here is a heuristic device. It suggests that this second conflict with Britain, as with the Revolutionary War, could have created a new type of Republican government, albeit the type that Fisher Ames feared. The resulting narrative justifying this war would blend our dominant historical narratives, with Mr. Madison's War giving rise to a successful Second War of Independence.

ALMOST LOSING THE WAR

The nearly fatal military crisis required for this scenario is easy to imagine and extrapolate from the history of the War of 1812. The Madison administration's grand strategy for prosecuting a conflict with Britain was a mismatch of political goals and military capabilities. It was designed to compel London to end its predatory maritime practices—namely, its Orders in Council and the practice of impressment—and its support for Native American tribes in the Northwest and Southeast by conquering Canada. London could have modified these policies, which it did after the assassination of Prime Minister Spencer Perceval in June 1812, but the Jeffersonian military establishment could not quickly conquer Canada. Despite Jefferson's boast that it would be a mere matter of marching, the United States relied on a distributed militia-based army that was slow to mobilize, poorly led, and tied to an ad hoc strategy of uncoordinated thrusts at Canada. Even War Hawk and former congressman Peter Porter of New York recognized the difficulties when he observed that declaring war was "an act of madness fatal to the administration . . . at this time, when, so far from being in a situation to conduct offensive operations, we are completely exposed to attacks in every quarter."[9] Moreover, rather than massing forces to cut the critical line of communication linking Upper and Lower Canada, the three-pronged strategy pursued in 1812 consisted of piecemeal attacks from Detroit, Niagara, and Lake Champlain. The first two efforts proved disastrous, and the latter directed at the St. Lawrence River and Montreal was late and undersized. The situation was so dire in early 1813 that Joseph Ellicott, surveyor and founder of Buffalo, New York, wrote, "From the Manner the War is conducted, there is much more Probability of this Part of the United States being conquered by and added to Canada than Canada be conquered by the United States."[10]

The situation in the following year was no better. Even most Republicans noted that the country was in a serious crisis, one more desperate than at any time since independence.[11] One House member later recalled, "The federal government was . . . in the last gasp of existence. But six months more and it [would have been] no longer . . . dissolved into its original elements."[12] After the British captured Washington, the Americans seriously considered moving the seat of government. The House decided to establish a committee to consider removing the capital to "a safer place," most likely a northern commercial city. Representative Jonathan Fisk of New York argued that doing so would bring the government closer to the "monied interests" at a time when financing the war was becoming increasingly problematic. Concurrently, municipal leaders in Philadelphia sent a memorial to Congress in late September 1814 offering to act as host to Congress should it decide to leave the District of Columbia.[13]

After the United States failed to attain an early victory while England was preoccupied with Napoleon, the war degenerated into a series of iterative efforts by both belligerents to gain parcels of territory that could be used as bargaining chips in negotiations. The odds shifted to favor London once Napoleon abdicated. It is not implausible to imagine that hypothetical British strategic victories at Plattsburgh, in New Orleans, and in the Chesapeake Bay would have split New England from the Union and the West from the Eastern Seaboard.

The British could have achieved victory at Plattsburgh in a number of ways. On Lake Champlain, Capt. George Downie's squadron could have bested Capt. Thomas Macdonough's vessels. Hotshot from Downie's HMS *Confiance* set Macdonough's flagship, USS *Saratoga*, on fire twice. Those fires could have resulted in secondary explosions that would have crippled his ship or damaged the lines that had been set to swing the ship around to bring its unused battery into action. Further, Macdonough, rather than Downie, could have been killed early in the battle. On land, Governor-General George Prévost could have listened to his regimental commanders, who had recently arrived from service with Wellington, and used his superior numbers to overwhelm Brig. Gen. Alexander Macomb's forces. Holding Plattsburgh would have given the British a point from which to threaten New England or Albany.

A British victory at New Orleans is as easily imaginable. Jackson might not have learned that New Orleans, instead of Mobile, was the primary target of Vice Adm. Alexander Cochrane's invasion. He would thus have left more of his forces at Mobile and been unable to defend New Orleans when the British landed. On that score, Jackson was lucky that he received timely reporting of the landing at Bayou Bienvenue and that the British waited to mass their forces instead of marching immediately on the city. The British conceivably would have taken the city or would have forced Jackson to burn it to the ground as he had threatened. The landing at Bayou Bienvenue could have been a ruse to lead Jackson out of the city while the main British force approached, as Jackson expected, from Lake Pontchartrain. In either case, Jackson would not have been able to supply Fort St. Philip, which was guarding the seaward approach to the city, and would have fallen back to Mobile with the British probably in pursuit. Moreover, losing the city would have been a severe blow to Washington and its ability to control the Mississippi River Valley.

Finally, if the British amphibious operations in the Chesapeake Bay had had better intelligence, Admiral Cochrane and General Ross would have bypassed Baltimore and taken the fleet to the Delaware River, captured Philadelphia, and burned Independence Hall. That city's defenses were weak and disorganized compared to the extensive fortifications that Gen. Samuel Smith constructed around Baltimore.[14] Following the raid on Washington, the loss of America's largest and most sophisticated urban center would have exacerbated the fissures in the Republican Party in Pennsylvania and turned a major component of Madison's party against him.

APRÈS MADISON: THE KING AND CLAY ADMINISTRATIONS

In the midst of or even after such military debacles, Madison could have resigned, perhaps using his poor health as an excuse. The president had feared that remaining in Washington during the summer of 1814 would cause another attack of the bilious fever that had nearly proved fatal the previous year. His wife, Dolley, also worried about his personal safety. During the war, Madison's government simultaneously faced a collapse of the country's financial system. Banks outside New England had suspended specie payment, and the lack of a national bank made it impossible to continue funding the war absent the unlikely prospect of additional taxes and loans. Madison lamented the nature of his difficulties to the newly elected governor of Virginia in November 1814:

> You are not mistaken in viewing the conduct of the Eastern States as the source of our greatest difficulties in carrying on the war; as it is certainly the greatest, if not the sole, inducement with the enemy to persevere in it. The greater part of the people in that quarter have been brought by their leaders, aided by their priests, under the delusion scarcely exceeded by that recorded in the period of witchcraft; and the leaders are becoming daily more desperate in the use they make of it. Their object is power. If they could obtain it by menaces, their efforts would stop there. These failing, they are ready to go to every length. . . . Without foreign cooperation, revolts and separation will hardly be risked. . . . The best may be hoped, but the worst ought to be kept in view.[15]

Indeed, this "worst" outcome could easily have come to fruition. Governor Caleb Strong of Massachusetts communicated with the British authorities in Halifax and attempted to arrange a separate peace and possible military assistance if the federal government attacked New England. The Hartford Convention was preparing to meet, and some Federalists believed on the basis of their electoral success in New York in 1813 that they were in a position to obstruct the war and possibly form a New York–New England confederation.[16] Both Strong's treasonous behavior and the convention's findings could have become more ominous if the British had won at Plattsburgh, Philadelphia, and New Orleans.

If Madison had resigned while the country experienced these setbacks, he could have triggered a succession crisis in fall of 1814. Had Madison resigned in September after Washington and Plattsburgh, Vice President Elbridge Gerry could have served as president until his death from natural causes on November 23, 1814. Then the country could have been left without both a president and a vice president. The law governing succession that had passed in March 1792 stated that in case of the removal, death, resignation, or inability of both the president and the vice president, the succession went to the president pro tempore of the Senate. If no such officer were available, the office went to the Speaker of the House of Representatives. In history, Senator John Galliard from South Carolina was elected president pro tempore after Gerry's death. A senator since 1805, Galliard had been president pro tempore in 1810 and would serve as such again through all but one of the next nine years, underscoring his favorable standing in the Senate and, for that matter, with the House as well.

If Gerry had died as president without a president pro tempore in the Senate, the office of chief executive would have gone to Speaker Langdon Cheves of South Carolina, a Republican Quid who was critical of many government policies. Langdon had been elected in January 1814 to replace the popular speaker Henry Clay, who had joined the American delegation negotiating with the British in Europe.

How such a succession crisis could have been resolved is far from clear. History suggests a number of possibilities. If the Senate with twenty-eight Democrats and eight Federalists had elected the president pro tempore of the Senate Gilliard, a southerner, to succeed Gerry as president, Clay's western supporters might have considered Gilliard illegitimate. The Senate also possibly could have elevated William Giles of Virginia to the presidency. During Madison's illness in the summer of 1813, Secretary of State Monroe had informed Jefferson at Monticello that Madison's enemies were counting on the presumed death of Madison and Gerry. He anticipated that Giles would be elected president of the Senate as soon as the vice president withdrew from the position after Madison's death. Giles was a member of the Invisibles, a nebulous group of Washington politicos who frequently opposed the policies of the

Madison administration. Senators John Randolph of Virginia, William Smith of Maryland, and Rufus King of New York also belonged to this group.

Federalists in the Senate supported King, who, like Gerry, was a native of Massachusetts, as their candidate for the presidency, hoping they could gain enough support from disaffected Democrats. King possessed sufficient credentials for the position of chief executive; indeed, he would become the Federalist candidate for president in the election of 1816. He had been a member of the Philadelphia Constitutional Convention, had served as the minister to Great Britain from 1796 to 1803 and settled disputes resulting from Jay's Treaty, and was the minority leader in the Senate in 1812 when some Republican newspapers advocating a coalition government proposed his appointment as secretary of state. King and other leading New York Federalists met with Republican Governor DeWitt Clinton that summer to suggest creating a Peace Party, but Clinton outwardly refused to support an open alliance with the Federalists, much less a bipartisan government. Again in the summer of 1814, prominent Republicans put considerable political pressure on the administration to broaden support for the war by appointing Federalists like King to the cabinet.[17]

King's attitude toward the war had changed substantially. At its outset, he had declared that "a war of party, & not country" might lead to an alliance with France.[18] However, after the British attack on Washington in August 1814, he lent his support to the war as a justifiable defensive action.

The worst outcome for this post-Madison succession crisis would have been if Clay, detained in Ghent, had claimed the presidency while at the same time a Republican-Federalist clique in the Senate had elected King as president pro tempore of the Senate and then elected or elevated him as a national unity president. King might have looked to James Monroe for support given the Virginian's dual-hatted role as secretary of state and of war following William Armstrong's dismissal/resignation after the British attack on Washington. Monroe, however, had his own presidential ambitions and allies in Congress, including Randolph, a member of the Invisibles. Further, Monroe would have possibly joined the national unity government as the secretary of war and angled for his long-sought appointment as commander of the U.S. Army, an ambition that had prompted Josiah Quincy of Massachusetts to accuse him of planning a military dictatorship to preserve Virginia's long-standing primacy.[19] By doing so, he could have insulated himself from the battlefield losses attributable to Armstrong. Even though the Federalists made gains in the 1814 congressional elections, Monroe could have bet his fortunes on a continuing

Republican majority and could have endeavored to bring along Virginia and the other southern states that were vulnerable to additional British amphibious attacks.

Such a political compact in Washington—particularly one that concluded a peace agreement with London on the basis of uti possideti, with each side retaining whatever territory it held at the war's end—might have triggered the formation of a countergovernment headed in absentia by Clay and supported by the political and military authorities in the middle and western states. Clay had advocated the continuation of the war and western secession, if necessary. As a commissioner to the peace talks, he remarked that continuing the war for three more years was better than subverting the national interest to the particular concerns of New England. Clay opined that because the Madison administration had been too willing "to sacrifice the interests of its best friends for those of its bitterest enemies . . . there might be a party for separation at some future day in the Western states too." Clay had also claimed in 1812 that Madison was "unfit for the storms of war," an opinion that could have helped him justify and rationalize his ascendance to the presidency.[20] If acclaimed by his fellow War Hawks, he would have been in a perfect position and had complete authority to negotiate with London. He might even have leveraged his isolation as a prisoner of the British as an effective propaganda message.

New York governor Daniel Tompkins and Pennsylvania governor Simon Snyder could have vied for control of the government in Clay's absence. These governors were men with ample ambition. Tompkins went on to become vice president during Monroe's eight years in office. Snyder was a runner-up for that position, and his state was the "keystone" of the Republican Party both in terms of Madison's election and the vote to declare war in 1812. Clay, however, would likely have preferred a westerner to rule in his stead.

William Henry Harrison, a former governor and a successful general, would have been a popular choice. Harrison, a military officer since the age of eighteen, was appointed governor of the Indiana Territory (comprising present-day Indiana, Illinois, Michigan, Wisconsin, and eastern Minnesota) in 1801. He resigned in 1812 and assumed command of the forces preparing to recapture Detroit. In this effort, he had Henry Clay's support and had chosen Clay's brother-in-law as his brigade inspector.[21] Clay wrote to Monroe at the time of Harrison's appointment, "If you will carry your recollection back to the age of the Crusades and of some of the most distinguished leaders of those expeditions, you will have a picture of the enthusiasm of existing in this country for the expedition to Canada, and for Harrison as the commander."[22] In 1813, he campaigned to clear British and hostile Indian forces south of Lake Erie, to retake Detroit, and to defeat British general Procter and Tecumseh at the Battle of the Thames. Subsequently, he hoped to gain a major command in the East, but he resigned when Armstrong thwarted his ambitions. Given his background and availability, Harrison would have been an obvious choice as vice and de facto acting president. A rump Senate that might have convened in Pittsburgh, a location safe from British attack and centrally located between the middle Atlantic and western states, could have elected him.

An important factor in Harrison's selection would have been the loyalties of the commanding officers of the military districts throughout the country. A review of the generals commanding these districts in late 1814 suggests that only three might have remained loyal to the King administration in Washington, based largely on their state affiliations. In this scenario, they would have honored the peace agreement that King had negotiated with the British. First, Maj. Gen. Henry Dearborn, native of New Hampshire, commanded the First Military District, which comprised his home state and Massachusetts. Although a Republican, he had been demoted to this position because of his vacillation in attacking Canada. His initial desire for an armistice early in the war and Governor Strong's negotiations with the British could have led him to remain loyal to Washington.

Next, Brig. Gen. Thomas Cushing, a native of Massachusetts, commanded the Second Military District consisting of Connecticut and Rhode Island. He had cordial relations with Federalist governor John Cotton Smith in New London, although they soured over the issue of Cushing's authority over the state militia, which outnumbered his federal troops. Possibly this predicament would have led him to support the King administration, particularly given the political climate in New England as evidenced in the Hartford Convention.

Last, Brig. Gen. William Winder of Maryland commanded the Tenth Military District comprising the District of Columbia and Maryland. As a Federalist, the nephew of Maryland governor Levin Winder, the unsuccessful defender of Washington in 1814, and the beneficiary of Monroe's patronage, he would have remained loyal to a King administration.

THE CRUCIBLE OF A LONG WAR
Midwest American political and military leaders of the Clay administration could have continued the war by pursuing three strategic military objectives.

The first would have been to dominate the Great Lakes in order to deny the British "control of the lakes," which Wellington recognized was the key to winning the war. The balance of power on Lake Ontario had shifted to the British in October 1814 when HMS *St. Lawrence* set sail, carrying 102 guns and carronades plus a pair of 68-pounder "smashers." With the Americans planning to launch their ship of the line, the USS *New Orleans*, carrying 110 guns and carronades in early 1815, the naval race between the two cautious fleet commanders, Commodores Chauncey and Yeo, certainly would have continued. Protecting Sackets Harbor would have become a major priority for Major Generals Brown and Izard, the commanders of the Left and Right Divisions, respectively. British plans to launch an offensive against that major naval base in 1815 would have shifted the center of the northern front from Lake Champlain to Lake Ontario.

Harrison probably would have taken personal charge of the second objective, controlling the Old Northwest and continuing to deny the British and their Indian allies access to western Upper Canada. American raids in 1814 had destroyed that region's mills and grain stores, making it incapable of supporting a British force of any size; thus, the number of operations requiring Harrison's attention would have been limited, allowing him time to coordinate operations to the north and south.

Jackson would have remained in charge of the southern front so long as he consented to fight a defensive strategy and prevent a British advance up the Mississippi River or into Alabama from Mobile. This third objective may have been the most difficult to accomplish given the long lines of communication from the ordnance factories in the Middle Atlantic states. Assuming that a surprise and rapid British advance on New Orleans had prevented Jackson from carrying out his promise to burn the Crescent City rather than let it fall, Jackson's aggressive nature could have compelled him to favor retaking New Orleans. He might have required and received assistance from Maj. Gen. Thomas Pinckney, commanding the Sixth Military District headquartered in Charleston, South Carolina.

The campaign of 1815 could have been shaped by two factors. First, Napoleon Bonaparte's return from exile at Elba could have led Britain to recall immediately those units that had been sent to North America, and the resulting transatlantic redeployment could have consumed the troops, supplies, and time required for a major offensive against Sackets Harbor. Second, American plans to fight on the defensive in northern New York and the Old Northwest could have been replaced with a multipronged offensive against Canada's central axis of communications running from Montreal through the Great Lakes. Harrison could finally have the chance that he was denied in 1813 to lead an attack up the St. Lawrence. Instead of following Major General Wilkinson's unsuccessful path along the north shore of the river, he could have chosen to split his forces. Harrison could have led the main element along the southern shore to Montreal and threatened the British garrison at Plattsburgh, while Brown and Izard turned west and marched on Kingston to destroy Yeo's base and his fleet.

Faced with this threat, Prévost might well have brushed off his earlier plans to abandon Montreal and retire to the Quebec City, leaving winter to hold off the Americans and hoping that reinforcements could arrive from Europe in the spring. Such American victories could have rallied the "Late Loyalists" of Upper Canada, who were American immigrants lured by the promise of cheap land and had arrived there well after the American Revolution. Although they had turned against the United States after General Hull's defeat in 1812 and the looting that had accompanied the U.S. invasions in 1813, American battlefield successes in 1815 could have won their loyalty. Meanwhile in the South, Jackson could have moved out from Mobile and encircled, probed, and harried New Orleans' defenses. Doing so could have kept pressure on the British while Pinckney took the opportunity to convince Jackson's former and now reluctant Indian allies of the weaknesses of the British and the new American commitment to return their lands.

American gains in Canada in 1815 could have significantly raised Harrison's political capital. Having captured Lake Ontario and Montreal, he might have been hailed as the new George Washington, undoubtedly eclipsing Clay's political capital as the de jure president, albeit the resident of a well-guarded estate in England along with his fellow commissioners. Even if London again proposed a peace agreement based on a return to the status quo antebellum—in point, the prewar boundaries—the rump government in Pittsburgh, with half of Canada in its possession, likely would not have approved of such terms. Even a deal to swap Upper Canada and Montreal for New Orleans, perhaps proffered through the King administration, would not have been tempting if Harrison and company believed they could complete the conquest of Upper and Lower Canada in 1816. Finally, American successes might have weakened the policies and political legitimacy of the King administration. British efforts to use King and Monroe to their benefit would have only further tarred the administration and their supporters as the "New Tories."

Meanwhile, the failure of negotiations in 1815 could have prolonged the war and strengthened the case of a martial government—not a Hamiltonian imitation of a European monarchical-armed state but a regime focused on a popular "strong man." A victory and a truncated election in 1816, as well as the weather, would have even further strengthened that case. For a variety of reasons, including unusually high volcanic activity, sunspots, and a deviation in weather patterns, 1816 became the only "year without a summer" in U.S. history. Winter persisted through May. Planting was delayed in some areas, and replanting made necessary in others. A terrible cold wave followed in early June, and snow fell in New England and New York. Boston recorded a near freezing low temperature on June 10, and more crops died in a hard frost that was harsh enough to destroy the fruit on trees.[23] Hence, a history of the final year of the war, its aftermath, and legacy might have read as follows.

1816: THE END OF THE WAR AND THE BIRTH OF A NEW REPUBLIC

Many Americans, particularly those in New England, took the weather as a sign of heavenly displeasure with the war. This argument was compelling until a June cold snap thwarted a British offensive to retake Montreal. Harrison and his men huddled inside their fortifications as British troops struggled through their attacks and found little to comfort them during the periodic storms. The Americans also benefited when weather-related delays in crossing the Atlantic forced Wellington to begin his offensive with fewer troops than planned. Unable to breach the city's defenses or to coax Harrison out into open combat, the victor of Waterloo met the victor of Tippecanoe and the Thames in the no-man's-land between their lines to discuss the following terms: Montreal would be exchanged for New Orleans; Britain would retain occupied territory in Maine, and the United States would keep Upper Canada; all prisoners would be immediately released; London would break off diplomatic contact with and cease all communication with the King administration; and no British warship or merchant vessel would enter any port in New England.

President Clay approved the agreement weeks later. He planned to board the frigate USS Constellation at Plymouth, England, for passage to Philadelphia. Governors Snyder of Pennsylvania and Tompkins of New York accompanied Harrison when he met Clay at the harbor entrance. The president and vice president disembarked and addressed a joint session of Congress at the newly reconstructed Constitutional Hall. A week later, both men boarded a steamboat for Baltimore to attend a meeting with King and Monroe, the latter having been elected the de jure vice president earlier that year by the rump Congress in Washington. After two weeks of negotiations, both presidents and vice presidents addressed a reunited Congress on Capitol Hill. National elections would take place in November. Clay announced he would return home to Kentucky for a much-needed visit with his family and that he fully expected Harrison to be the next president of the United States. King and Monroe announced that they would neither seek nor accept election to national office. Brown and Jackson were present but silent. Harrison spoke briefly, noting that the conflict had proven the need for a "necessary and competent" army and navy under an experienced commander in chief. The nation could expect and demand no less.

In the run-up to the elections, Harrison submitted to Congress three constitutional amendments designed to ensure that the nation would never again find itself so unprepared for war with a foreign power. The first mandated that candidates for president, vice president, and the national Senate must have attained the rank of colonel in the U.S. Army or Marines Corps or captain in the U.S. Navy or general in the state militia. The second directed the Senate to elect a vice president should the office become vacant because of the death, resignation, or impeachment of the sitting office holder. It also gave the vice president direct responsibility for managing the military, Indian affairs, and internal improvements—most important, roads, canals, and ports. In Harrison's words, "Such a high office should not exist only to address a President's death." The third amendment charged each of the individual states and territories with maintaining sufficient military forces for self-defense.

In promoting these changes, Harrison forcefully argued that Republican ideals were an insufficient foundation for national defense. He routinely quoted Brig. Gen. Edmund P. Gaines, who was with him at the Battle of the Thames and later successfully defended Fort Erie: "The ordinary operation of civil affairs, in our beloved country, is as deadly hostile to every principle of military discipline, as a complete military government would be to a democracy. . . . Every individual composing [the army] must leave at home all of what are considered to be the choicest fruits of republicanism."[24]

Subsequent enabling legislation defined these state forces as an infantry brigade, an artillery battery, and a troop of cavalry. State revenues used to maintain these forces allowed the federal government to focus on the expansion of the navy and Marine Corps. These reforms remedied the young republic's failure to create an effective standing army and a well-maintained militia after the War of Independence. Efforts to create a rational and sustainable military establishment in the wake of General St. Clair's disastrous campaign, Shay's Rebellion, the Whiskey Rebellion, the threat of a French invasion, and the growing crisis with Britain had all proven incomplete and ineffective. Harrison's reforms closed this sad chapter in American history. [25]

The Harrison republic did not create a military junta; rather, it established a new arrangement between the political and military spheres, or what in today's parlance would be regarded as a "soft coup." It created a stronger network of military and civilian leaders and sparked a revival of the Society of the Cincinnati, which Maj. Gen. Henry Knox and other Revolutionary War officers founded in 1783. This society proved useful in addressing several fundamental problems of the growing republic by forging bonds across regional and cultural issues that divided European Americans. Over the next several decades, the new political military elite found peaceful solutions to the assimilation of the Native American tribes and the emancipation of African American slaves. The linkages between the two issues—that is, the greater weight given to "northern" views with the incorporation of several states created out of Upper Canada and the retention of large land holdings by the Creeks and other southwestern tribes—effectively smothered the growth of a slave-agricultural economy in the South. Full emancipation, without a civil war, was attained in all of the continental states in time for the national centennial celebration of 1876.

At the same time, the emergence of a larger and more effective military establishment increased official U.S. involvement in Latin America during the collapse of the Spanish Empire. Avoiding both the Mexican War of Independence and concurrent conflicts in the Viceroyalty of New Granada, the Harrison republic seized Cuba and the Spanish West Indies to strengthen America's commercial power and to improve its strategic presence in the Caribbean. Military governors ruled these new territories and helped draw off elements of American society that favored the perpetuation of slave-based agriculture in the South. The annexation of Texas and the Mexican-American War followed, facilitated by the continuous existence of a standing military force that trained and modernized on a regular basis and by law avoided the minimal funding and organization of the pre-1812 period.

Finally, the new civil-military balance gave the republic's democracy a martial character. It restored the aristocratic model of society that the Federalists clung to and that the Jeffersonian Republicans found appalling, but it substituted a new military class for the old gentry that the original English colonists had established. Active and former military officers became the leading elements of society and took commanding positions not only in politics but also in manufacturing, commerce, and education. Deference vied with popular democracy as a core political virtue, with the military becoming a bridge across political parties and a more important pillar of the republic. Service as a commissioned officer was also considered to be the foundation of a successful career and high standing in

polite society. "Governor-general" became the official title of many state governors, and
"president-general" was officially recognized as the formal title of the chief executive of
the United States. After his election, Andrew Jackson became the first president-general,
followed by Winfield Scott and Jefferson Davis.

The existence of state armies also changed the tone and character of civil society.
Governors used them largely as a corps of engineers and as an arm of law enforcement.
The need for roads and canals to serve as the arteries of immigration and commerce
provided continuous opportunities for military engineers to apply their skills and for
combat officers to keep their troops employed and their units' (and often personal) coffers
filled. Less frequently, state armies took part in preventing civil disturbances and, when
that failed, restoring the peace. State armies also proved to be an effective institution of
political socialization and integration for freed slaves and new immigrants.

COUNTERFACTUAL AND COUNTER-COUNTERFACTUAL ARGUMENTS

Every counterfactual historical projection gives rise to a counter-counterfactual
argument as to why key events and dominant trends would have pushed aside
such imagined happenings. In this case, the history of the United States shows
the strength and persistence of the inherited English antipathy to a standing
army that are reinforced by such historical events as the Boston Massacre of
1770, which led to the Revolutionary War. The U.S. Army has remained a relatively small military force throughout much of the nation's history. Its expansion during the Civil War (including the use of martial law in the former
Confederacy during Reconstruction) and the Second World War were exceptions to this rule of rapid demobilization, which ceased to be in force after the
outbreak of the Korean War. The militarization of the U.S. Cold War strategy
of containment against the backdrop of the nuclear arms race gave rise to
President Dwight Eisenhower's warning about the rise of the "military-industrial
complex." Eisenhower's counsel suggests how unlikely and difficult it would
have been for a militarized republic to emerge from the War of 1812 given the
rapid rise of the Jeffersonian republicanism.

Yet, some wars in American history have been transformational events that
have led to significant domestic political discontinuities. For example, the
American Revolution created an independent confederation that quickly
transformed itself into a more unified federation. The Civil War led to the

Emancipation Proclamation and the Fourteenth Amendment. The Second World War necessitated a massive reorganization and growth of the national security apparatus. The Vietnam War helped spark the social counterculture revolution of the 1960s and 1970s.

This chapter's worst-case counterfactual history suggests that a slight chance existed that the War of 1812 could have been such a transformational event. This outcome would have had a larger impact because it took place early in the republic's history, as the country was poised to expand across the continent. Moreover, the social narrative constructed to legitimize the war's outcome in this scenario would have combined elements of Mr. Madison's War and the Second War of Independence, again pointing out their complementary natures. Clay and Harrison would have eclipsed Madison in American history, with these Western politicians being associated with the victory and the author of the Constitution with the battlefield failures through 1814. King and Monroe, as well as the governors and military district commanders who supported them, in the short term would have been relegated to a status akin to what Jefferson Davis held in the first decades following the Civil War. As the decades passed, undoubtedly a period of national reconciliation would have seen their historical status reassessed and rehabilitated, much as Robert E. Lee has been treated favorably in most histories of the American Civil War.

In considering this counterfactual, we should recall that some historians judge that the historic War of 1812 gave Americans "a national character" and proved the durability of the "grand republican experiment."[26] Military historians of the period also observe that the war convinced the country's political elite to renounce the radical view of the Jeffersonians and to embrace the moderate Whig view, which was favorable to establishing an army and navy that could adequately defend the country.[27] This worst-case scenario suggests that this evolution of civil-military affairs could have gone further had the country suffered more severe political and military crises during the conflict. Perhaps this alternative outcome of a more martial republic should come to mind each time we hear Francis Scott Key ask, "O! say does that star-spangled banner yet wave, / o'er the land of the free and the home of the brave?"

— 9 —

WHAT IF THE WAR OF 1812
HAD NEVER OCCURRED?

Historical events were not inevitable. Their complicated origins, evolution, and conclusions allow us to recognize that situations could have turned out otherwise. Students of history understand that major landmarks of the past were neither preordained nor occurrences of random chance. Rather, they are the unique products of specific decisions, events, and trends that historians strive to uncover and understand. Yet as previous chapters have discussed about the War of 1812, understanding the significance of the past is not complete until we explore what could have but did not happen. This work requires speculation, which does not attempt to prove what "would have happened" but offers instead a heuristic perspective on what "might have happened" that helps us understand and appreciate the significance of the historical events and trends tied to the War of 1812.

Two separate tasks are involved in answering the question, What if the War of 1812 had never occurred? The first task is to identify specific historical events that, had they occurred differently or not at all, could have led America and Britain to avoid the war. The best candidates are those episodes that turned on a narrow margin and from which we can plausibly argue that history could have proceeded in a direction that avoided the War of 1812. The second task is to explore what might have happened to American society and U.S.-British relations without the war. Identifying key historical personalities and movements that benefited from the war is the first step in this exercise. Imagining how they would have developed without the war is the second.

A SWORD NOT DRAWN

The presidential election of 1800 is a prime candidate for a historical turning point that could have set the United States on a path of pacific relations with

Britain in the first decades of the nineteenth century. President John Adams lost the election by the narrowest margin. Although he ran third in the electoral count of all sixteen states with 65 votes—Thomas Jefferson and Aaron Burr each had 73, and Charles Pinckney had 64—as the incumbent Adams had come very close to winning. With a difference of only 250 popular votes in New York City, President Adams would have defeated the other contenders with an electoral count of 71.

As historian David McCullough notes, had the news of the peace agreement with France ending the Quasi War arrived a few weeks earlier, it too could have been critical for Adams.[1] His decision to send a second peace mission to France cost him support among Federalists and probably the election. The first attempt in early 1798 ended with the XYZ Affair as French officials demanded substantial bribes to begin negotiations. Based on assurances that Paris was ready to negotiate, Adams announced in February 1799 that he was sending a minister plenipotentiary to France. He patiently resisted calls, largely from fellow Federalists, for waging an all-out war with France, and his efforts led in October 1800 to the Convention of Mortefontaine, which restored peaceful relations. The first report of the convention appeared in a Baltimore paper on November 7, too late to affect the election.

Had Adams won a second term, his diplomatic and executive experience likely would have set the country on a path that avoided war with London. Adams was not an Anglophile, but he consistently evidenced patience with the British because he thought the young republic would be put at risk in any war with Britain or France. As the first American minister plenipotentiary to the Court of St. James from 1785 to 1788, Adams had firsthand experience dealing with the British over contentious diplomatic issues. He spent much of his time on trade and on the implementation of the Treaty of Paris concerning debts, treatment of Loyalists, compensation for confiscated property and slaves seized by the British, and the continued presence of British troops in North America. But London did not consider appointing an ambassador to the United States necessary and held the nascent American government in low regard. Adams left London in March 1788 with assurances from King George III that whenever the United States fulfilled its obligation under the treaty, he would fulfill his. Five years later when the Royal Navy began seizing American vessels and impressing sailors whom they claimed were British citizens, Vice President Adams cast a negative vote and broke a tie in the Senate on a bill that would have suspended all trade with Britain. Adams also supported the

Jay's Treaty of 1795 because it avoided war even though it yielded to London on almost all points of dispute.

Similarly, in 1798 Adams favored limiting the conflict with France to an undeclared naval war. By leaving the door open to peace, he alienated High Federalists who wanted a declaration of war. Adams opposed Inspector General of the Army Alexander Hamilton's plan to conquer Spanish Florida and Louisiana. It is fair to conclude that Adams's experience in avoiding an "unnecessary war" with France probably would have helped manage U.S.-British relations after war resumed on the Continent in 1803.

Clearly, a key factor in this alternative history is the degree to which Adams could have continued what historian Bradford Perkins termed the First Rapprochement between Britain and the United States, one that lasted for a decade. In a second term, Adams might have concluded an agreement similar to the Monroe-Pinkney Treaty of 1806, which Jefferson refused to submit to the Senate for ratification. Aimed at resolving issues that arose after the Peace of Amiens collapsed in 1803 and European hostilities resumed, the Monroe-Pinkney Treaty in many ways was more favorable to Washington than Jay's Treaty was. The British agreed not to interfere with the reexport trade between the United States and its West Indies colonies as long as American ships paid a small transit duty on their stopover in the United States. The British also agreed to narrow the definition of contraband, to stop interfering with shipping within five miles of the American coast, and to give proper notice of blockades. In exchange, Washington's negotiators offered a promise of benevolent neutrality. As historian Donald Hickey notes:

> The rejection of the Monroe-Pinkney Treaty was a great turning point in the Age of Jefferson. Republicans would later claim that the only options the United States had in this era were submission, commercial sanctions, or war. But the Monroe-Pinkney Treaty offered another alternative, that of accommodation. By rejecting this treaty, the United States missed an opportunity to reforge the Anglo-American accord of the 1790s and to substitute peace and prosperity for commercial restrictions and war.[2]

Hickey also observes that in the spring of 1812 a Baltimore newspaper circulated a rumor that a special diplomatic mission would be sent to London to avert war. The rumor was deemed credible at the time and was reported on both sides of the Atlantic. It included the notion that Britain had offered to resurrect the Monroe-Pinkney Treaty with modifications more favorable to the United States. Although nothing came of the rumor, its popularity suggests such an agreement was considered plausible at the eleventh hour before the war and perhaps would have been a more likely outcome in a second Adams administration.

A key element in Adams's strategy for maintaining pacific relations with Britain was to create and maintain a navy sufficient to deter European powers from waging hostilities with the young republic. In 1794, Congress approved the Act to Provide a Naval Armament, allocating funds to man and equip three frigates built during the Washington administration. In 1798, Congress moved further to create an independent Department of the Navy. In less than two years, the navy grew to fifty ships and more than five thousand officers and sailors. David McCullough argues that "Adams's insistence on American naval strength proved decisive in achieving peace with France in 1800."[3]

The Jefferson administration subsequently allowed the fleet to wither. It halted the construction of the ships of the line and decommissioned most of the frigates. With others lost to rot and other causes, by 1812 only seven ships survived. Adm. Alfred Mahan points to the dilapidated state of the U.S. Navy as a direct cause of the War of 1812. Mahan notes that Vice President Adams and Federalist statesman Gouverneur Morris strongly advocated building a navy of sufficient size to deter France and Britain from molesting U.S. interests. In his analysis of the war of 1812, he cited Morris's cost-benefit analysis and prophecy from 1794:

> I believe that we could now maintain twelve ships-of-the-line, perhaps twenty, with a due proportion of frigates and smaller vessels. And I am tolerably certain that while the United States of America pursue a just and liberal conduct, *with twenty sail-of-the-line at sea* [Morris's emphasis], no nation on earth will dare to insult them. I believe also, that, not to mention individual losses, five years of war would involve more national expense than the support of a navy for twenty years. One thing I am thoroughly convinced of, that, if we do not render ourselves respectable, we shall continue to be insulted.

Mahan then opines, "Had Morris's navy existed in 1800, we probably should have had no War of 1812; that is, if Jefferson's passion for peace, and abhorrence of navies could have been left out of the account."[4]

The composition of British naval forces stationed off the North American East Coast supports this view. The Royal Navy had a total of 5 ships of the line, 19 frigates, 41 brigs, and 16 schooners at Halifax, Newfoundland, Jamaica, and the Leeward Islands in 1812, or a fraction of its 150 ships of the line, 164 frigates, and 134 sloops. Morris's imagined American fleet would have easily overmatched this British fleet.

If not avoiding the conflict, a stronger navy might have given greater weight to the option of pursuing an undeclared naval war against Britain over the issues of impressment and trade. Among the various motions that the Senate debated in June 1812 to limit the conflict's dimensions was a maritime war commensurate with the British depredations on the high seas that were cited as the principal grievance requiring an armed response. For Federalists, a naval war would have been the lesser of two evils, the other being the full-scale conflict that Henry Clay and the War Hawks promoted. A war bill authorizing warships and privateers to make reprisals against Britain was at first approved by a 17–13 vote on June 8, but three days later a modified bill reported from committee failed by a tied 16–16 vote. Subsequent efforts to amend the war bill and restrict combat to the high seas also failed.

As with a second term for President John Adams, the restoration of Louisiana to France in 1800 could have pivoted Anglo-American relations away from the trajectory that led to the War of 1812. When rumors emerged in 1798 of Spain's decision to return the territory to France, a number of American officials advocated a preemptive war. Senior British officials indicated they would support such a venture, and American minister Rufus King and British foreign secretary Baron Hawkesbury discussed the issue in 1801 when it appeared that France might also gain control of the Floridas. The backdrop for these discussions was Gen. Victor-Emmanuel Leclerc's arrival in Haiti with twenty-five thousand French troops to defeat the slave rebellion led by Pierre Dominique Toussaint L'Overture and to reassert French control.

In early 1802, President Madison wrote to Robert Livingston, the American minister in Paris, famously noting, "The day that France takes possession of N. Orleans fixes her sentence which is to restrain her forever within her low water mark. It seals the union of two nations who in conjunction can maintain exclusive possession of the ocean. From that moment we must marry ourselves to the British Fleet and nation."[5] Jefferson's cabinet also discussed the idea of an alliance with Britain in April. The secretary of the British legation in Philadelphia subsequently reported that Jefferson spoke openly of a possible military response to

French designs in North America. The secretary noted that if the United States could not expel the French from Louisiana, it would seek assistance from foreign powers, including Great Britain. Secretary of State Madison also instructed Livingston to warn France against occupying the territory and to invite it to sell New Orleans and the Floridas to the United States. He told the American envoys sent to Paris to negotiate the purchase, however, that they were also empowered to open consultations with the British on military cooperation if the French were determined to deny the United States free navigation of the Mississippi. Britain, meanwhile, was simultaneously attempting to avoid hostilities with France in Europe and did not emphasize its concerns over the potential French threat to Canada and the West Indies. In early 1803, though, London considered unilaterally seizing New Orleans to keep it from falling into French hands, after which the British would negotiate its transfer to the Americans.

Napoleon's effort to dispose of Louisiana as quickly as possible cut these plans short. Disease and combat had so significantly reduced Leclerc's forces in Haiti that any prospect of a French occupation and defense of Louisiana was doomed. Meanwhile, war clouds loomed on the Continent, giving the French emperor a more immediate reason to dispense with his dreams of the New World empire. Documents transferring possession of Louisiana to the United States were signed in April 1803. Nevertheless, had Paris not taken such a prudent move, Britain and the United States in 1803 probably would have created a de facto alliance that would have helped manage and possibly resolve the impressment and neutral trade issues that contributed to the drift toward war later in the decade.

Even as those issues complicated bilateral relations, events in Britain still could have defused the maritime issues that led to the War of 1812. While the War Hawks in Congress led the call to arms, the Whigs in Parliament made a concerted effort to have the Orders in Council revoked. Their opposition to the orders and their calls for free trade reflected important segments of the British economy: the Birmingham hardware district, Staffordshire potteries, cutlers of Sheffield, Lancashire and Yorkshire cotton centers, Worcester's porcelain and glass manufacturers, Leicester's framework knitters, Liverpool's shipping industry, and Scottish manufacturers in Glasgow, Dunfermline, and Paisley. As British historian Jon Latimer observes, the opposition was so strong that a change in the government's position was anticipated in the spring of 1812.[6]

But then a random act intervened. On May 11, John Bellingham assassinated the prime minister and author of the controversial Orders in Council,

Spencer Perceval, albeit for personal and not political reasons. Opposition to the orders increased after Perceval's death, but no effective government existed until June 8 when Robert Banks Jenkinson, Second Earl of Liverpool, became prime minister. His government rescinded the orders on June 23, but the announcement did not reach the United States until after Congress had declared war. Had such news arrived earlier—either because Bellingham had acted sooner or the British had assembled a new government more quickly— it would have reversed the impact of the disappointing report that the USS *Hornet* delivered to New York City on May 19 that the Perceval government had not softened its policies. This dispatch set in motion Madison's war message and Congress's declaration of war in June. Madison later lamented that if the notice of the repeal had arrived earlier, he would have either recalled the declaration of war or sought an immediate armistice. However, at that crucial moment in early July, Secretary of the Treasury Gallatin crafted an agenda that combined limited attacks on Canada from Detroit and across the Niagara River while delaying a campaign to capture Montreal pending further war preparations and renewed negotiation with London.[7]

Concurrently, British intentions and actions left open a way to avoid general war. Lord Castlereagh informed Jonathan Russell, the American minister in London, that the British government had "great hopes . . . of the favorable effect" that the repeal of the Orders in Council would have on American policy.[8] The British government also ordered the Royal Navy to ignore attacks from American privateers that had been sent to sea before news of the repeal had reached the United States. London waited ten weeks after receiving the American declaration of war, or until October 13, before authorizing general reprisals against the United States. It also instructed Vice Adm. Sir John Borlase Warren, the new naval commander on the American station, to propose an armistice on the basis of status quo antebellum, which ironically were the same terms in the Ghent Treaty two years later.

Meanwhile, the British commander of Lower Canada Lt. Gen. Sir George Prévost sent a dispatch to London informing the government that "unless the safety of the Provinces entrusted to my charge should require them, no measures shall be adopted by me to impede the speedy return to those accustomed relations of amity and goodwill which it is the mutual interest of both countries to cherish and preserve."[9] He quickly sent a subordinate to arrange an armistice with Maj. Gen. Henry Dearborn, who on August 9 agreed only to an informal arrangement where both sides conducted defensive operations, as well as movements of supplies and reinforcements, pending an official termination of hostilities by their respective governments.

It took six days for Dearborn's letter informing the government of this arrangement to reach Washington. Madison rejected the armistice at this point because the repeal of the orders did not end the impressment of American sailors or the blockading of enemy ports to neutral—that is, American—shipping. Unaware that Minister Russell was en route to the United States, Madison and Secretary of State Monroe also brushed off the efforts of the remaining British diplomats in Washington to renew negotiations, saying they preferred to pursue discussion through their minister in London. On August 25, Dearborn sent a message to Prévost informing him that the armistice should be considered terminated. Three days later, news of Brig. Gen. William Hull's surrender at Detroit reached Washington. Now, Madison needed victories to restore America's honor and to justify the war to what would soon become an increasingly dubious public.

THE COURSE OF ANGLO-AMERICAN RELATIONS
WITHOUT WAR

Had Britain and the United States avoided the War of 1812, they quite possibly would have established and maintained a tradition of resolving their disputes peacefully through the first half of the nineteenth century. The First Rapprochement would have become permanent, based on Britain's recognition of American primacy in North America and on the Americans' desire for profitable commercial relations with the British Empire. This counterfactual history is roughly how actual events unfolded in the first half of the nineteenth century as, time after time, Washington and London resolved their differences without resorting to arms.

A number of agreements that were signed after the war might well have occurred in the absence of hostilities. The Rush-Bagot Agreement of 1817 provided for a gradual naval disarmament on the Great Lakes, essentially returning matters to where they had been before the war prompted naval races on Lakes Ontario and Erie. More important was the Anglo-American Convention in 1818, which signaled a new era of cooperation. It redefined the rights of American fishermen along the coasts of Newfoundland and Labrador in a corrective measure designed to reestablish most of the privileges that had been granted to the United States in the 1783 Treaty of Paris but, in British eyes, were forfeited after declaring war in 1812. The convention also fixed the boundary between Canada and the Louisiana Purchase at the forty-ninth parallel, but it put off settling conflicting claims over the Oregon Territory.

Along the border with Canada, peaceful relations were maintained despite several crises and contentious negotiations over the border from the Great Lakes to the Pacific. The first of these crises began in 1837 with a rebellion in Upper Canada against British rule. William Mackenzie led fellow American immigrants, who called themselves Patriots, in an uprising that was quickly crushed. Fleeing to Buffalo, New York, Mackenzie gathered additional volunteers and occupied a Canadian island above Niagara Falls. When Canadian militiamen attacked and sank the SS *Caroline*, an American steamboat carrying supplies and reinforcements to the island, a major international incident erupted. President Martin Van Buren, eager to continue good relations with London, sent Brig. Gen. Winfield Scott to Buffalo to enforce "peace with honor." Scott calmed the public and convinced Mackenzie to withdraw from the island. His followers went underground to organize "hunting lodges," but they resumed operations the next year, burning a Canadian vessel in American waters and launching two filibustering expeditions. Both failed.

Another territorial dispute, this time along the border between Maine and New Brunswick, was also peacefully resolved. President John Tyler also summoned Scott to resolve the dispute over timber rights along the Aroostook and St. John Rivers, where local militiamen had reinforced armed logging camps. Scott was succinct in his assessment: "Mr. President, if you want war, I need only look on in silence. The Maine people will make it for you fast and hot enough. But if peace be your wish, I can give no assurance of success."[10] Tyler's and Secretary of State Daniel Webster's wish for peace was delivered when the government in London changed, and Britain's bellicose foreign secretary Lord Palmerston was replaced with Lord Aberdeen, who wanted this quarrel resolved quickly. Negotiations led to the Webster-Ashburton Treaty of 1842, awarding the United States some seven thousand acres and Canada a little more than five thousand acres. The treaty also demarcated the then imprecise border between Minnesota and Canada.

Similarly, the contending claims over the Oregon Territory were resolved in 1846 when both sides agreed to extend the forty-ninth parallel boundary to the Pacific Ocean but left Vancouver Island to Canada. The agreement followed tense negotiations as the Democratic platform of 1844 endorsed the slogan "Fifty-Four Forty or Fight" and demanded the whole of Oregon and a boundary at that latitude west of the Continental Divide. When the British envoy to Washington overplayed his instructions, President James Polk called upon Congress to pass a declaration in 1846 serving Britain with one year's notice that Washington would abrogate the existing joint occupation agreement. He did so knowing that Whigs who wanted British investment capital and southern Democrats who valued Britain as a cotton market were unwilling to risk a confrontation with London. Congress added an amendment to the declaration that called for an amicable settlement, which was reached only a few months after the declaration was passed.

American and British interests along the southern boundaries of the United States were also settled amicably. In March 1818, Maj. Gen. Andrew Jackson invaded Spanish Florida with seventeen hundred men, ostensibly to end Indian attacks on American soil. Jackson captured two British citizens and, without waiting for Washington's instructions, court-martialed and executed them for aiding Indian enemies of the United States. Although Charles Bagot, the British minister in Washington, lodged an official protest, Foreign Secretary Lord Castlereagh assured Washington that neither of the executed men had government sanction for their activities and only requested a full record of the court-martial. Months later, Castlereagh claimed credit for avoiding war over the executions: "Such was the temper of Parliament, and such the feeling of the country that . . . WAR MIGHT HAVE BEEN PRODUCED BY HOLDING UP A FINGER; and . . . an address to the Crown might have been carried for one, BY NEARLY A UNANIMOUS VOTE."[11] Yet, public and political outrage soon gave way to consideration of trade issues and a growing recognition of American power. Moreover, by early 1819 Washington and Madrid had signed a treaty agreeing to transfer Florida to the United States, although ratification did not occur until 1822.

London and Washington also reached a common position over the independence of Spain's other colonies in the Western Hemisphere. London initially hoped Madrid would retain control under a loose system, but trade opportunities and Spanish resistance to such an arrangement led London to take a hands-off attitude, warning other European powers not to interfere. In late 1823, Britain and France, which had intervened in the Spanish civil war and thus raised the prospect of French intervention in Latin America, defused the prospect for European involvement. Separately, President Monroe decided to act independently on the matter and issued a proclamation that became known as the Monroe Doctrine, refusing Britain's offer of a limited alliance that would have made Washington appear as a junior partner to London.

British-American competition in Texas was similarly resolved peacefully. London agreed to diplomatic recognition and a trade agreement with the Lone Star Republic's second president, Mirabeau Buonaparte Lamar, contingent on his rescinding the republic's request for annexation by the United States. When the first president of Texas, Sam Houston, returned to office in 1841, he hoped London would persuade Mexico City to recognize Texas's independence. At the same time he used the prospect of an Anglo-Texas alliance to tempt Washington into agreeing to annexation. In 1843, Prime Minister Lord Aberdeen promised the House of Lords that he would promote Mexican recognition of Texas and the abolition of slavery in that new republic. Britain, in fact, had investments in both countries and supported a peaceful reconciliation between the two. Moreover, Britain's antislavery movement hoped to use this economic leverage to end slavery in Texas. At the same time, former president Jackson issued a public letter encouraging Congress to annex Texas to prevent the British from using the prospective state as a foothold from which to attack New Orleans and incite slave rebellions.

Tyler, as well as Jackson's protégé and presidential nominee James Polk, made annexation a central issue in the 1844 election. Democrats framed Texas as a national security interest threatened by British designs, and the Whigs argued that annexation would bring war with Mexico and antagonize sectional interests in the United States. Polk's emergence as the Democratic nominee and subsequent narrow victory in the general election gave President Tyler an opportunity to settle the matter before the inauguration. He did so with Polk's consent. Warning of a potential new war with Mexico, as well as British and French intrigues, Tyler exhorted Congress to act quickly. By a slim margin, it passed a resolution committing the United States to defend Texas and to admit it to the Union upon the consent of the Texans and the new American president.

Polk moved quickly after taking office and sent a delegation to convince the Texans to accept annexation. He also ordered Zachary Taylor to move four thousand troops from Corpus Christi past the Nueces River and to the Rio Grande, placing U.S. forces in territory contested by Mexico and Texas. Meanwhile, the Mexican government offered to recognize Texas if it remained independent and accepted the Nueces River, instead of the Rio Grande, as a boundary. A special convention in Texas rejected the Mexican offer and accepted U.S. statehood, rendering moot a joint British-French offer to mediate an agreement between Texas and Mexico, which had welcomed the offer and severed ties with Washington. The Mexicans, however, had moved troops to the border and on April 25, 1846, clashed with Taylor's force, triggering the Mexican-American War.

The counter-counterfactual argument to the notion of an extended rapprochement for Washington and London is that the War of 1812 served as an object lesson and helped prevent numerous bilateral disagreements from becoming armed conflicts through the first half of the nineteenth century. Absent that lesson, the postrevolutionary generation of American leaders might have found another opportunity to claim the fervor of the American Revolution. Moreover, Republicans would have looked for opportunities to prove, as their predecessors did in 1812, that their party's egalitarian approach to politics and government was equally, if not more, capable of defending the nation in times of war. On the other side of the equation, London could have continued to press its interests in North America—including the defense of Canada, commercial ambitions, and unresolved territorial claims—and resorted to arms. Jeffersonian defense policies that hollowed out the army and the navy and placed unwarranted trust in state militias for national defense could have reinforced the less than full recognition that British leaders accorded to American independence and was evidenced in the sobriquet "Cousin Jonathan." The prospects for a clash of arms between London and Washington might have increased once the entente formed at the Congress of Vienna gave way to disputes over the balance of power in Europe and the disposition of former Spanish colonies in the New World. This increased tension, in turn, could have caused the British again to rely on their naval supremacy to blockade European ports and interfere with neutral—that is, American—oceanic commerce.

This argument, however, ignores the shift in relative power that took place in the first half of the nineteenth century. Whereas England ruled the seas, American demographic and economic growth provided the basis for military power that the United States could use to conquer and hold the North American continent. Had the object lesson of 1812 not been learned early in the century, the British would not have needed to revisit it decades later, assuming they had made the same calculations about avoiding war with the United States during the Napoleonic wars. The United States with its interior lines of communication, advanced by the rail and telegraph networks, would have had a decided advantage over British leaders located an ocean away and confronted with long-standing continental considerations in Europe.

AMERICA WITHOUT THE WAR OF 1812

The War of 1812 affected the trajectory of American development in three ways. First, it elevated Andrew Jackson to national prominence. Second, Jackson, first as military commander and then as president, accelerated the removal of Native Americans from their ancestral lands east of the Mississippi. Third, this exodus opened much of the Deep South to cotton cultivation, vastly expanding slavery and setting the stage for the American Civil War. Hence, the absence of the War of 1812 would have wrought significant changes on American politics and society.

Nothing in Andrew Jackson's prewar biography suggests he would have been a major figure in American history. Born into frontier poverty on the border between North and South Carolina, Jackson was orphaned early in life and matured, as Daniel Walker Howe writes, "with an eye on the main chance and just enough book learning to practice law."[12] For a person with humble beginnings, Jackson moved up quickly in society as a lawyer and politician. By the time he turned thirty-one in 1798, Jackson had been a member of the U.S. House of Representatives and a U.S. senator from the state of Tennessee and then became a judge on the Tennessee Supreme Court. Jackson's record as a national legislator was extremely limited. As a member of the lower chamber of Congress, he focused on getting the federal government to reimburse the Tennessee militia for an expedition against the Cherokees. As a member of the upper chamber, Jackson was, as Robert Remini notes, "out of his depth in the senate, and he knew it."[13] He served for only one session. He resigned, returned to Nashville in 1798, and was appointed a judge of the state's superior court, where he served for the next six years.

Jackson used this time to build political connections, particularly with officers of the state militia. In 1802, he was narrowly elected as major general of the Tennessee militia. Jackson performed admirably in this capacity and learned his duties, including maintaining the peace between the white and Indian communities and protecting the latter within their lands. During this time he became a proponent of removing the Indian tribes to lands west of the Mississippi River to reduce the friction between whites and Indians, to make room for more settlers, and to remove the temptation for European powers—Britain, France, and Spain—to support Indian resistance.

When the United States declared war in 1812, Jackson was ordered to take some two thousand volunteers to New Orleans. Departing in January 1813, Jackson's forces had moved five hundred miles when he received orders from the secretary of war to dismiss his volunteers and turn over his arms and supplies to General Wilkinson in New Orleans. Rather than dismissing his troops, Jackson led them on an arduous journey back to Tennessee, during which time he earned his nickname "Old Hickory" for his determination. In September the government ordered Jackson to call out the militia again after the Native Americans' attack on Fort Mims. His campaign during the Creek War lasted until March 1814, culminating at the Battle of Tohopeka (Horseshoe Bend). His victories earned him an appointment as a major general in the U.S. Army and command of the Seventh Military District.

Jackson's appointment came with authority to arrange a peace settlement with the Indians, and he used this opportunity to represent the interests of land-hungry westerners. At Fort Jackson on August 1, 1814, he demanded some twenty-three million acres—representing half of the land that friendly and hostile Creeks occupied and three-fifths of present-day Alabama and Georgia—and four million acres of Cherokee lands to create a buffer zone with Spanish Florida (and British influence). Jackson's terms were much harsher than those that the Creeks received from Gen. Thomas Pinckney and Indian agent Benjamin Hawkins, whom Secretary of War Armstrong previously had appointed as treaty commissioners.[14]

Subsequently, Jackson marched his army to Louisiana, where he won a stunning victory over invading British forces. This victory, which lionized Jackson as the "Hero of New Orleans" and made him a national figure, was a necessary but not sufficient event leading to his historic presidency. His 1817–1818 campaign against the Seminole Indians in Spanish Florida was tarnished by his exercising his less-than-clear authority and his summary execution of two British citizens, leading to a formal congressional investigation. Then, radicals in Congress forced his resignation as the junior of the U.S. Army's two major generals, and when President Monroe appointed him as the governor of the Florida Territory, he lasted only eleven weeks before he returned to Tennessee. There, he declined an offer to run for governor but accepted the state legislature's nomination to run for president as a stalking horse. Historian Sean Wilentz notes, "Had everything proceeded as planned, Andrew Jackson might be remembered today as a minor footnote to presidential history."[15] Jackson's 1824 campaign capitalized on his standing as a national figure after the sectional debate over Missouri's status as a slave or free state, and on the sectional character of the other candidates. His outsider status and military accomplishments added to his appeal, which also benefited from a post-1812 political trend toward greater participatory democracy. Jackson received more than 40 percent of the vote but lost the election in the House of Representatives to John Quincy Adams. The following October, the Tennessee legislature again nominated Jackson for president in 1828. In that election, with 68 percent of the electoral vote and 56 percent of the popular vote, he handily defeated Adams.

Jackson's presidency involved numerous controversies over core issues of national importance that shaped the growth of the still-young republic. Jackson, according to Howe, ultimately viewed major decisions through the paradigm of his personal power, which he "zealously maintained."[16] Hence, it is easy to imagine other outcomes had "King Andrew I," as some detractors dubbed him at the time, not been chief executive. Jackson's conflict with the Second Bank of the United States and his defense of national sovereignty in the nullification crisis with South Carolina were the two most important crises during his presidency. Jackson had been a critic of the bank before his election in 1828. He had made it a basic issue of his reelection in 1832, and "Jackson himself doubtless counted his ultimate victory over 'the Monster' his greatest single accomplishment."[17] Critics, however, maintain that destroying the bank was irresponsible and did incalculable harm to the country's development. In particular, without a central bank and its controls, state banks and loans proliferated, creating a speculative boom in land prices and led to the Panic of 1837.

Jackson's stance on the South Carolina nullification crisis is more positively understood through the lens of the Civil War. Jackson, through force of arms, upheld and defended the primacy of the Union during his first term. Vice President John C. Calhoun wrote the essay "The South Carolina Exposition and Protest," charging that Congress had gone beyond its constitutional writ in passing such legislation as the tariff of 1828, and that individual states could pass laws nullifying such acts and blocking their enforcement. Jackson responded to a South Carolina law that forbade state and federal officers from enforcing the tariffs by sending a warship and revenue cutters to Charleston and threatening to lead federal forces in the field if necessary. After the South Carolina legislature and Congress escalated the situation by passing respective resolutions to "repel force by force" and to authorize the president to use the army and navy to enforce the laws, Henry Clay and John Calhoun worked out a compromise tariff in 1833 that defused the crisis. Jackson's reputation as a decisive commander undoubtedly bolstered his threats. Without such a compelling threat, which was similar to George Washington's decision to march troops into Pennsylvania in 1794 and put down the Whiskey Rebellion, a more serious crisis or the weakening of the Union might have transpired.

In addition, the removal of Indian tribes from lands east of the Mississippi might not have been pursued so consistently and thoroughly had Jackson not risen to the presidency. After the Treaty of Ghent, Indians living in the Old Northwest were quickly stripped of their lands, and by 1821, most of Indiana, Illinois, and much of the Michigan Territory had been ceded to white settlers. In the South, however, the Five Civilized Tribes—Creek, Cherokee, Choctaw, Chicksaw, and Seminole—still held significant lands and enjoyed considerable autonomy. This situation remained the case even after the Treaty of Fort Mims relieved the Creek and Cherokee tribes of considerable real estate. Geographer Jedidiah Morse's 1822 report on the nation's Indian tribes lauded the economic and educational progress of the Five Civilized Tribes, which practiced agriculture and animal husbandry as their white neighbors did. He recommended that the Indians be allowed to remain in place. The federal government promoted this way of life and under-mined the prevalent expectation among white settlers that these lands would be available as the Indians tribes became extinct or were forced off their lands.

The controversy surrounding the Treaty of Indian Springs, which was con-cluded late in the Monroe administration to obtain remaining Creek lands in what later became Alabama and Mississippi, suggests this amicable situation might have remained absent Andrew Jackson. When the Creeks refused to rat-ify the treaty and assassinated the chief who had been bribed to sign it, the administration of John Quincy Adams nullified the treaty after determining that the federal commissioners who had drafted it had colluded with Georgian officials. Jackson, however, encouraged the Georgians to continue to fight for the treaty, and a federal-state battle was avoided only when the Creeks agreed to a new treaty more favorable to them. Southerners concluded from this expe-rience that Andrew Jackson would secure the expropriation of these lands. When Jackson was elected in 1828, Georgia's legislature unilaterally declared that starting in 1830 state laws would extend over the Cherokee nation. Concurrently at the federal level, the Indian Removal Bill became Jackson's top legislative priority. Reversing the assimilation policies of the Washing-ton, Adams, and Monroe administrations, Jackson called for a new round of treaties that would culminate in removing Native American commu-nities to lands west of the Mississippi. The bill led to a national debate that pitted pro-Indian evangelical groups and their supporters in Congress against the administration and southern state governments.

The act passed in the Senate on a 28–19 party line vote but more narrowly in the House, 102–97. The votes were highly sectional: representatives from slave states voted in favor by 61–15, while those from free states voted to oppose the measure by 41–82. Ironically, voting on Indian affairs proved to be the most consistent predictor of partisan affiliation as the second party system took shape, suggesting that Jackson's emphasis on Indian removal helped produce an alternative to his party. Tragically, the subsequent forced migrations, including the infamous Trail of Tears' removal of the Cherokees in 1838–1839, led to a high morality rate with some four thousand out of twelve thousand people estimated to have perished. This policy also affected the remaining northern tribes and led to the Black Hawk War in 1832. Before the end of Jackson's two terms, federal and state authorities had expelled some forty-six thousand Native Americans.

To this day, historians disagree on the motives behind Jackson's Indian policies but not on his critical role in their formulation and implementation. Howe writes, "During the Removal process the president personally intervened frequently, always on behalf of haste, sometimes on behalf of economy, but never on behalf of humanity, honesty, or careful planning. . . . Indian Removal reveals much more about Jacksonian politics than just its racism. In the first place, it illustrates imperialism, that is, a determination to expand geographically and economically, imposing an alien will upon subject peoples and commandeering their resources."

Biographer Remini, however, puts Jackson's intentions and actions in a positive light. He argues that of the courses of action available to addressing the fundamental issues between European and Native Americans, only removal was practical. No one, he notes, seriously argued for genocide. He also contends that most Indians and whites did not favor integration, with the former preferring their long-standing customs and lifestyles and the latter unwilling to accommodate an interracial society. Enforcing the existing treaties, meanwhile, would only have perpetuated the periodic violence between the Native Americans and the growing white population, which tripled from five million to fifteen million people in the first quarter of the nineteenth century. Remini contends that removing tribes to lands opened by the Louisiana Purchase was the only realistic option to keep the remaining tribes east of the Mississippi from suffering the fate of the many tribes that had disappeared since the European colonization of North America. Remini further argues that Jackson expected the Indians to thrive in their new surroundings. "To his dying day on June 8, 1845, Andrew Jackson genuinely believed that what he had accomplished rescued these people from inevitable annihilation. And although that statement sounds monstrous, and although no one in the modern world wishes to believe it, that is exactly what he did. He saved the Five Civilized Nations from probable extinction."[18]

The removal of the Indian populations from the Old Southwest (or the Deep South) immediately following the War of 1812 opened the land to the rapid expansion of slave-based cotton agriculture. Alabama (1819) and Mississippi (1817) were admitted to the Union as thousands of white settlers, most from neighboring states, arrived. This great migration—which for African American slaves constituted a "Second Middle Passage" following their forced passage across the Atlantic—focused on the so-called black belt portion of the Tennessee River Valley in northern Alabama that was known for its rich dark soil. The southern population boom was prompted when the wars in Europe and North America ended and the demand—and prices—for cotton rose. Short-staple cotton enjoyed a relatively long growing season in the region, and U.S. cotton production soared tenfold in the first two decades of the nineteenth century. Cotton production in the South stimulated textile production and industrial expansion in the Northeast, where capital and industries had sat idle during the U.S. trade embargoes and British blockades, respectively, before and during the War of 1812.

Consequently, the South became more committed to slavery after the War of 1812. The Missouri debates of 1819 over the status of slavery in the new territories seeking statehood generated polarizing votes in the House of Representatives similar to those regarding the Indian removal acts, with northern representatives voting 80–14 in favor of gradual emancipation and southern representatives voting 64–2 in opposition. The Missouri Compromise of 1820 prohibited north of the 36°30' parallel until the South secured repeal of the restriction by the Kansas Nebraska Act of 1854. In between, the nation grew more divided on the issues of slavery expansion and emancipation.

CONCLUSION

The War of 1812 gave rise to Andrew Jackson who, as a national political figure, was instrumental in rapidly removing Native Americans from lands in the Old Southwest that white settlers then expropriated to establish a cotton-slave economy. Had the war not elevated Jackson to greatness, the region might have developed more slowly, maintaining its complex ethnic and racial character, and avoided the quick expansion of the cotton culture that led to decades of sectional strife and the dissolution of the Union. In a less compressed time frame, the country might have made more gradual adjustments and perhaps moved in step with Britain toward the abandonment of slavery, which Britain and its colonies abolished with the Slavery Abolition Act of 1833. The Old Southwest might have evolved a more heterogeneous and egalitarian culture, with the original southern states along the Atlantic Seaboard alone preserving their "peculiar institution" and maintaining a cultural distinction similar to Quebec's status in Canada.

Absent a second war with Britain, the United States could have begun an extended rapprochement with Britain that replaced the Second War of Independence narrative in our history. The shift in power in North America toward the United States would have been characterized as a more cooperative, and less competitive, period with Britain. Internally, Andrew Jackson might not have accelerated the Indian removal policies in the Old Southwest; thus, the area would not have been so quickly or thoroughly open to slave-based plantation farming. Indeed, the United States could have been more inclined to follow Britain's abandonment of slavery in 1833.

A counter-counterfactual argument to this what-if history of an America without the War of 1812 is that the same demographic, economic, political, and technological factors would have still driven Euro-American westward expansion into the Old Northwest, the Louisiana Territory, and Florida. The steady constriction of Indian lands in the Old Northwest would have been paralleled, in time, by a similar movement across the Old Southwest. The hunger for land and the white settlers' well-established means for acquiring it through unfair treaties imposed by threats to and bribes for key tribal leaders in time would have accomplished as much as the national policy of Indian removal backed by federal troops did.

Moreover, the notion that the United States would eventually dominate the North American continent, and possibly the entire hemisphere, was a well-established narrative for the young republic's future well before the term "Manifest Destiny" was popularized in 1845 in the effort to annex Texas. In that year, the Jacksonian *Democratic Review* argued that the acquisition of Texas would be "the fulfilment [sic] of our manifest destiny to overspread the continent allotted by Providence for the free development of our yearly multiplying millions." Yet more than twenty years earlier, Secretary of State John Quincy Adams more fully articulated the same sentiment in a cabinet meeting when he said that the world should

> be familiarized with the idea of considering our proper dominion to be the continent of North America. From the time when we became an

independent people it was as much a law of nature that this should become our pretension as that the Mississippi should flow to the sea. Spain had possessions upon our southern and Great Britain upon our northern border. It was impossible that centuries should elapse without finding them annexed to the United States; nor that any spirit of encroachment or ambition on our part renders it necessary, but because it is a physical, moral, and political absurdity that such fragments of territory, with sovereigns at fifteen hundred miles beyond [the] sea, worthless and burdensome to their owners, should exist permanently contiguous to a great, powerful, enterprising, and rapidly-growing nation.[19]

Leaders and political parties, however, need to translate such aspirations into policies and actions. Without someone of Jackson's stature, the West might not have been conquered as systematically and inevitably as it appears from today's perspective. Andrew Jackson was as important to the growth of the United States as George Washington was to its independence. His role in consolidating the republic east of the Mississippi in the War of 1812 and in securing the Louisiana Purchase laid the foundation for subsequent expansions into the Oregon Territory and former Mexican territories. Without the War of 1812, "King Andrew" would never have had the opportunity to accomplish so much.

CHRONOLOGY

	NORTH AMERICA		EUROPE
	POLITICAL	**MILITARY**	
1803			
Apr 30			Louisiana Purchase Treaty
May 16			Britain and France resume hostilities
1804			
Dec 2			Napoleon's coronation
1805			
May	*Essex* Decision		
Oct 19			Ulm surrenders
Oct 21			Battle of Trafalgar
Dec 2			Battle of Austerlitz
1806			
Oct 14			Battles of Jena & Auerstadt
Nov 21			Berlin Decree
Dec 31	Monroe-Pinkney Treaty signed		
1807			
Jan 7			Orders in Council
Jun 22		*Leopard* v. *Chesapeake*	
Jul 7–9			Treaties of Tilsit
Nov–Dec			France invades Portugal
Nov 11			Orders in Council
Dec 17			Milan Decree
Dec 22			Embargo Act
Mar			France invades Spain
Aug 1			Wellington in Portugal

(continued)

	NORTH AMERICA		EUROPE
	POLITICAL	**MILITARY**	
1807 *(continued)*			
Sep			Britain invades Spain
Dec 4			Napoleon captures Madrid
1809			
Mar 1	Repeal of Embargo		
Mar 1	Non-Intercourse Act		
Apr 19	Erskine Agreement		
May 13			Napoleon captures Vienna
Jul 5–6			Battle of Wagram
Jul 28			Battle of Talavera
Oct 19			Treaty of Schönbrunn, Austria joins Continental System
1810			
May 1	Macon's Bill #2		
Nov 2	Macon's Bill #2 Invoked		
1811			
May 16		*President* v. *Little Belt*	
Nov 7		Battle of Tippecanoe	
1812			
Mar 9	John Henry letters released		
Apr 4	Embargo signed		
May 11			Perceval assassinated
Jun 1	Madison's war message		
Jun 4	House votes for war		
Jun 16	Orders in Council withdrawn		
Jun 18			France invades Russia
Jun 22	Baltimore riots begin		
Jul 12		Hull invades Canada	
Jul 17		British capture Mackinac	
Jul 22			Battle of Salamanca
Aug 16		British capture Detroit	
Aug 19		*Constitution* v. *Guerrière*	
Sep 7			Battle of Borodino
Sep 14			Napoleon in Moscow
Oct 13		Battle of Queenston	
Oct 25		*United States* v. *Macedonian*	
Dec 29		*Constitution* v. *Java*	

(continued)

NORTH AMERICA			EUROPE
POLITICAL		MILITARY	
1813			
Jan 18–22		Battle of Frenchtown	
Feb–Mar			Britain, Russia, Prussia, & Sweden form new coalition
April 15		U.S. seizes Mobile, West Florida	
Apr 27		Battle of York	
Apr 28–May 9		Battle of Ft. Meigs	
May 2			Battle of Lützen
May 21–22			Battle of Bautzen
May 27		Battle of Fort George	
May 29		Battle of Sacket's Harbor	
Jun 1		*Shannon* v. *Chesapeake*	
Jun 4–Aug 16			Armistice between France and Coalition
Jun 6		Battle of Stoney Creek	
Jun 12			French evacuate Madrid
Jun 21			Battle of Vitoria
Jun 22		Battle of Craney Island	
Jul 26–Aug 1			Battle of Sorauren
Jun 24		Battle of Beaver Dams	
Jun 25–26		Battle/sack of Hampton	
Jul 27		Battle of Burnt Corn Creek	
Aug 10		Battle of St. Michaels	
Aug 26–27			Battle of Dresden
Aug 29			Battle of Kulm
Aug 30		Battle of Ft. Mims	
Sep 9			French surrender San Sebastian
Sep 10		Battle of Lake Erie	
Oct–Nov			Wellington invades France
Oct 5		Battle of the Thames	
Oct 16–19			Battle of Leipzig
Oct 26		Battle of Chateauguay	
Oct 30–31			Battle of Hanau
Nov 1		Battle of French Creek	
Nov 3		Battle of Tallushatchee	
Nov 9		Battle of Talladega	
Nov 11		Battle of Crysler's Farm	
Nov 29		Battle of Autosse	

(continued)

NORTH AMERICA			EUROPE
POLITICAL		MILITARY	
1813 *(continued)*			
Dec 10		U.S. burns Newark	
Dec 18		British capture Ft. Niagara	
Dec 19		British burn Lewiston	
Dec 29		British burn Black Rock & Buffalo	
1814			
Jan 22–27		Battles of Emuckfau, Enitachopco, and Calabee Creeks	
Feb 27			Battle of Orthez
Mar 17			British seize Bordeaux
Mar 27		Battle of Tohopeka (Horseshoe Bend)	
Mar 28		*Phoebe & Cherub v. Essex*	
Mar 30		Battle of La Colle Mill	
Apr 10			Battle of Toulouse
Apr 11			Napoleon abdicates
May 6		Battle of Oswego	
May 15		U.S. burns Port Dover	
May 30		Battle of Sandy Creek	
Jul 3		Battle of Fort Erie	
Jul 5		Battle of Chippewa Creek	
Jul 25		Battle of Lundy's Lane	
Aug 3		Battle of Conjocta Creek	
Aug 8			Ghent negotiations begin
Aug 9	Treaty of Fort Jackson		
Aug 9–11		Battle of Stonington	
Aug 15		Siege of Ft. Erie	
Aug 24		Battle of Bladensburg	
Aug 24		British occupy Washington, DC	
Aug 31		Battle of Caulk's Field	
Sep 1		British capture Castine	
Sep 11		Battle of Plattsburgh	
Sep 12–13		Battle of Baltimore	
Sep 15		British attack on Ft. Bowyer	
Oct 19		Battle of Cook's Mill	
Nov 7		U.S. captures Pensacola	
Dec 15– Jan 5	Hartford Convention		

(continued)

	NORTH AMERICA		EUROPE
	POLITICAL	**MILITARY**	
1814 *(continued)*			
Dec 23		Battle of Villeré Plantation	
Dec 24			Treat of Ghent signed
1815			
Jan 8		Battle of New Orleans	
Feb 11		British capture Ft. Bowyer	
Feb 16	U.S. Senate ratifies Treaty of Ghent		
Feb 20		*Constitution v. Cyane & Levant*	
Feb 26			Napoleon escapes Elba
Jun 18			Battle of Waterloo

NOTES

Introduction

1. John Whiteclay Chambers II, ed., *The Oxford Companion to American Military History* (New York: Oxford University Press, 1999); John Keegan, *Fields of Battle: The Wars for North America* (New York: Alfred A. Knopf, 1996), 202; and Kevin Phillips, *The Cousins' Wars: Religion, Politics, and the Triumph of Anglo-America* (New York: Basic Books, 1999).
2. Gordon S. Wood, *Empire of Liberty: A History of the Early Republic, 1789–1815* (New York: Oxford University Press, 2009), 659.

1. The Need for New Narratives

1. Edward James Wagner II, "Federal-State Relations during the War of 1812" (PhD diss., Ohio State University, 1963), 184.
2. J. C. A. Stagg, *Mr. Madison's War: Politics, Diplomacy, and Warfare in the Early American Republic, 1783–1830* (Princeton, NJ: Princeton University Press, 1983), 391, 395.
3. Bradford Perkins, *Prologue to War: England and the United States, 1805–1812* (Berkeley: University of California Press, 1961), 46.
4. Donald R. Hickey, *The War of 1812: A Forgotten Conflict* (Urbanna: University of Illinois Press, 1989), 38.
5. Roger H. Brown, "Who Bungled the War of 1812?," *Reviews in American History* 19 (1991): 181–87.
6. See John M. Stahl, *"The Invasion of the City of Washington": A Disagreeable Study in and of Military Unpreparedness* (New York: Van Trump, 1918), 27–28; and Francis F. Beirne, *The War of 1812* (New York: E. P. Dutton, 1949), 389–90.
7. Wood, *Empire of Liberty*, 278.
8. Walter A. McDougall, *Freedom Just around the Corner: A New American History, 1585–1828* (New York: HarperCollins, 2004), 321.
9. Wood, *Empire of Liberty*, 669.
10. George G. Herring, *From Colony to Superpower: U.S. Foreign Relations Since 1776* (New York: Oxford University Press, 2008), 93.

11. Walter R. Borneman, *1812: The War That Forged a Nation* (New York: HarperCollins, 2004), xi.

12. Phillips, *The Cousins' Wars*, 333–36. Rutland is quoted in George G. Herring, *From Colony to Superpower*, 126.

13. Walter Russell Mead, *Special Providence: American Foreign Policy and How It Changed the World* (New York: Alfred A. Knopf, 2001), 227. Mead's analysis also suggests that these wars may reflect a now defunct "Davisonian" culture (named after President of the Confederacy Jefferson Davis) that expanded U.S. territory to preserve and extend slavery; see page 92. See also Frank Lawrence Owsley Jr., *Struggle for the Gulf Borderlands: The Creek War and the Battle of New Orleans, 1812–1815* (Tuscaloosa: University of Alabama Press, 2000), 192.

14. Bradford Perkins, ed., *The Causes of the War of 1812: National Honor or National Interest?* (New York: Holt, Rinehart and Winston, 1962).

15. Stagg, *Mr. Madison's War*, 39–40.

16. Mark Zuehlke, *For Honour's Sake: The War of 1812 and the Brokering of an Uneasy Peace* (Toronto: Vintage Canada, 2006), 70, 72.

17. Ibid., 54, 89; and Alan Taylor, *The Civil War of 1812: American Citizens, British Subjects, Irish Rebels, & Indian Allies* (New York: Alfred A. Knopf, 2010), 133.

18. Hickey, *War of 1812*, 75.

19. Stagg, *Mr. Madison's War*, 374; and Wagner, "Federal-State Relations," 73.

20. Wagner, "Federal-State Relations," 141.

21. Sean Wilentz, *The Rise of American Democracy: Jefferson to Lincoln* (New York: W. W. Norton, 2005), 110; and Robert Remini, *Andrew Jackson and His Indian Wars* (New York: Viking, 2001), 93.

22. Donald E. Graves, *Where Right and Glory Lead! The Battle of Lundy's Lane, 1814* (Toronto: Robin Brass Studio, 2003), ix.

23. James Madison, *Special Message to Congress on the Treaty of Ghent, February 18, 1815*, www.millercenter.org.

24. Richard V. Barbuto, *Niagara, 1814: America Invades Canada* (Lawrence: University Press of Kansas, 2000), 322.

25. Both quotes from David McCullough, *John Adams* (New York: Simon & Schuster, 2001), 606.

26. Daniel Walker Howe, *What Hath God Wrought: The Transformation of America, 1815–1848* (New York: Oxford University Press, 2007), 423.

27. Ibid.

28. Ibid., 365.

29. Ibid., 790.

30. Ibid., 809; and Walter A. McDougall, *Throes of Democracy: The American Civil War Era, 1829–1877* (New York: HarperCollins, 2008), 297.

31. Frederick Jackson Turner, *The Frontier in American History* (New York: Henry Holt, 1921).

2. A Classical View of the Military Balance in the War of 1812

1. Taylor, *Civil War of 1812*, 157.
2. Beirne, *The War of 1812*, 249.
3. Hickey, *The War of 1812*, 153.
4. Thomas Jefferson, *The Jeffersonian Cyclopedia*, ed. John P. Foley (New York: Funk & Wagnalls, 1900), 762.
5. Samuel B. Griffith, *Sun Tzu: The Art of War* (Oxford, UK: Oxford University Press, 1963).
6. Keegan, *Fields of Battle*, 200.
7. Richard Glover, *Peninsular Preparation: The Reform of the British Army, 1795–1809* (London: Cambridge University Press, 1963), 76ff.
8. Quoted in Zuehlke, *For Honour's Sake*, 354.
9. Jarvis Hanks et al., *Soldiers of 1814: American Enlisted Men's Memoirs of the Niagara Campaign*, ed. Donald E. Graves (Youngstown, NY: Old Fort Niagara Association, 1995), 14.
10. Walter Lord, *The Dawn's Early Light* (New York: W. W. Norton, 1972), 181; and Robin Reilly, *The British at the Gates: The New Orleans Campaign in the War of 1812* (Toronto: Robin Brass Studio, 2002), 238.
11. Wesley B. Turner, *British Generals in the War of 1812: High Command in the Canadas* (Montreal: McGill-Queen's University Press, 1999), 18, 142–46. Turner's analysis also takes into account common shortcomings, such as a failure to gather intelligence; a lack of knowledge of history or theory, of planning, and of understanding of the common soldier; insubordination; a neglect of duty; and being absent without leave.
12. Jon Latimer, *1812: War with America* (Cambridge, MA: Harvard University Press, 2007), 388.
13. Andro Linklater, *An Artist in Treason: The Extraordinary Double Life of General James Wilkinson* (New York: Walker Publishing, 2009), 282.
14. Stagg, *Mr. Madison's War*, 320.
15. Ibid., 269.
16. Linklater, *An Artist in Treason*, 308.
17. Carl Benn, *The Iroquois in the War of 1812* (Toronto: University of Toronto Press, 1998), 67.
18. J. Mackay Hitsman, *The Incredible War of 1812: A Military History* (Toronto: Robin Brass Studio, 1999), 36.
19. Glover, *Peninsular Preparation*, 180.
20. Stagg, *Mr. Madison's War*, 155–59.
21. Glover, *Peninsular Preparation*, 122.
22. For a discussion of this issue, see Brent Nosworthy, "Light Infantry and Skirmishing," in *With Musket, Cannon and Sword, Battle Tactics of Napoleon and His Enemies* (New York: Sarpedom, 1996).

23. Wade G. Dudley, *Splintering the Wooden Wall: The British Blockade of the United States, 1812–1815* (Annapolis, MD: Naval Institute Press, 2003), see chapter 8, 131ff.

3. Invasions of 1814 and 1863

1. This comparative history is based primarily on Graves's *Where Right and Glory Lead!* and Stephen W. Sears's *Gettysburg* (New York: Houghton Mifflin, 2004).

2. Hinkley, *The War of 1812*, 287ff.

3. Doris Kearns Goodwin, *Team of Rivals: The Political Genius of Abraham Lincoln* (New York: Simon & Schuster, 2005), 315. Subsequent unsuccessful efforts included the Niagara Falls peace talks in the summer of 1864 and the Hampton Roads peace talks in January 1865.

4. Sears, *Gettysburg*, 77, 116.

5. Stagg, *Mr. Madison's War*, 400.

6. Robert Malcomson, *Lords of the Lake: The Naval War on Lake Ontario, 1812–1814* (Annapolis, MD: Naval Institute Press, 1998), 286–87.

7. Graves, *Where Right and Glory Lead!*, 23.

8. Sears, *Gettysburg*, 7. The U.S. Marine Corps' Fleet Marine Force Manual (FMFM) 1-1 *Campaigning* (Washington, DC: Department of the Navy, January 1990), 18, uses Lee's advance into Pennsylvania as an negative object lesson: "The South's political objectives would seem to indicate a military strategy of attrition based on prolonging the war as a means to break Northern resolve—as had been George Washington's strategy in the Revolution. In fact, this was the strategy preferred by Confederate President Jefferson Davis. Lee, however, chose to concentrate his army in Virginia. This was due in part to a perspective much narrower than Grant's and the fact that he was constrained to defend Richmond. But it was also due to Lee's insistence on offensive strategy—not merely an offensive-defensive as early in the early stages of the war, but eventually an ambitious offensive strategy in 1862 and '63 aimed at invading the North as a means to breaking Northern will. Given the South's relative weakness, Lee's strategy was questionable at best—both as a viable means of attaining the South's policy aims and also in regard to operational practicability, particularly the South's logistical ability to sustain offensive campaigns."

9. For these quotations regarding Stuart's orders, see Sears, *Gettysburg*, 104–5.

10. Graves, *Where Right and Glory Lead!*, 75.

11. Ibid., 92.

12. Sears, *Gettysburg*, 73–74.

13. Graves, *Where Right and Glory Lead!*, 97–98.

14. Stagg, *Mr. Madison's War*, 402–3.

15. Graves, *Where Right and Glory Lead!*, 103.

16. Ibid., 104.

17. Stagg, *Mr. Madison's War*, 402.

18. Graves, *Where Right and Glory Lead!*, 125.

19. Sears, *Gettysburg*, 223–28, 233. After the war, Ewell was compared unfavorably with Stonewall Jackson, who many believed would have taken Cemetery Hill had he still been alive and in command of the corps. Sears judges that "absent any help from Hill's Corps—a decision entirely Lee's—it is highly unlikely that even Stonewall could have conquered Cemetery Hill on July 1."
20. Ibid., 292, 345.
21. Graves, *Where Right and Glory Lead!*, 174.
22. Ibid., 208–9.
23. Sears, *Gettysburg*, 359.
24. Graves, *Where Right and Glory Lead!*, 228.
25. Sears, *Gettysburg*, 471.
26. Ibid., 475.
27. Wolfgang Schivelbusch, *The Culture of Defeat: On National Trauma, Mourning, and Recovery*, trans. Jefferson Chase (New York: Henry Holt, 2003), 66–67.

4. The Men Who Governed America during the War of 1812

1. A notable exception is C. Edward Skeen's *Citizen Soldiers in the War of 1812* (Lexington: University Press of Kentucky, 1999), which provides a thematic analysis of the American militia during the war and numerous references to the efforts of these governors.
2. Henry Adams, *The Jeffersonian Transformation: Passages from the "History"* (New York: The New York Review of Books, 2007), 109–10.
3. Charles D. Lowery, *James Barbour: A Jeffersonian Republican* (Tuscaloosa: University of Alabama Press, 1984), 66.
4. See Myron F. Wehtje, "Opposition in Virginia to the War of 1812," *Virginia Magazine of History and Biography* 78, no. 1 (January 1970): 65–86.
5. Wagner, "Federal-State Relations," 17–18, 110.
6. Lowery, *James Barbour*, 71.
7. Wagner, "Federal-State Relations," 121.
8. Lowery, *James Barbour*, 78.
9. Adams, *Jeffersonian Transformation*, 90.
10. Ray W. Irwin, *Daniel D. Tompkins, Governor of New York and Vice President of the United States* (New York: The New York Historical Society, 1968), 65.
11. Ibid., 71–73, 134.
12. Wagner, "Federal-State Relations," 16–17.
13. Ibid., 92–93.
14. Irwin, *Daniel D. Tompkins*, 173.
15. Taylor, *Civil War of 1812*, 269–70; and Wagner, "Federal-State Relations," 101.
16. Wagner, "Federal-State Relations," 97–98.
17. Ibid., 108–10.
18. Irwin, *Daniel D. Tompkins*, 196.
19. Ibid., 202.

20. Adams, *Jeffersonian Transformation*, 104. John Adams was far more critical in his assessment of Maryland when he visited in 1777: "The Manners of Maryland are somewhat peculiar. . . . They have but few Merchants. . . . The Lands are cultivated, and all Sorts of Trades are exercised by Negroes, or by transported convicts, which has occasioned the Planters and Farmers to assume the title of Gentlemen, and they hold their Negroes and convicts, that is all labouring People and Tradesmen, in such Contempt, that they think themselves a distinct order of Beings. Hence, they will never suffer their sons to labour or learn any Trade, but they bring them up in Idleness or, what is worse, in Horse Racing, Cock fighting, and Card Playing." Quoted in Linklater, *An Artist in Treason*, 8.

21. Frank A. Cassell, "Baltimore in 1813: A Study of Urban Defense in the War of 1812," *Military Affairs* 33, no. 3 (December 1969): 351.

22. Wagner, "Federal-State Relations," 118–20.

23. Adams, *Jeffersonian Transformation*, 60–61.

24. Richard Buel Jr., *America on the Brink: How the Political Struggle over the War of 1812 Almost Destroyed the Young Republic* (New York: Palgrave Macmillan, 2005), 147.

25. Wagner, "Federal-State Relations," 34, 41,45.

26. Ibid., 58, 65, 66.

27. J. S. Martell, "A Side Light on Federalist Strategy during the War of 1812," *American Historical Review* 43, no. 3 (April 1938): 553–66.

28. Donald R. Hickey, "Federalist Party Unity and the War of 1812," *Journal of American Studies* 12, no. 1 (April 1978): 34.

29. Adams, *Jeffersonian Transformation*, 117.

30. Sarah McCulloh Lemmon, *Frustrated Patriots: North Carolina and the War of 1812* (Chapel Hill: University of North Carolina Press, 1973), 18.

31. Ibid., 27.

32. Ibid., 77.

33. Ibid., 134.

34. Wagner, "Federal-State Relations," 153.

35. Adams, *Jeffersonian Transformation*, 91.

36. See Victor Sapio, *Pennsylvania and the War of 1812* (Lexington: University Press of Kentucky, 1970), 59; and Sanford W. Higginbotham, *The Keystone in the Democratic Arch: Pennsylvania Politics, 1800–1816* (Harrisburg: Pennsylvania Historical and Museum Commission, 1952), 253, 256.

37. Higginbotham, *Keystone in the Democratic Arch*, 272–75.

38. Wagner, "Federal-State Relations," 17.

39. Ibid., 99.

40. Higginbotham, *Keystone in the Democratic Arch*, 295–97.

41. Emerson Lee Derr, "Simon Snyder, Governor of Pennsylvania, 1808–1817" (Master's thesis, University of Pennsylvania, 1960), 201–2.

42. William C. Davis, *Look Away! A History of the Confederate States of America* (New York: Free Press, 2002), see chapter 11: "The States in Their Sovereignty."

5. Dueling Narratives: Henry Adams's Alternative History of the War of 1812

1. Henry Adams, *The War of 1812*, ed. H. A. DeWeerd (New York: Cooper Square Press, 1999).

2. Robert Sobel, *For Want of a Nail: If Burgoyne Had Won at Saratoga* (London: Greenhill Books, 1977). See also Robert Crowley's *What If? The World's Foremost Military Historians Imagine What Might Have Been* (New York: Berkley Publishing Group, 2001); and *What If? 2: Eminent Historians Imagine What Might Have Been* (New York: Berkley Publishing Group, 2002). None of the other eight alternative histories in this series covers the War of 1812.

3. Steve Tally, *Almost America: From the Colonists to Clinton: A "What if" History of the U.S.* (New York: HarperCollins, 2000); David Fitz-Enz, *Redcoats' Revenge: An Alternate History of the War of 1812* (Washington, DC: Potomac Books, 2008); and Eric Flint, *1812: The Rivers of War* (New York: Ballantine Books, 2005).

4. Adams, *The War of 1812*.

5. John Elting, *Amateurs, to Arms! A Military History of the War of 1812* (New York: Da Capo Press, 1995), 331.

6. David Hackett Fischer, *Historians' Fallacies: Toward a Logic of Historical Thought* (New York: Harper & Row, 1970), 15–16.

7. Ibid., 16.

8. Garry Wills, *Henry Adams and the Making of America* (New York: Houghton Mifflin, 2005), 36. See also pages 7 and 392.

9. Adams, *The War of 1812*, 18.

10. Ibid., 20, 22.

11. Elting, *Amateurs, to Arms!*, 34.

12. Latimer, *1812*, 63.

13. Adams, *The War of 1812*, 19.

14. Ibid., 47.

15. Turner, *British Generals in the War of 1812*, 32–33.

16. Adams, *The War of 1812*, 28.

17. Turner, *British Generals in the War of 1812*, 33.

18. Adams, *The War of 1812*, 38–39.

19. Theodore Roosevelt, *Naval War of 1812* (New York: The Modern Library, 1999), 45.

20. Adams, *The War of 1812*, 56.

21. Ibid., 57.

22. Sandy Antal, *A Wampum Denied: Procter's War of 1812* (Ottawa: Carleton University Press, 1997), 169–71.

23. Ibid., 174.

24. Adams, *The War of 1812*, 58.

25. Antal, *A Wampum Denied*, 154, 177.

26. Beverly W. Bond Jr., "William Henry Harrison in the War of 1812," *Mississippi Valley Historical Review* 13, no. 4 (March 1927): 516.

27. Adams, *The War of 1812*, 71.

28. Ibid., 86.

29. Elting, *Amateurs, to Arms!*, 4.

30. Adams, *The War of 1812*, 99.

31. Ibid., 98.

32. Elting, *Amateurs, to Arms!*, 150.

33. Donald E. Graves, *Field of Glory: The Battle of Crysler's Farm, 1813* (Toronto: Robin Brass Studio, 1999), 285.

34. Ibid., 317.

35. Adams, *The War of 1812*, 151–52, 159, 161.

36. Dudley, *Splintering the Wooden Wall*, 155.

37. Adams, *The War of 1812*, 165–66.

38. Antal, *A Wampum Denied*, 219.

39. Robert Remini, *The Battle of New Orleans* (New York: Viking, 1999), 86.

40. Adams, *The War of 1812*, 295.

41. Ibid., 322–23.

42. Elting, *Amateurs, to Arms!*, 290; and Reilly, *The British at the Gates*, 210–11.

43. Owsley, *Struggle for the Gulf Borderlands*, 118, 170.

44. Adams, *The War of 1812*, 301, 303.

45. Owsley, *Struggle for the Gulf Borderlands*, 125–26.

46. Elting, *Amateurs, to Arms!*, 295.

47. Remini, *The Battle of New Orleans*, 254–55.

48. Adams, *The War of 1812*, 181.

49. Barbuto, *Niagara, 1814*, 211–12.

50. Adams, *The War of 1812*, 185–86.

51. Graves, *Where Right and Glory Lead!*, 127, 209. Also see Barbuto, *Niagara, 1814*, 218.

52. Adams, *The War of 1812*, 191.

53. Turner, *British Generals in the War of 1812*, 140–41; and Barbuto, *Niagara, 1814*, 238, 239–40.

54. Adams, *The War of 1812*, 212–14.

55. Barbuto, *Niagara, 1814*, 285, 292.

56. Taylor, *Civil War of 1812*, 403.

57. Adams, *The War of 1812*, 220.

58. Ibid., 221.

59. Elting, *Amateurs, to Arms!*, 199; Lord, *Dawn's Early Light*, 26; and Anthony S. Pitch, *The Burning of Washington: The British Invasion of 1814* (Annapolis, MD: Naval Institute Press, 1998), 18; and Latimer, *1812*, 309–10.

60. Adams, *The War of 1812*, 234, 235.

61. Latimer, *1812*, 303–9; and Pitch, *The Burning of Washington*, 55.

62. Cassell, "Baltimore in 1813," 351.

63. Adams, *The War of 1812*, 237.

64. Elting, *Amateurs, to Arms!*, 261; Latimer, *1812*, 359; and David G. Fitz-Enz, *The Final Invasion: Plattsburgh, the War of 1812's Most Decisive Battle* (New York: Cooper Square Press, 2001), 51.

65. Fitz-Enz, *Final Invasion*, 51; Hitsman, *Incredible War of 1812*, 267; and Zuehlke, *For Honour's Sake*, 323.

66. Adams, *The War of 1812*, 239.

67. Frances Diane Robotti and James Vescovi, *The USS* Essex *and the Birth of the American Navy* (Holbrook, MA: Adams Media, 1999), 200.

68. Roosevelt, *Naval War of 1812*, 163.

69. Adams, *The War of 1812*, 330.

70. Zuehlke, *For Honour's Sake*, 361, 364.

71. Bradford Perkins, *Castlereagh and Adams: England and the United States, 1812–1823* (Los Angeles: University of California Press, 1964), 125.

72. Adams, *The War of 1812*, 347.

73. Zuehlke, *For Honour's Sake*, 349, 380; and Perkins, *Castlereagh and Adams*, 138.

6. The Battle of Bladensburg: Could Washington Have Been Saved?

1. John C. Fredriksen, *The United States Army in the War of 1812: Concise Biographies of Commanders and Operational Histories of Regiments, with Bibliographies of Published and Primary Resources* (Jefferson, NC: McFarland, 2009), 11.

2. Alan Lloyd, *The Scorching of Washington: The War of 1812* (New York: R. B. Luce, 1974), 153.

3. Charles C. Muller, *The Darkest Day: 1814, the Washington-Baltimore Campaign* (Philadelphia: J. B. Lippincott, 1963), 59.

4. Stagg, *Mr. Madison's War*, 40–48, 413–15.

5. Stahl, "Invasion of the City of Washington," 215–16.

6. The American military interpretation of the principles of war that originated during the Napoleonic period include objective, offensive, mass, economy of force, maneuver, unity of command, security, surprise, and simplicity.

7. Stahl, "Invasion of the City of Washington," 184.

8. John S. Williams, *History of the Invasion and Capture of Washington, and of the Events Which Preceded and Followed* (New York: Harper & Brothers, 1857), 196.

9. Stagg, *Mr. Madison's War*, 207–10, 277, 281.

10. Williams, *History of the Invasion*, 154–55; and Stahl, "The Invasion of the City of Washington," 178.

11. A fictional account of such a battle on Capitol Hill is described in Flint, *1812*.

12. William M. Marine, *The British Invasion of Maryland, 1812–15* (Baltimore: Society of the War of 1812 in Maryland, 1913), 115; and Stahl, "The Invasion of the City of Washington," 161.

13. Williams, *History of the Invasion*, 167–68.

14. This account is based on Joseph A. Whitehorne, *The Battle for Baltimore: 1814* (Baltimore: Nautical & Aviation Publishing Company of America, 1997), 175ff.

15. British flag officers were fairly conspicuous on the battlefield, drawing the attention of enemy sharpshooters. Ross led from the front, as did General Brock, who was killed leading a charge at the Battle of Queenston, Ontario, in 1812. In the words of one American on the battlefield, "General Ross was one of the finest looking men that I ever saw on horseback. Before being killed at North Point, Ross had his horse shot out from under him as he entered Washington. Earlier that day, Cockburn suffered two near misses when a bullet struck his saddle and a marine standing beside him was killed by roundshot a moment later." See Latimer, *1812*, 307, 314–15.

7. Victory or Defeat, and for Whom? Alternative Outcomes for the War of 1812

1. Hickey, *The War of 1812*, 73.
2. Zuehlke, *For Honour's Sake*, 301.
3. See Lawrence Wilkinson, "How to Build Scenarios," *Global Business Network*, 2004.
4. British authors tend to place more emphasis on the linkages between the European and North American conflicts. See Jeremy Black, *The War of 1812 in the Age of Napoleon* (Norman: University of Oklahoma Press, 2009), 113–99; and J. P. Riley, *Napoleon and the World War of 1813: Lessons in Coalition Warfighting* (London: Frank Cass Publishers, 2000), 115. Also see Buel, *America on the Brink*, 182–84.
5. Stagg, *Mr. Madison's War*, 319–20.
6. Riley, *Napoleon and the World War of 1813*, 107ff.
7. See John G. Gallaher, "Victory at Kulm: The 1813 Campaign," in *The Napoleon Options: Alternate Decisions of the Napoleonic Wars*, ed. Jonathan North (London: Greenhill Books, 2000). This essay depicts a French victory in 1813 resulting in a second peace agreement at Tilsit between France, Prussia, and Russia.
8. Jay Luvaas, ed., *Napoleon on the Art of War* (New York: Free Press, 1999), 61; Yeo quoted in C. P. Stacey, "An American Plan for a Canadian Campaign," The American Historical Review 46, no. 2 (January 1941): 348; Hickey, *The War of 1812*, 90; and Riley, *Napoleon and the World War of 1813*, 443.
9. Wood, *Empire of Liberty*, 266, 268.
10. Ron Chernow, *Alexander Hamilton* (New York: Penguin Press, 2004), 552–66.

8. A Worst-Case Scenario for the War of 1812

1. Chernow, *Alexander Hamilton*, 548.
2. Seth Ames, ed., *The Works of Fisher Ames*, vol. 12 (Boston: Little, Brown, 1854), 382.
3. R. Ernest Dupuy and Trevor N. Dupuy, *The Harper Encyclopedia of Military History: From 3500 BC to the Present* (New York: HarperCollins, 1993), 816.
4. Letter from Samuel Adams to James Warren, January 7, 1776, http://www .themoralliberal.com/2010/09/25/samuel-adams-to-james-warren-on-militias -and-standing-armies/.
5. Chernow, *Alexander Hamilton*, 578.

6. Wood, *Empire of Liberty*, 698.
7. Ibid., 700.
8. Adams, *The War of 1812*, 208, 289, 347.
9. Taylor, *Civil War of 1812*, 132.
10. Ibid., 147.
11. Stagg, *Mr. Madison's War*, 271.
12. Wagner, "Federal-State Relations," 212.
13. Stagg, *Mr. Madison's War*, 429–30.
14. Derr, "Simon Snyder," 201–2.
15. Ralph Ketchum, *James Madison: A Biography* (Charlottesville: University of Virginia Press, 1998), 593.
16. Stagg, *Mr. Madison's War*, 285.
17. Ibid., 428.
18. Harvey Strum, "New York Federalists and Opposition to the War of 1812," *World Affairs* 142, no. 3 (Winter 1980): 173.
19. Stagg, *Mr. Madison's War*, 281–82.
20. Ibid., 273; and Zuehlke, *For Honour's Sake*, 360, 364.
21. Stagg, *Mr. Madison's War*, 218.
22. Zuehlke, *For Honour's Sake*, 154.
23. C. Edward Skeen, *1816: America Rising* (Lexington: University Press of Kentucky, 2003), 3.
24. Taylor, *Civil War of 1812*, 319.
25. See Lawrence D. Cress, *Citizens in Arms: The Army and the Militia in American Society to the War of 1812* (Chapel Hill: University of North Carolina Press, 1982).
26. Wood, *Empire of Liberty*, 699–700.
27. Don Higginbotham, "The Early American Way of War: Reconnaissance and Appraisal," *William and Mary Quarterly* 44, no. 2 (April 1987): 270.

9. What if the War of 1812 Had Never Occurred?

1. David McCullough, *John Adams* (New York: Simon & Schuster, 2001), 556.
2. Bradford Perkins, *The First Rapprochement: England and the United States, 1795–1805* (Los Angeles: University of California Press, 1967); and Hickey, *The War of 1812*, 16.
3. McCullough, *John Adams*, 566.
4. Capt. Alfred Thayer Mahan, *Sea Power in Its Relations to the War of 1812* (London: Sampson Low, Marston, 1905), volume 1. See page 72 for the Morris quote and page 74 for Mahan's observation.
5. Perkins, *First Rapprochement*, 160.
6. Latimer, *1812*, 33.
7. Stagg, *Mr. Madison's War*, 259.
8. Hickey, *The War of 1812*, 282.
9. Zuehlke, *For Honour's Sake*, 119.
10. McDougall, *Throes of Democracy*, 255.

11. Perkins, *Castlereagh and Adams*, 209.

12. Howe, *What Hath God Wrought*, 328.

13. Remini, *Andrew Jackson and His Indian Wars*, 43.

14. Owsley, *Struggle for the Gulf Borderlands*, 87.

15. Wilentz, *Rise of American Democracy*, 244.

16. Howe, *What Hath God Wrought*, 367.

17. John M. Blum et al., *The National Experience: The History of the United States to 1887*, 2nd ed. (New York: Harcourt, Brace, and World, 1968), 237.

18. Howe, *What Hath God Wrought*, 421; and Remini, *Andrew Jackson and His Indian Wars*, 281. Historian Andro Linklater argues that the key turning point for the Native Americans living east of the Mississippi occurred in 1797 when Congress reduced the size of the Legion of the United States. Under "Mad" Anthony Wayne, the Legion won the Battle of Fallen Timbers and established order in the Old Northwest based on an inclusive policy articulated by President Washington and Secretary of War Henry Knox. Knox had proposed that "instead of exterminating a part of the human race by our modes of population," the government should extend "our Knowledge of cultivation, and of the arts, to the Aboriginals of the Country by which the source of future life and happiness [might be] preserved and extended." Linklater says of the Legion, "Neither settler nor Indian could have ignored that overwhelming force. Had it remained in existence, it might have made possible a coherent, organized westward expansion that did not sweep aside the rights of Native American owners. That at least was the president's dream." See Linklater, *An Artist in Treason*, 124–25, 160–61.

19. The *Democratic Review* is quoted in Howe, *What Hath God Wrought*, 703; and Adams is quoted in Perkins, *Castlereagh and Adams*, 278.

BIBLIOGRAPHIC NOTE
AND SOURCES

This note describes the sources used in this study. It begins with general histories of the early United States, followed by monographs and reference works on the War of 1812. The note then presents works on military forces, individual military theaters, battles, and other specific topics. A standard bibliography listing sources by author concludes this section.

Students of American history are blessed with a number of recent sweeping histories on the early republic. Two recent additions to the Oxford History of the United States—Gordon Wood's *Empire of Liberty: A History of the Early Republic, 1789–1815* and Daniel Walker Howe's *What Hath God Wrought: The Transformation of America, 1815–1848*—use the end of the War of 1812 as a point of demarcation. The first two installments of Walter McDougall's history of the United States—*Freedom Just around the Corner: A New American History, 1585–1828* and *Throes of Democracy: The American Civil War Era, 1829–1877*—cover a broader period. Sean Wilentz's *The Rise of American Democracy: Jefferson to Lincoln* provides an equally sweeping account but focuses more on political developments.

Histories of the War of 1812 are similarly in plentiful supply. It is useful to read and compare the perspectives and conclusions of American, British, and Canadian authors, such as Donald R. Hickey's *The War of 1812: A Forgotten Conflict*; Jon Latimer's *1812: War with America*; and J. Mackay Hitsman's *The Incredible War of 1812: A Military History*, respectively. Other long-standing single-volume accounts include Henry Adams's *The War of 1812*; Francis F. Beirne, *The War of 1812*; John K. Mahon, *The War of 1812*; John Elting's *Amateurs, to Arms! A Military History of the War of 1812*; and J. C. A. Stagg's *Mr. Madison's War: Politics, Diplomacy, and Warfare in the Early American*

Republic, 1783–1830. Alan Taylor's recent *The Civil War of 1812: American Citizens, British Subjects, Irish Rebels, & Indian Allies* provides a unique cultural and social account of the war. Carl Benn's "essential history," *The War of 1812*, is an excellent and well-designed introductory volume. As for the war's international context, see Jeremy Black's *The War of 1812 in the Age of Napoleon* and J. P. Riley's *Napoleon and the World War of 1813: Lessons in Coalition Warfighting*.

Monographs on individual theaters and campaigns are equally numerous. Pierre Berton's two-volume popular history of this front—*The Invasion of Canada, 1812–1813* and *Flames Across the Border, 1813–1814*—are "gateway" readings on the northern theater and on the War of 1812. Richard Barbuto's *Niagara, 1814: America Invades Canada* is probably the most comprehensive account of the war's central front. In covering the Niagara frontier in the last year of the war, Barbuto sets the broader strategic context in which operations took place across the U.S.-Canadian border. Donald Graves's *Field of Glory: The Battle of Crysler's Farm, 1813* and *Where Right and Glory Lead! The Battle of Lundy's Lane, 1814* are also excellent. Other books covering individual battles include David G. Fitz-Enz, *The Final Invasion: Plattsburgh, the War of 1812's Most Decisive Battle*; Robert Malcomson, *A Very Brilliant Affair: The Battle of Queenston Heights, 1812*; and Joseph A. Whitehorne, *While Washington Burned: The Battle for Fort Erie, 1814*. Finally, notable works focusing on the Native American experiences of the War of 1812 in the north include Sandy Antal's *A Wampum Denied: Procter's War of 1812*; Carl Benn's *The Iroquois in the War of 1812*; and John Sugden's *Tecumseh: A Life*.

The British campaign in the Chesapeake Bay is, however, the most frequently visited and revisited by historians, no doubt because of the spectacular burning of the White House and the Capitol in Washington and the stalwart defense of Fort McHenry as captured in the American national anthem. See Alan Lloyd, *The Scorching of Washington: The War of 1812*; Walter Lord, *The Dawn's Early Light*; William M. Marine, *The British Invasion of Maryland, 1812–15*; Charles C. Muller, *The Darkest Day: 1814, the Washington-Baltimore Campaign*; Anthony S. Pitch, *The Burning of Washington: The British Invasion of 1814*; John M. Stahl, *"The Invasion of the City of Washington": A Disagreeable Study in and of Military Unpreparedness*; and Joseph A. Whitehorne, *The Battle for Baltimore, 1814*. Two British accounts are James Pack, *The Man Who Burned the White House, Admiral Sir George Cockburn, 1772–1853* and Andrew Tully, *When We Burned the White House*.

Similarly, the Battle of New Orleans has drawn considerable attention. Robin Reilly's *The British at the Gates, The New Orleans Campaign in the War of 1812* and Robert Remini's *The Battle of New Orleans* cover the strategic and operational aspects of the southwest and the particulars of the battle. Frank Lawrence Owsley Jr.'s *Struggle for the Gulf Borderlands: The Creek War and the Battle of New Orleans, 1812–1815*, however, is probably the best single volume on this theater. Robert Remini's *Andrew Jackson and His Indian Wars* provides considerable follow-on context regarding the harsh terms Jackson imposed equally on his Indian opponents and allies.

Coverage of the naval war of 1812 is anchored by two classics—Capt. Alfred Thayer Mahan's *Sea Power in Its Relations to the War of 1812* and Theodore Roosevelt's *Naval War of 1812*. Wade G. Dudley, *Splintering the Wooden Wall: The British Blockade of the United States, 1812–1815* provides a more contemporary assessment of the British and American oceanic naval strategies. Individual warship histories include Frances Diane Robotti and James Vescovi's *The USS Essex and the Birth of the American Navy*. Three books provide detail on the naval engagements on the Great Lakes: Robert Malcomson's *Lords of the Lake: The Naval War on Lake Ontario, 1812–1814*; David Curtis Skaggs and Gerard T. Altoff's *A Signal Victory: The Lake Erie Campaign, 1812–1813*; and Barry Gough's *Through Water, Ice & Fire: Schooner* Nancy *of the War of 1812*.

Reference works on the War of 1812 include John C. Fredriksen's *The United States Army in the War of 1812: Concise Biographies of Commanders and Operational Histories of Regiments, with Bibliographies of Published and Primary Resources*; David S. Heidler and Jeanne T. Heidler's *Encyclopedia of the War of 1812*; Donald R. Hickey, *Don't Give Up the Ship! Myths of the War of 1812*; and Robert Malcomson, *The A to Z of the War of 1812*. On the naval war, see Howard I. Chapelle, *The History of the American Sailing Navy: The Ships and Their Development*.

Sources

Adams, Henry. *The Jeffersonian Transformation: Passages from the "History."* New York: The New York Review of Books, 2007.

———. *The War of 1812*. Edited by H. A. DeWeerd. New York: Cooper Square Press, 1999.

Ames, Seth, ed. *The Works of Fisher Ames*. Vol. 12. Boston: Little, Brown, 1854.

Antal, Sandy. *A Wampum Denied: Procter's War of 1812*. Ottawa: Carleton University Press, 1997.

Barbuto, Richard V. *Niagara, 1814: America Invades Canada*. Lawrence: University Press of Kansas, 2000.

Beirne, Francis F. *The War of 1812*. New York: E. P. Dutton, 1949.

Benn, Carl. *The Iroquois in the War of 1812*. Toronto: University of Toronto Press, 1998.

———. *The War of 1812*. Oxford, UK: Osprey Publishing, 2002.

Berton, Pierre. *Flames Across the Border, 1813–1814*. New York: Penguin Books, 1981.

———. *The Invasion of Canada, 1812–1813*. New York: Penguin Books, 1980.

Black, Jeremy. *The War of 1812 in the Age of Napoleon*. Norman: University of Oklahoma Press, 2009.

———. "A British View of the Naval War of 1812." *Naval History Magazine* 22, no. 4 (August 2008).

Blum, John M., William S. McFeely, Edmund S. Morgan, and Arthur M. Schlesinger Jr. *The National Experience: The History of the United States to 1887*. 2nd ed. New York: Harcourt, Brace, and World, 1968.

Bond, Jr., Beverly W. "William Henry Harrison in the War of 1812." *Mississippi Valley Historical Review* 13, no. 4 (March 1927): 499–516.

Borneman, Walter R. *1812: The War That Forged a Nation*. New York: HarperCollins, 2004.

Brown, Roger H. "Who Bungled the War of 1812?" *Reviews in American History* 19 (1991).

Buchholz, Heinrich Ewald. *Governors of Maryland: From the Revolution to the Year 1908*. Baltimore: Williams & Wilkins, 1908.

Buel, Jr., Richard. *America on the Brink: How the Political Struggle over the War of 1812 Almost Destroyed the Young Republic*. New York: Palgrave Macmillan, 2005.

Carter-Edwards, Dennis. "The War of 1812 along the Detroit Frontier: A Canadian Perspective." *Michigan Historical Review* 13 (Fall 1987): 25–50.

Cassell, Frank A. "Baltimore in 1813: A Study of Urban Defense in the War of 1812." *Military Affairs* 33, no. 3 (December 1969): 349–61.

Chambers II, John Whiteclay, ed. *The Oxford Companion to American Military History*. New York: Oxford University Press, 1999.

Chapelle, Howard I. *The History of the American Sailing Navy: The Ships and Their Development*. New York: W. W. Norton and Company, 1949. Reprinted by Konecky & Konecky, 1949.

Chernow, Ron. *Alexander Hamilton*. New York: Penguin Press, 2004.

Cress, Lawrence D. *Citizens in Arms: The Army and the Militia in American Society to the War of 1812*. Chapel Hill: University of North Carolina Press, 1982.

Crowley, Robert. *What If? The World's Foremost Military Historians Imagine What Might Have Been.* New York: Berkley Publishing Group, 2001.

———. *What If? 2: Eminent Historians Imagine What Might Have Been.* New York: G. P. Putnam's Sons, 2002.

Davis, William C. *Look Away! A History of the Confederate States of America.* New York: Free Press, 2002.

de Kay, James Tertius. *Chronicles of the Frigate Macedonian, 1809–1822.* New York: W. W. Norton, 1995.

Derr, Emerson Lee. "Simon Snyder, Governor of Pennsylvania, 1808–1817." PhD diss., University of Pennsylvania, 1960.

Dudley, Wade G. *Splintering the Wooden Wall: The British Blockade of the United States, 1812–1815.* Annapolis, MD: Naval Institute Press, 2003.

Dupuy, R. Ernest, and Trevor N. Dupuy. *The Harper Encyclopedia of Military History: From 3500 BC to the Present.* New York: HarperCollins, 1993.

Elting, John. *Amateurs, to Arms! A Military History of the War of 1812.* New York: Da Capo Press, 1995.

Fischer, David Hackett. *Historians' Fallacies: Toward a Logic of Historical Thought.* New York: Harper & Row, 1970.

Fitz-Enz, David. *The Final Invasion: Plattsburgh, the War of 1812's Most Decisive Battle.* New York: Cooper Square Press, 2001.

———. *Redcoats' Revenge: An Alternate History of the War of 1812.* Washington, DC: Potomac Books, 2008.

Flint, Eric. *1812: The Rivers of War.* New York: Ballantine Books, 2005.

Fredriksen, John C. *The United States Army in the War of 1812: Concise Biographies of Commanders and Operational Histories of Regiments, with Bibliographies of Published and Primary Resources.* Jefferson, NC: McFarland, 2009.

Gallaher, John G. "Victory at Kulm: The 1813 Campaign." In *The Napoleon Options: Alternate Decisions of the Napoleonic Wars*, edited by Jonathan North. London: Greenhill Books, 2000.

Glover, Richard. *Peninsular Preparation: The Reform of the British Army, 1795–1809.* London: Cambridge University Press, 1963.

Goodwin, Doris Kearns. *Team of Rivals: The Political Genius of Abraham Lincoln.* New York: Simon & Schuster, 2005.

Gough, Barry. *Through Water, Ice & Fire: Schooner* Nancy *of the War of 1812.* Toronto: The Dundurn Group, 2006.

Graves, Donald E. *Field of Glory: The Battle of Crysler's Farm, 1813.* Toronto: Robin Brass Studio, 1999.

———. *Where Right and Glory Lead! The Battle of Lundy's Lane, 1814.* Toronto: Robin Brass Studio, 2003.

Griffith, Samuel B. *Sun Tzu: The Art of War*. Oxford, UK: Oxford University Press, 1963.

Hanks, Jarvis, Amadiah Ford, and Alexander McMullen. *Soldiers of 1814: American Enlisted Men's Memoirs of the Niagara Campaign*. Edited by Donald E. Graves. Youngstown, NY: Old Fort Niagara Association, 1995.

Heidler, David S., and Jeanne T. Heidler, eds. *Encyclopedia of the War of 1812*. Santa Barbara, CA: ABC-CLIO, 1997.

Herring, George G. *From Colony to Superpower: U.S. Foreign Relations Since 1776*. New York: Oxford University Press, 2008.

Hickey, Donald R. *Don't Give Up the Ship! Myths of the War of 1812*. Toronto: Robin Brass Studio, 2006.

———. "Federalist Defense Policy in the Age of Jefferson, 1801–1812." *Military Affairs* 45, no. 2 (April 1981): 63–70.

———. "Federalist Party Unity and the War of 1812." *Journal of American Studies* 12, no. 1 (April 1978): 23–39.

———. "New England's Defense Problem and the Genesis of the Hartford Convention." *The New England Quarterly* 50, no. 4 (December 1977): 587–604.

———. *The War of 1812: A Forgotten Conflict*. Urbana: University of Illinois Press, 1990.

———. "The War of 1812: Still a Forgotten Conflict?" *Journal of Military History* 65 (July 2001): 741–69.

Higginbotham, Don. "The Early American Way of War: Reconnaissance and Appraisal." *William and Mary Quarterly* 44, no. 2 (April 1987): 230–73.

Higginbotham, Sanford W. *The Keystone in the Democratic Arch: Pennsylvania Politics, 1800–1816*. Harrisburg: Pennsylvania Historical and Museum Commission, 1952.

Hitsman, J. Mackay. *The Incredible War of 1812: A Military History*. Toronto: Robin Brass Studio, 1999.

Howe, Daniel Walker. *What Hath God Wrought: The Transformation of America, 1815–1848*. New York: Oxford University Press, 2007.

Irwin, Ray W. *Daniel D. Tompkins, Governor of New York and Vice President of the United States*. New York: The New York Historical Society, 1968.

Jefferson, Thomas. *The Jeffersonian Cyclopedia*. Edited by John P. Foley. New York: Funk & Wagnalls, 1900.

Jones, William Devereux. "A British View of the War of 1812 and the Peace Negotiations." *The Mississippi Valley Historical Review* 45, no. 3 (December 1958): 481–87.

Kaplan, Lawrence S. "France and Madison's Decision for War, 1812." *The Mississippi Valley Historical Review* 50, no. 4 (March 1964): 652–71.

Kastor, Peter J. "Toward 'the Maritime War Only': The Question of Naval
Mobilization, 1811–1812." *Journal of Military History* 61, no. 3 (July 1997):
455–80.

Keegan, John. *Fields of Battle: The Wars for North America.* New York: Alfred A.
Knopf, 1996.

Keller, Kenneth W. "Cultural Conflict in Early Nineteenth-Century
Pennsylvania Politics." *The Pennsylvania Magazine of History and Biography*
110, no. 4 (October 1986): 509–30.

Ketchum, Ralph. *James Madison: A Biography.* Charlottesville: University of
Virginia Press, 1998.

Latimer, Jon. *1812: War with America.* Cambridge, MA: Harvard University
Press, 2007.

Leckie, Robert. *From Sea to Shining Sea: From the War of 1812 to the Mexican War,
the Saga of America's Expansion.* New York: HarperCollins, 1993.

Lemmon, Sarah McCulloh. *Frustrated Patriots: North Carolina and the War of
1812.* Chapel Hill: University of North Carolina Press, 1973.

Linklater, Andro. *An Artist in Treason: The Extraordinary Double Life of General
James Wilkinson.* New York: Walker Publishing, 2009.

Lloyd, Alan. *The Scorching of Washington: The War of 1812.* New York: R. B.
Luce, 1974.

Lord, Walter. *The Dawn's Early Light.* New York: W. W. Norton, 1972.

Lowery, Charles D. *James Barbour: A Jeffersonian Republican.* Tuscaloosa:
University of Alabama Press, 1984.

Luvaas, Jay, ed. *Napoleon on the Art of War.* New York: Free Press, 1999.

Mahan, Capt. Alfred Thayer. *Sea Power in Its Relations to the War of 1812.*
London: Sampson Low, Marston, 1905.

Mahon, John K. *The War of 1812.* New York: Da Capo Press, 1972.

Malcomson, Robert. *The A to Z of the War of 1812.* Lanham, MD: Scarecrow
Press, 2009.

———. *Lords of the Lake: The Naval War on Lake Ontario, 1812–1814.*
Annapolis, MD: Naval Institute Press, 1998.

———. *A Very Brilliant Affair: The Battle of Queenston Heights, 1812.* Annapolis,
MD: Naval Institute Press, 2003.

Marine, William M. *The British Invasion of Maryland, 1812–15.* Baltimore:
Society of the War of 1812 in Maryland, 1913.

Martell, J. S. "A Side Light on Federalist Strategy during the War of 1812."
American Historical Review 43, no. 3 (April 1938): 553–66.

McCullough, David. *John Adams.* New York: Simon & Schuster, 2001.

McDougall, Walter A. *Freedom Just around the Corner: A New American History,
1585–1828.* New York: HarperCollins, 2004.

————. *Throes of Democracy: The American Civil War Era, 1829–1877*. New York: HarperCollins, 2008.

Mead, Walter Russell. *Special Providence: American Foreign Policy and How It Changed the World*. New York: Alfred A. Knopf, 2001.

Morison, Samuel Eliot. "Our Most Unpopular War." *Proceedings of the Massachusetts Historical Society* 80 (1968): 38–54.

Muller, Charles C. *The Darkest Day: 1814, the Washington-Baltimore Campaign*. Philadelphia: J. B. Lippincott, 1963.

North, Jonathan, ed. *The Napoleon Options: Alternate Decisions of the Napoleonic Wars*. London: Greenhill Books, 2000.

Nosworthy, Brent. *With Musket, Canon, and Sword: Battle Tactics of Napoleon and His Enemies*. New York: Sarpedon, 1996.

Owsley, Jr., Frank Lawrence. *Struggle for the Gulf Borderlands: The Creek War and the Battle of New Orleans, 1812–1815*. Tuscaloosa: University of Alabama Press, 2000.

Pack, James. *The Man Who Burned the White House: Admiral Sir George Cockburn, 1772–1853*. Hampshire, UK: Kenneth Mason, 1987.

Perkins, Bradford. *Castlereagh and Adams: England and the United States, 1812–1823*. Los Angeles: University of California Press, 1964.

————, ed. *The Causes of the War of 1812: National Honor or National Interest?* New York: Holt, Rinehart and Winston, 1962.

————. *The First Rapprochement: England and the United States, 1795–1805*. Los Angeles: University of California Press, 1967.

————. *Prologue to War: England and the United States, 1805–1812*. Berkeley: University of California Press, 1961.

Phillips, Kevin. *The Cousins' Wars: Religion, Politics, and the Triumph of Anglo-America*. New York: Basic Books, 1999.

Pitch, Anthony S. *The Burning of Washington: The British Invasion of 1814*. Annapolis, MD: Naval Institute Press, 1998.

Pratt, Julius W. "Western Aims in the War of 1812." *The Mississippi Valley Historical Review* 12, no. 1 (June 1925): 36–50.

Reilly, Robin. *The British at the Gates: The New Orleans Campaign in the War of 1812*. Toronto: Robin Brass Studio, 2002.

Remini, Robert. *Andrew Jackson and His Indian Wars*. New York: Viking, 2001.

————. *The Battle of New Orleans*. New York: Viking, 1999.

Riley, J. P. *Napoleon and the World War of 1813: Lessons in Coalition Warfighting*. London: Frank Cass Publishers, 2000.

Robotti, Frances Diane, and James Vescovi. *The USS Essex and the Birth of the American Navy*. Holbrook, MA: Adams Media, 1999.

Roosevelt, Theodore. *Naval War of 1812*. New York: The Modern Library, 1999.

Rutland, Robert Allen. *The Presidency of James Madison*. Lawrence: University Press of Kansas, 1990.

Sapio, Victor. *Pennsylvania and the War of 1812*. Lexington: University Press of Kentucky, 1970.

Schivelbusch, Wolfgang. *The Culture of Defeat: On National Trauma, Mourning, and Recovery*. Translated by Jefferson Chase. New York: Metropolitan Books, 2003.

Sears, Stephen W. *Gettysburg*. New York: Houghton Mifflin, 2004.

Skaggs, David Curtis, and Gerard T. Altoff. *A Signal Victory: The Lake Erie Campaign, 1812–1813*. Annapolis, MD: Naval Institute Press, 1997.

Skeen, C. Edward. *Citizen Soldiers in the War of 1812*. Lexington: University Press of Kentucky, 1999.

———. *1816: America Rising*. Lexington: University Press of Kentucky, 2003.

Sobel, Robert. *For Want of a Nail: If Burgoyne Had Won at Saratoga*. London: Greenhill Books, 1977.

Stacey, C. P. "An American Plan for a Canadian Campaign." *The American Historical Review* 46, no. 2 (January 1941): 348–58.

Stagg, J. C. A. "James Madison and the 'Malcontents': The Political Origins of the War of 1812." *The William and Mary Quarterly* 33, no. 4 (October 1976): 557–85.

———. *Mr. Madison's War: Politics, Diplomacy, and Warfare in the Early American Republic, 1783–1830*. Princeton, NJ: Princeton University Press, 1983.

Stahl, John M. *"The Invasion of the City of Washington": A Disagreeable Study in and of Military Unpreparedness*. New York: Van Trump, 1918.

Stewart, Richard W., ed. *The United States Army and the Forging of a Nation, 1775-1917*. 2nd ed. Washington, DC: Center of Military History, United States Army, 2009.

Strum, Harvey. "New York Federalists and Opposition to the War of 1812." *World Affairs* 142, no. 3 (Winter 1980): 169–87.

Sugden, John. *Tecumseh: A Life*. New York: Henry Holt, 1997.

Tally, Steve. *Almost America: From the Colonists to Clinton: A "What if" History of the U.S.* New York: HarperCollins, 2000.

Taylor, Alan. *The Civil War of 1812: American Citizens, British Subjects, Irish Rebels, & Indian Allies*. New York: Alfred A. Knopf, 2010.

Tully, Andrew. *When We Burned the White House*. London: Anthony Gibbs & Phillips, 1960.

Turner, Frederick Jackson. *The Frontier in American History*. New York: Henry Holt, 1921.

Turner, Wesley B. *British Generals in the War of 1812: High Command in the Canadas*. Montreal: McGill-Queen's University Press, 1999.

U.S. Marine Corps' Fleet Marine Force Manual, (FMFM) 1-1 Campaigning. Washington, DC: Department of the Navy, January 1990.

Wagner II, Edward James. "Federal-State Relations during the War of 1812." PhD diss., Ohio State University, 1963.

Wehtje, Myron F. "Opposition in Virginia to the War of 1812." *Virginia Magazine of History and Biography* 78, no. 1 (January 1970): 65–86.

Whitehorne, Joseph A. *The Battle for Baltimore, 1814*. Baltimore: Nautical & Aviation Publishing Company of America, 1997.

———. *While Washington Burned: The Battle for Fort Erie, 1814*. Baltimore: Nautical & Aviation Publishing Company of America, 1992.

Wilentz, Sean. *The Rise of American Democracy: Jefferson to Lincoln*. New York: W. W. Norton, 2005.

Wilkinson, Lawrence. "How to Build Scenarios." Global Business Network, 2004.

Williams, John S. *History of the Invasion and Capture of Washington, and of the Events Which Preceded and Followed*. New York: Harper & Brothers, 1857.

Wills, Garry. *Henry Adams and the Making of America*. New York: Houghton Mifflin, 2005.

Wood, Gordon S. *Empire of Liberty: A History of the Early Republic, 1789–1815*. New York: Oxford University Press, 2009.

Zuehlke, Mark. *For Honour's Sake: The War of 1812 and the Brokering of an Uneasy Peace*. Toronto: Vintage Canada, 2006.

INDEX

ABOUT THE AUTHOR

William Weber was born and raised in Buffalo, New York, and holds a PhD and MA in foreign affairs from the University of Virginia and a BA in history from Canisius College. Following his graduate schoolwork, he was an assistant professor of political science at James Madison University in Harrisonburg, Virginia. He recently completed a thirty-year career as an intelligence analyst working on political-military issues and lives in Northern Virginia.